Organization Design

A well-designed organization is an effective organization. Decisions about organization design determine the shape and form of the organization – not only the reporting structure and authority relations, but also the number and size of sub-units and the interfaces *between* the sub-units. Indirectly, such decisions affect individual productivity as well as the organization's ability to attain strategic goals.

Organization Design equips the reader with advanced tools and frameworks, based on both research and practical experience, for understanding and re-designing organizations. Particular emphasis is placed on how one can improve effectiveness by simplifying complex roles, processes, and structures.

Readers will find thorough conceptual explanations combined with examples from different industries. This updated second edition includes a new chapter about traditional organizational forms, and is complemented by a companion website.

This textbook will be essential reading for students, scholars, and practitioners.

Nicolay Worren is an Associate Professor at the Norwegian University of Life Sciences, Norway. Before entering academia in 2015, he was a management consultant and participated in more than 25 organization re-design projects. He holds a Master's degree in psychology from McGill University and received his doctorate in management studies from Oxford University. He writes a blog: www.organizationdesign.net

Organization Design
Simplifying Complex Systems

SECOND EDITION

Nicolay Worren

Routledge
Taylor & Francis Group

LONDON AND NEW YORK

Second edition published 2018
by Routledge
2 Park Square, Milton Park, Abingdon, Oxon, OX14 4RN

and by Routledge
711 Third Avenue, New York, NY 10017

Routledge is an imprint of the Taylor & Francis Group, an informa business

First edition published by Pearson Education Limited 2012

British Library Cataloguing-in-Publication Data
A catalogue record for this book is available from the British Library

Library of Congress Cataloging-in-Publication Data
Names: Worren, Nicolay A. M., 1966- author.
Title: Organization design: simplifying complex systems / Nicolay
    Worren.
Other titles: Organisation design
Description: Second Edition. | New York: Routledge, 2018. |
    Revised edition of the author's Organisation design, c2012. |
    Includes index.
Identifiers: LCCN 2017056719 | ISBN 9781138502857 |
    ISBN 9781138502864 | ISBN 9781315145112 (eISBN)
Subjects: LCSH: Delegation of authority. | Line and staff
    organization. | Hierarchies. | Workflow. | Personnel
    management. | Complex organizations.
Classification: LCC HD50 .W67 2018 | DDC 658.4/02—dc23 LC
    record available at https://lccn.loc.gov/2017056719

ISBN: 978-1-138-50285-7 (hbk)
ISBN: 978-1-138-50286-4 (pbk)
ISBN: 978-1-315-14511-2 (ebk)

Typeset in Minion
by RefineCatch Limited, Bungay, Suffolk

Visit the companion website: www.routledge.com/worren

Contents

List of figures

List of tables

Preface

Purpose

This book is written at a time when the field of organization design is experiencing a revival. Yet despite an increasing interest among both practitioners and scholars, there are only a handful of textbooks in this area, and – to my knowledge – none that have been published recently. It is therefore my hope that this book will fill a gap and prove useful to those that want to learn more about this important and fascinating field of research and practice.

The book aims to be:

- Focused – in concentrating on the core elements of organization design
- Current – in addressing key challenges facing organizational leaders today
- Rigorous – in advocating the use of systematic, data-based approaches
- Pragmatic – in developing prescriptions for action.

Audience

This book is primarily intended for:

- *MBA and other master-level students*, either as the core or supplementary text in courses
- *Participants in executive education programs*
- *Graduate students* who are in the process of identifying topics for their research projects
- *Internal and external consultants* and *project managers* who assist leaders in (re)designing organizations.

Although the book has been written to provide an integrated and complete treatment of the core elements of organization design, it is also possible to use individual chapters and combine these with chapters from books in related fields such as strategic management, organization theory, or operations management.

Approach

Organization design is sometimes considered the applied variant of organizational theory. Unfortunately, organizational theory is a diverse and fragmented field with many competing paradigms. In addition, scholars in many other disciplines – including law and economics, strategic management, operations management, engineering, sociology, and psychology – carry out research that may have a bearing on organization design issues.

For a textbook to be focused, and reasonably coherent theoretically, one faces some choices as an author. The basic orientation that I have adopted has led me to include some theories and frameworks, while leaving out others. I realize that some readers may have a different view of the field. I still hope that they accept my choices as logical, given the aims of the book.

The approach taken in this book is mainly inspired by systems theory as defined by Russell Ackoff (Ackoff and Emery, 1972). Ackoff emphasized that the study of systems is a *transdisciplinary* undertaking. He defined systems as sets of interrelated elements. He argued that human systems are purposeful, that is, goal-seeking, and have some degree of autonomy in being able to selects goals as well as the means by which to pursue them.

We may add that the elements in question are roles (or groups of roles, i.e., units) rather than individuals (Jaques, 1990). This differentiates organization design from organizational behavior, which mainly focuses on the individuals in the organization, as opposed to the roles that they hold.

Among systems theorists, there are some who put more emphasis on learning about the nature of real-world systems, while others concentrate on developing methodologies to intervene and change systems (Jackson, 2000).

My thinking on this issue has been influenced by Chris Argyris, who argued that it should be the goal of social scientists to produce knowledge that can help people change the status quo. As he said: "The most powerful empirical tests for theories are provided when predictions are made about changing the universe, not simply describing it" (Argyris, 2005, p. 424).

Argyris goes on to say that one must specify causal and testable propositions about how to create change in order to produce actionable knowledge. I attempt to heed this advice by deriving specific design propositions that can be used as a basis for interventions.

The common theme through the different chapters is *organizational complexity*. The key assumption is that it should be the goal to minimize complexity in organization design, as complexity reduces the probability that a system will achieve its mission and goals.

In selecting topics to cover, I have prioritized those areas where I believe the book can make a contribution. As an example, I do describe the change management aspects of organization re-design in one chapter (Chapter 8), but the issues that receive the most attention are those that are specifically related to the design process (particularly the early phases when the key choices are made). This in no way assumes that other aspects of change management are unimportant – but in my judgment, they have already been well covered in existing texts.

Key features

Chapter overviews. Every chapter begins with an overview that briefly describes the background and current situation with regard to the chapter topic, the key challenges, the questions that these challenges raise, and the proposed solutions.

Extensive use of examples. Every chapter features one or more examples that are used to illustrate the key conceptual ideas of the chapter. For the most part the examples represent real cases, but in some chapters hypothetical cases have been developed for pedagogical purposes (but these are still based on observations that have been made in organizations).

Tools and frameworks. There are numerous tables and illustrations that summarize and visualize the key concepts being discussed.

Review questions. The review questions are intended to aid the reader both in remembering the content and in reflecting upon the implications of the issues that are discussed.

Resources for lecturers

Brief cases. Lecturers who use the book will have access to brief cases that illustrate the key concepts in each chapter. www.routledge. com/worren

Teaching aids. A slide set and teaching notes are also available to lecturers.

Simulation. A simulation for students, based on a real re-design project, is under development. It will be made available from a separate website.

Resources for practitioners

Design propositions. Every chapter includes a list of actionable principles that practitioners can use as the basis for interventions in organizations.

Blog. The author writes a blog, www.organizationdesign.net, that describes new trends and offers advice to managers and consultants.

Resources for researchers

Research questions. Every chapter contains a list of research questions that identify important areas for further research in the field.

List of articles and books. Some of the key references that are used in this book have been shared as a Mendeley file: https://www.mendeley.com/community/organization-design-references/

Chapter structure

This book contains nine chapters, which may be divided into four parts:

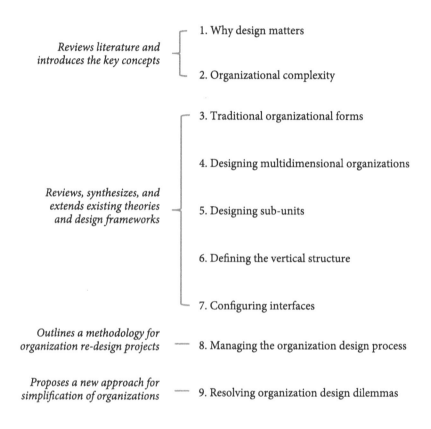

Reviews literature and introduces the key concepts

1. Why design matters

2. Organizational complexity

Reviews, synthesizes, and extends existing theories and design frameworks

3. Traditional organizational forms

4. Designing multidimensional organizations

5. Designing sub-units

6. Defining the vertical structure

7. Configuring interfaces

Outlines a methodology for organization re-design projects

8. Managing the organization design process

Proposes a new approach for simplification of organizations

9. Resolving organization design dilemmas

Chapter 1 and 2 review existing theory and research and thus provide the background for the remaining chapters. Chapter 1 covers some key elements of organizational theory that have implications for organization design in general. Chapter 2 focuses more specifically on theory and research related to organizational complexity.

Chapter 3 to 7 provide in-depth discussions of the core elements of organization design. The chapters in this part roughly follow the sequence of an actual re-design project. As Russell Ackoff used to point out in his speeches, an architect draws the house (the whole), before he adds the rooms (the parts). We thus begin, in Chapter 3 and 4, by discussing various ways in which to design the overall structure of an organization. We proceed, in Chapter 5, by considering how sub-units are designed. We then look at the definition of roles and the placement of roles at different hierarchical layers in Chapter 6. Chapter 7 discusses how to improve interfaces, with the main emphasis on frameworks that are relevant once a sub-unit has been established.

In Chapter 8, we review a methodology that can be used to plan and manage organizational re-design projects.

Chapter 9 is slightly more experimental, in presenting a new approach to identify, analyze, and simplify complex organizational designs. The chapter is based on fairly detailed descriptions of five specific cases drawn from client engagements.

The chapter structure is primarily intended for those who read all chapters consecutively. But I also wanted the book to be usable for those who prefer another sequence or are only interested in one or a few of the chapters. To make them readable as stand-alone chapters, I have sometimes repeated basic concepts. The downside is that there is a bit of content overlap, but I hope it is not too much.

A note on terminology

In this book, all of the chapters make use of the concepts of *functional requirements* and *design parameters*.

There is a certain precedent for the use of the term *design parameters*: Henry Mintzberg (1979) used it in his book and defined it as "the basic elements used in designing organizational structures" (p. 14). But the term *functional requirement* is new (in this context). Some readers will find it odd that such technical terms are used in a book about social systems, which consist of people.

However, I agree with Suh (2001) that design (in any field, technical or social) is fundamentally about finding design parameters (means) that satisfy functional requirements (ends). And I have found more commonly used terms to be less precise when writing about the topic. Nonetheless, one should probably use other words in practice. When discussing this topic with people who are unfamiliar with the terminology, one may, for example, substitute "mandate," "mission," or "goal" for functional requirement, and "accountable unit" for design parameter.

To minimize confusion, I have included a glossary where these and other key terms are defined.

Your feedback

I welcome communication from readers. Readers may contact me directly via email or by using the contact form on my blog.

Ackoff, R.L. and Emery, F. E. (1972). *On Purposeful Systems*. Chicago: Aldine-Atherton.

Argyris, Ch. (2005). Actionable knowledge. In Tsoukas, H., & Knudsen, Ch. (Eds.), *Oxford Handbook of Organization Theory* (pp. 423–452). New York: Oxford University Press.

Jackson, M.C. (2000). *Systems Approaches to Management.* London: Springer.

Jaques. E. (1990). *Creativity and Work.* Madison, CT: *International Universities Press.*

Mintzberg, H. (1979). *The Structuring of Organizations.* Englewood Cliffs, NJ: Prentice-Hall.

Suh, N. P. (2001). *Axiomatic Design: Advances and Applications.* Oxford: Oxford University Press.

About the author

Nicolay Worren is an associate professor at the Norwegian University of Life Sciences. Before entering academia in 2015, he was a management consultant and participated in more than 25 organization re-design projects. He holds a Master's degree in psychology from McGill University and received his doctorate in management studies from Oxford University. He writes a blog: www.organizationdesign.net

Acknowledgments

I have benefited from ideas and suggestions from numerous people in writing this book. I have learned a lot about this topic from my clients, from my former colleagues in Accenture, PA Consulting Group, and Deloitte, and from my current academic peers.

I would like to thank Andrew Campbell (Ashridge), Roberto Dandi (LUISS Business School), and one anonymous reviewer for very helpful reviews of the book. Roberto Dandi also proposed adding a new chapter on traditional organizational forms, which appears in this edition.

Christopher Brown (Worcester Polytechnic Institute) patiently responded to my e-mails regarding the intricacies of axiomatic design theory. Ken Shepard at the Global Organization Design Society provided feedback on the original version of the chapter on vertical structuring. My students at the Norwegian University of Life Sciences also provided helpful feedback after using the book in my course. I also wish to thank Ron Sanchez, former professor at the Copenhagen Business School, for allowing me to use some material in Chapter 7 that we developed in collaboration.

The first edition of this book was published by Pearson Education, and I am grateful to Gabrielle James, former acquisitions editor, for having supported the project from the start. Now with Routledge, I wish to thank Natalie Tomlinson for initiating the revision of the book and the editorial team that took over (Lucy McClune and Judith Lorton) for guidance through the process.

The writing process has demanded a lot of time that would otherwise have been spent with the family. My gratitude goes to my wife, Maria, and to our children, Alvaro, Joaquim, Catalina, Tomas, and Julia, for their patience and understanding.

Nicolay Worren

1 Why design matters

Chapter overview

Background	• Organization design is part of every manager's job.
	• Empirical research confirms the potential impact of organization design on the functioning and performance of organizations.
	• Four foundational concepts in the literature are hierarchical decomposition, task uncertainty, coordination cost, and alignment between strategy and structure.
Challenges	• Business schools have historically placed little emphasis on organization design.
	• Management education has generally focused on *decision making* as opposed to the creation of decision alternatives (i.e., design).
	• With the exception of some economics-based theories, academic research has generally failed to influence the actual design of organizations.
	• Well-known business "gurus" have also downplayed the role of formal structure in creating effective organizations.
Key question	• How can the discipline of organization design be revitalized in order to ensure that it has stronger impact on managerial practice – without losing academic rigor?
Proposed approach	• Reaffirm the strategic importance of design.
	• Adopt a "design attitude" as a complement to the "decision attitude."
	• Use *organizational architecture* as the over-arching concept.

- Incorporate an explicit focus on purpose and functional requirements.

- Develop prescriptive knowledge to bridge the gap between research and practice.

Introduction

A sales unit has grown to more than 25 people. The manager responsible for the unit feels that she spends too much time on administration and supervision of employees. She concludes that there needs to be two or three teams, each led by a manager that can be responsible for handling day-to-day responsibilities. On the other hand, she is not sure how they should be subdivided. Should they be grouped according to geography, with one team for each main region, or by product, with one team for each main product category?

A project manager is recruited to the corporate staff of a large divisionalized firm to run a project charged with the implementation of a new IT system. During the first week in the new role, he discovers that there are three other IT projects, at the divisional level of the firm, that are configuring software solutions that will deliver functionality that partly overlaps with functionality that his project is supposed to deliver. He is pondering how the projects could be aligned with each other. As a first step, he draws a simple diagram that he intends to show to his manager to illustrate how the three projects interrelate.

The CEO of an oil company asks his leadership team to consider how to organize its drilling teams. The company consists of several operating units, each responsible for the operations on a particular oil field. Each unit has its own drilling team, which is called on when new oil wells need to be drilled. Several members of the leadership team argue that this organization is inefficient, as it is difficult to utilize capacity effectively across assets: At times, drilling teams in one unit have been idle while there have been insufficient resources to perform the work required in other units. The CEO challenges his team to come up with an alternative model.

What these stories have in common is that they portray managers who, for various reasons, find themselves in the role of *organizational designer*: attempting to make sense of, and improve, the functioning of complex organizations through the creation or adjustment of roles, processes, and structures. This is also the topic of this book, which will review concepts and frameworks for re-designing complex organizations. This introductory chapter introduces some key concepts that will serve as a foundation for the remaining chapters. It also reviews the status of organization design – as a field of research and as a practical discipline – both its achievements, and some of its challenges and limitations. It then discusses how we can develop the field further to ensure that it provides research-based and useful knowledge that contributes to enhance the effectiveness of organizations.

As the stories above suggest, organization design is part of every manager's job. In fact, most managers are faced with organization design challenges on an almost daily basis. Managers constantly design and re-design individual roles, define new projects (including their structure and reporting relationships), and contemplate better ways to coordinate organizational processes with multiple internal stakeholders. Periodically they may also make more fundamental changes to the structure of sub-units or entire organizations, or participate in adapting and implementing high-level designs developed by others.

Many, if not most, professionals engage in design activities: Engineers design products. Architects design buildings. Art directors design advertising campaigns. The main difference is the "materials" by which one designs – in designing organizations, managers create, or re-define, *roles, processes, and structures*. Unlike products, buildings, and ad campaigns, the outputs of organization design processes are abstract and invisible artifacts (Kennedy, 2002). Nonetheless, they are real enough for the people that work in the organizations and that are being affected. Choices made during organization design processes may to a large extent define people's roles and responsibilities, determine who they will collaborate with, and either broaden or limit the career paths available to them.

Design is, as Romme (2003) formulated it, "inquiry into systems that do not yet exist" (p. 558). The starting point is usually a problem or opportunity for which there is no self-evident solution, which triggers a process of search, aimed at identifying or developing a new solution that will work in the specific case that one is confronted with. For a manager, the problem or opportunity may have emerged as the result of external events (e.g., a merger) or may be the result of internal events (e.g., a decision to expand the business). The basic condition is that the manager, or a group of stakeholders, perceives that there is a potential for improvement, and initiates a design process to change the existing situation into a preferred one (Simon, 1996).

At times, *organization design* and *organization theory* are treated as synonymous to each other. However, it may be useful to draw a distinction between the two. Organization theory is essentially a *descriptive* field of study. Organizational theorists build theories to understand organizational functioning and carry out empirical research to test the validity of the theories (for example, examining whether the adoption of a certain corporate structure has an effect on the financial performance of firms). The term organization design, on the other hand, more often refers to a body of *prescriptive* (or normative) knowledge – knowledge about what *one should do* in different situations in order to attain a given objective (Romme, 2003). The goal for many of those working in this field is to develop tools and frameworks that are *pragmatically valid* – that is, usable by practitioners attempting to create new organizations or re-design existing organizations (Worren, Moore, & Elliott, 2002).

Despite these differences, organization design and organization theory are certainly closely related. Indeed, there are several ideas developed by organizational theorists that have gained widespread acceptance, and that also inform organization design methodology and practice. In the following we will briefly review three concepts that are central to both organization theory and organization design: Hierarchical decomposition, task uncertainty, coordination cost; and fit or alignment (between strategy, environment, and structure).

Foundational concepts

Hierarchical decomposition

In designing organizations, one sub-divides the organization into, for example, divisions, departments, teams, or roles. The basic process of dividing a system, composed of interacting elements, into units and sub-units is called *decomposition*. In this process, one decides which tasks, roles, or processes should be grouped together in the same unit, and implicitly separates other tasks, roles, and work functions. Depending on how far one decomposes the organization, one also creates a hierarchical structure (Figure 1.1). One may choose to define a relatively flat structure (with many units at the same level, but few levels between the top and bottom) or may create a more pyramidal form (few units at the same level, but many levels between the top and bottom).

Decomposition creates several effects. The most immediate effect is *division of labor*, or specialization. The basic idea of division of labor was first introduced by Smith (1776/1977), who described it as a key condition for increasing productivity. Smith explained that a worker who carries out one specific task repeatedly will likely develop greater skill, and perform the task faster, than a worker who switches between different tasks that he or she is not accustomed to performing. The same is true for sub-units of the organization that focus on one functional area or one particular activity in a work process. Over time, specialization allows the sub-unit to build up knowledge pertaining to the specific functional area or activity in the work process that it is responsible for. It may also spur innovation, if the sub-unit has been granted the necessary operational autonomy to introduce changes to improve the performance of its work processes (Sanchez, 1995; Jacobides, 2006).[1]

1 Baldwin & Clark (2000) attributed the rapid innovations that have happened in the computer industry during the last four decades to the modularization of both product and organizational structures (i.e., the creation of semi-independent sub-units within an overall architecture).

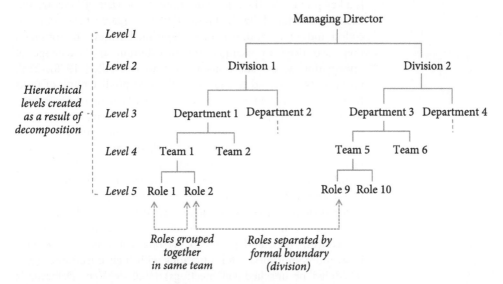

Figure 1.1 Hierarchical decomposition of an organization.

There is another, related term used in the literature: *Grouping* (e.g., Galbraith, 2002; Nadler & Tushman, 1997). Compared to the term decomposition, one here takes the "bottom up" perspective: Instead of focusing on how one sub-divides a large systems into smaller parts, grouping involves the aggregation of parts (e.g., roles) that have already been defined into larger units. For example, one may define a set of roles, focused, on say, marketing, and decide that these should be grouped together in a new unit called "the marketing department." Another set of roles, related to sales, may be grouped together to form "the sales department."

Integration, on the other hand, is the process of achieving unity of effort among the various sub-systems of the organization (Lawrence & Lorsch, 1969, p. 34). This will usually require that one develop relationships *across* the formal boundaries that separate the different sub-units that have been defined. Once it has been decided that sales and marketing should be handled by two separate departments, the next question is how they can coordinate. For example, how can we ensure that the sales and the marketing departments agree on branding and pricing policies, and communicate the same message to the customers? In the parlance of organization theory, this is a question of which "coordination mechanism" they should use (i.e., which tools, procedures, or processes the two departments should make use of to coordinate).

Task uncertainty

The particular coordination mechanism that is appropriate depends on the *uncertainty* of the tasks that one is faced with. This is a key premise in the *information processing view* of organization design, introduced by Galbraith (1974). Organizations need to collect and interpret information about the business environment; they also need to facilitate the distribution and exchange of information across sub-units (Tushman & Nadler, 1978). Task uncertainty is related to the variability and predictability of tasks (it may also be defined as the degree to which there are known solutions to problems). Galbraith (1974) stated that "the greater the task uncertainty, the greater the amount of information that must be processed among decision makers during task execution in order to achieve a given level of performance" (p. 4). Different coordination mechanisms vary in the degree of information that they transmit (Daft & Lengel, 1984). There is a continuum from impersonal coordination mechanisms, with limited "bandwidth," and which is suitable for routine tasks (e.g., establishing common procedures, rules, and plans) to personal coordination mechanisms, more appropriate for situations with high uncertainty (e.g., scheduled or unscheduled meetings) (Van de Ven, Delbecq, & Koenig, 1976). Integration may also be supported by establishing structural linkages across sub-units: One may define a cross-functional process that ensures that information is shared and that work is coordinated across sales and marketing; or one may alter the formal structure by having one manager oversee both departments.

Alignment between structure and strategy

There are many different ways of decomposing an organization and many ways of integrating different sub-units. To understand the rationale guiding different choices, we first need to consider the relationship between the organizational structure and the firm's strategy. This relationship was first systematically studied by Chandler (1962), in his analysis of the historical development of large firms during the years 1850–1920. During this time period, new national and international markets emerged. In response to these external developments, some firms were able to grow rapidly in size by developing new products and scaling up their production facilities. Chandler observed that as firms adopted a diversification strategy, moving into new product or geographical areas, they moved from a functional to a divisional structure (see Figure 1.2) (This observation was later supported by the empirical research carried out by Rumelt, 1974.) Unlike the more centralized functional structure, the multidivisional structure allowed relatively autonomous divisional executives to pursue growth within a given market segment, coordinated by a centralized executive office responsible for broad policies and coordination across the divisions. Chandler concluded that the multidivisional structure was a key innovation that simplified the management of diversity.

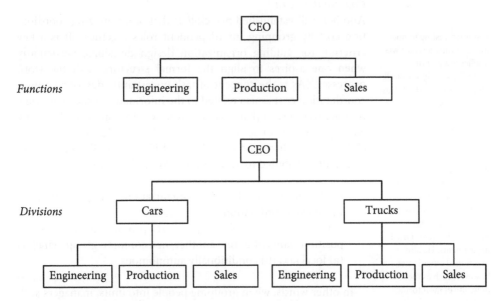

Figure 1.2 Comparison between functional and divisionalized structure[2].

The overall implication is that the structure of the organization needs to be aligned with new strategies that are formed in response to changes in the business environment. This insight generated a lot of research, particularly during the 1960s and 1970s. This line of research is referred to as *contingency theory* (for a review, see Donaldson, 2001). A key assumption is that high performing firms are those that find the right fit between the way their organizations are designed and the environmental contingencies that they face. For example, in stable, mature markets, consumers typically value reliable but low cost products. Firms in such market environments may thus succeed by focusing on efficient production. Work processes in these firms may be characterized by a high degree of formalization (i.e., operating procedures that are documented and standardized). The formal structure may be relatively centralized and the responsibilities of different units and individual jobs may be both stable and clearly defined. More dynamic market environments, on the other hand, require firms to innovate in order to provide new product features and/or adapt their strategies to respond to the actions of both existing competitors and new entrants. In such market environments, firms need to develop internal flexibility to succeed; they need a capability to respond to changing customer preferences, emerging technologies, or competitor actions. One element of this capability is an organizational structure that is easy to reconfigure. This may involve, among other things, allowing more autonomy to operating units (i.e., more decentralization), use of temporary project teams, and more reliance on quick and informal communication to achieve coordination across units.[3]

2 In the example shown in Figure 1.2, the divisions are based around product or product category; however divisions may also be defined based on geography or customer segments (see Chapter 3).

3 Although most scholars would probably support the overall tenet of contingency theory, there has been considerable debate about the specific linkage between environmental contingencies and organizational characteristics. Different studies have produced somewhat inconsistent results. See Donaldson (2001), Mintzberg (1979), and Pfeffer (1997) for detailed discussions.

Coordination cost

Another well-established principle is that of minimizing coordination cost by grouping interdependent roles together.[4] It is a key criterion for guiding organization design decisions, particularly when one aspires to align the formal structure with the work processes. (As is the concept of task uncertainty, described above, coordination cost is also related to the information processing view of organizations, in that it concerns how information is shared by employees within or across sub-units in the organization.) The principle was first discussed in Gulick and Urwick (1937) but is more frequently attributed to Thompson (1967), who stated (p. 57):

> Under norms of rationality, organizations group positions to minimize coordination costs.
>
> Organizations seek to place reciprocally interdependent positions tangent to one another, in a common group, which is (a) local and (b) conditionally autonomous.

In other words, when grouping people into units, managers seek (or should seek) to put the people that need to interact most frequently with each other (or most intensively) in the same sub-unit.[5] If a company expands into a new geographical region, it may make sense to place the people who are responsible for sales in that region in the same team, as they will probably need to coordinate with each other frequently. Similarly, if a company decides to implement a new IT system, it may make sense to place those responsible for configuring and rolling out the system in a separate project team.

The underlying assumption is that the cost of coordination is lower *within* than *across* a unit. In most cases, people who belong to the same unit coordinate effectively because they report to the same boss, pursue the same goals and priorities, share the same resources, and usually work on the same physical premises. Over time, members of a sub-unit are likely to develop a shared culture, further facilitating collaboration. On the other hand, if one is dependent upon other units to perform one's work, it will require coordination with people who usually report to another manager, pursue different goals and priorities, work on a different site, and who may hold different norms and assumptions. It goes without saying, then, that it is important to place the boundaries between units in the right places.

Key challenges facing the discipline

Although some organization design concepts are by now well established, the discipline has, on the whole, exerted much less of an impact than one would expect. Today, several scholars concede that the field was marginalized during a long period as a result of a general neglect of the importance of design, combined with a

4 It is interesting to note that coordination cost was implicitly a part of Chandler's analysis as well: One of his key insights was that a functional structure would lead to higher coordination cost than a multidivisional structure in a firm that pursues a diversification strategy, as functional departments such as sales and production would have to interact with a large number of other internal departments. He also mentioned other issues, however, such as the difficulty of monitoring performance in diversified, functional organizations.

5 Thompson described the grouping of "positions," but the same principle is also relevant at higher levels. For example, executives of a large multinational company, consisting of various business units and subsidiaries, may seek to minimize coordination costs by grouping related business units and subsidiaries into divisions or business areas.

disconnect between theory and practice in management research and teaching.

Until recently, few business schools offered courses in organization design as part of their undergraduate or MBA curriculums. The main focus has been on other subjects, such as corporate strategy, finance, and organizational behavior. More generally, Boland and Collopy (2004) contend that a "decision attitude" has prevailed in management education. Case studies often portray managers facing a set of alternative courses of action from which a choice must be made. Similarly, management techniques such as net present value analysis seem to assume that it is easy to come up with alternatives to consider, but difficult to choose among them. Boland and Collopy argue that the decision attitude is useful in stable situations where the feasible alternatives are well known, but that a "design attitude" is needed in more uncertain and demanding situations that require novel solutions.

As for research, despite the more than 30 years that have passed, Thompson's book from 1967 is still the most frequently cited book in the field (Heath & Staudenmayer, 2000). According to Jeffrey Pfeffer (1997), a leading management theorist, the key reason for this neglect is the general lack of interest in applied issues among business school faculty. A large number of studies are being published each year on organizational issues, but most of them are focused on extending or testing existing theories rather than on resolving issues facing practicing managers. The result is that managers rarely turn to academic research for guidance when considering how to design their organizations (Rynes, Brown, & Colberg, 2002). Pfeffer notes that there are some lines of research, such as contingency theory, that initially focused on issues that were managerially relevant. But even this research lost its relevance over time as it gradually employed more abstract, high level theoretical constructs that were further removed from the "design variables" that a manager can manipulate directly (see also Miller, Greenwood, & Prakash, 2009).

One possible cause of this problem is that traditional management research (particularly that published in leading US journals) is modeled on the natural sciences, adopting rigorous, quantitative methods in describing organizational functioning. Bettis (1991) argued that this research paradigm only leads to *explanation* but not to meaningful *prescription*:

> What would we think for example, of medical schools whose research did not address the treatment of disease, or electrical engineering departments whose research did not aim at the improvement of integrated circuit design and manufacture, or law schools whose research did not address the interpretation of the U.S. Constitution by the courts?
>
> (Bettis, 1991, p. 317)

Bettis concluded that business schools should be modeled on other professional schools and that business school faculty to a greater extent should undertake "problem driven" as opposed to "theory driven" research. He also believes that one needs to encourage the development of prescriptive implications based on the research, i.e., principles that managers can employ to re-design their organizations.

The lack of interest in organization design has also been related to a more general skepticism toward "structure" and toward hierarchical structures in particular. Hierarchies have been associated with a top-down, control-oriented management style (Leavitt, 2005). Indeed, a vast management literature has emerged since the 1950s that criticizes (hierarchical) structure and advocates more informal and "humane" ways of directing and coordinating work. Some of the most well-known concepts include participative management, transformational leadership, social networks, and self-managing teams. The advent of modern information systems reinforced the impression that hierarchical structures would be supplanted by new and flatter organizational forms. (One of the effects of hierarchy is to regulate information flow. With modern information systems, information could be transferred at low cost; one of the key predictions by management theorists was thus that modern information systems would lead to a radical decentralization of large hierarchies.) Well-known management gurus are among the most vocal opponents of (traditional) organizational designs. Tom Peters (2006) argued that the best companies are the most disorganized ones. Michael Hammer (2001), the originator of the term "Re-engineering," stated in his 2001 book that the goal should be to create a "structureless organization."

Managers who are influenced by this rhetoric may underestimate the importance of the formal aspects of organizing. Even if most managers accept that some structural forms are inappropriate in certain contexts, many have assumed that you can easily compensate for an inappropriate structure by encouraging informal collaboration across formal boundaries. For example, two product divisions that want to sell an integrated solution that includes both of the divisions' products may, instead of making any formal changes to their organization, simply create an ad hoc project team charged with developing and selling the integrated solution to customers. Unfortunately, after having performed several studies on this subject, Hansen (2009) found that as many as two-thirds of all attempts at informal collaboration across formal organizational boundaries fail to produce a positive return. Campbell (2012) concluded that informal collaboration is less effective than using teams with a formal mandate and an appointed manager.

The story of Oticon, a Danish hearing aid manufacturer, is a case in point. In 1990, it introduced a radical new organizational form called the "spaghetti organization." According to the then CEO,

Lars Kolind, the new organization should consist of "knowledge centres . . . connected by a multitude of links in a non-hierarchical structure" (Foss, 2003, p 333). The new organization only consisted of two formal layers: A management group of 10 people, and the employees, working in temporary projects. The goal was to remove the need for management intervention and create a self-organizing company. For example, employees could join whichever projects they wanted, and project managers were free to manage the projects in their preferred way, once the project was ratified in a management committee. Oticon was able to introduce several new products during the 1990s (such as in-the-ear hearing aids) and experienced increased growth and financial performance. It was hailed by Tom Peters – as well as several business magazines – as a prime example of a network-based, innovative company.[6] Just like Michael Hammer, the message seemed to be: "Structure is out."

A few years later, however, a Danish researcher, Nicolai Foss (2003), decided to examine the Oticon organization in more detail. His version is quite different from the story about Oticon that was created by business journalists and management gurus. First, he discovered that the organizational model was far from as decentralized as one was made to believe. In fact, the CEO, through his role as chairman of the so-called Projects and Products committee, retained ultimate decision-making authority, as no project would receive funding without the committee's approval. However, the real problem appeared after a project had been ratified: It became clear that the committee could at any time halt, change, or even close projects, and that this kind of intervention took place frequently. The result was frustration among project managers, who felt that their projects could be interrupted in arbitrary ways, and declining motivation among employees in general, because of the gap between the official rhetoric of delegation and the actual manner of governance in the firm. A second problem that Foss observed was related to competition for employees. Managers had no guarantee that they could actually carry their projects to an end, because of the risk that key team members would leave and instead join other projects. Oticon gradually realized that the organization was not working as intended, and made several changes to the model starting in 1995, including introducing a more layered organization. As Foss dryly concludes his paper: "the spaghetti organization may have been beset by organizational costs that came to dominate the benefit aspects" (Foss, 2003, p. 332).

In fairness, we should note that even management gurus learn and adjust their message accordingly. In a subsequent article, Michael Hammer acknowledged that unclear accountability is a common cause of failure in process improvement efforts (Hammer, 2004). Since structure basically can be defined as an accountability hierarchy (a system for allocating roles and responsibilities), Hammer seems to concede that being structureless may not be such

6 Peters has cited Oticon as a role model in several presentations and at the time of printing of this book still referred to the company on his web site: http://tompeters.com/columns/one-thousand-people-one-thousand-careers/

a good idea after all. Moreover, it should be emphasized that the morale of the Oticon case is not that we should stop experimenting with new ways of organizing. Indeed, Oticon introduced a number of important concepts, which we should try to study and refine. Importantly, Nicolai Foss notes in his paper that the spaghetti organization might have been a viable organizational form, had it been more carefully designed.

Even as traditional organization theory has yielded increasingly little influence on managerial practice (Miller, Greenwood, & Prakash, 2009), and much of the rhetoric directed at managers has focused on other issues than design, there is one notable exception from this general state of affairs, namely *organizational economics* (Williamson, 1981; Jensen, 1983). As pointed out in Pfeffer (1997), economists have recently displayed an eagerness to take on topics traditionally left to psychologists and sociologists. Economic models and methods have been used to study such organizational issues as the effects of rewards and incentives on performance, the boundaries between firms and markets, and the advantages and disadvantages of different organizational structures.

However, the import of economics-based models into organization theory and the use of such models in providing guidance to managers are controversial. A number of well-known scholars have argued that these models are ill suited as a prescriptive frameworks (Ghoshal, 2005; Pfeffer, 1997; Davis et al., 1997).[7] The economics-based models are based on somewhat pessimistic assumptions about human nature, as they assume that people are primarily driven by self-interest, and will act "opportunistically," that is, seek to maximize their own "utility function" rather than that of the organization of which they are a member. One concern is that the application of these ideas will lead to control-oriented management practices, where the main task is seen as using surveillance, monitoring, and authority to curb opportunistic behavior. There is also only mixed empirical support for many of the key predictions made in economics-based theories (Donaldson, 1995; Pfeffer, 1997; Ghoshal, 2005).

We may add that this perspective is also of limited value in illuminating some of the more prosaic challenges that organizational designers must deal with. For example, the organizational economics literature has focused on conflicts of interest between the principal and the agent,[8] assuming the principal and agent are already known. If one were to apply this approach at a lower level in an organization, the initial problem would probably be to define who the principals and the agents actually are. Organizational designers will frequently encounter situations where these roles are poorly defined or where the same individual plays both the role of agent and principal in different processes, or where that the same agent is responsible toward multiple and poorly coordinated principals.

7 For an opposing viewpoint, see Felin & Foss (2009).

8 An agent is a person who acts on behalf of others, and the principal is the person or group who authorizes an agent to act on their behalf. In the organizational economics literature, the typical issue is the relationship between the chief executive (the agent), who acts on behalf of the shareholders.

The value of effective designs

Given the challenges described, there is a need to consider how the organization design discipline can best adapt to stay relevant. How can we ensure that managers fully exploit the potential of effective design? How can we develop design knowledge that can be of help to those that seek to improve the effectiveness of their organizations? What can we do to generate more attention to organization design among business school faculty?

In the following, some important developments are described that may contribute to revitalizing the discipline: The adoption of a *design attitude*, the introduction of the term *architecture* as an overarching concept, a stronger focus on purpose and requirements in design methodologies, and the introduction of a new, solutions-oriented research paradigm that can improve the interface between research and practice. But the first priority should probably be to reaffirm the importance of the concept itself.

It is clear that organization design decisions have a major impact on how an organization functions and performs. The most obvious examples may be decisions regarding the vertical layering of organizations. Such decisions define the hierarchical structure – in particular, the number of vertical layers, which in turn determines the size of units and the span of control for each manager (the number of direct reports per manager and the size of sub-units) and the hierarchical placement of different functions and roles (for example, whether different staff functions are placed at the corporate level, or decentralized to the divisional level). The vertical structuring of a firm also has a direct impact on costs: A flatter organization will have fewer managers (which usually are the more expensive resource). Indeed, one explanation for why organizations are pyramidal in shape is the fact that resources become more expensive the higher you go in the hierarchy.[9] Decisions regarding vertical structure may also have longer term, more indirect effects on both work processes and individual jobs. Flat structures generally have smaller status differences and provide more autonomy for the individual worker. On the other hand, flat structures require that managers spend more time to resolve differences and coordinate the efforts of their many subordinates (Mintzberg, 1979). Flat structures also provide fewer ladders in the internal career paths available to employees (i.e., a reduced chance of promotion).

There are a number of empirical studies that evaluate the impact of organizational design on organizational functioning. Some studies have investigated the effects of grouping decisions. These studies generally show, as would be expected, that people belonging to the same formal unit communicate more frequently with each other than with people in other units (Egeberg, 1989; Scharpf, 1977, cited in Mintzberg, 1979). The introduction of communication technologies such as e-mail has not changed these patterns. Kleinbaum (2008)

9 Of course, in practice this issue is more complicated, as managers provide value by supervising employees and coordinating work processes. So in practice, the basic trade-off in terms of designing the vertical structure is the value versus the cost of management.

used data from a large firm's e-mail server to examine e-mail messages sent by more than 30,000 people over a three-month period. After excluding some types of messages, such as mass mailings, Kleinbaum looked at who people were most likely to communicate with via e-mail. If formal structure played no role, one would expect there to be equally frequent communication across different units in the firm. Yet even when controlling for other factors such as gender and salary, he found that people were 10 times more likely to communicate with someone within their own business unit than with someone belonging to a different business unit.

It is also well documented that organization design has an impact on individual motivation and productivity. Several studies have looked at sources of stress, and concluded that it is not only the workload or pace of work that create stress, but the design of the job itself (Wong et al., 2007). In particular, employees may experience stress due to role conflicts and role ambiguity, which in turn is related to the existence of (and nature of) interdependencies. Employees may be subject to conflicting expectations from different parties, or face uncertainty about with whom or what they need to coordinate. As we will consider in greater depth in the following chapters, these are typical symptoms of complex organizations, and reflect managerial decisions regarding the definition of individual roles, allocation of responsibility, and grouping of sub-units.

There are also a number of studies that consider the effect of organization design on organizational level performance. It is well established that choices with regards to structure can have an impact on quality, customer satisfaction, and productivity, as well as on financial outcomes such as revenue growth and profitability. Burton, Lauridsen, and Obel (2002) studied 224 small and medium sized firms. Building on contingency theory (Donaldson, 2001), they reasoned that firms need to be designed in accordance with the situational demands. More specifically, they hypothesized that firms with organizational designs that were not in accordance with the external business environment or other contingencies (i.e., "misfits") would suffer a performance loss. They developed 24 hypotheses related to different misfits. One example of a misfit would be a firm that has a highly centralized organization, in an environment that is highly uncertain. According to organizational theory, an uncertain environment requires an organization that can adapt to changes, something that requires a willingness to delegate decisions to lower levels of the organization (i.e., decentralization). Another example of a misfit would be a large organization with an informal structure without sub-units or departments. According to organization theory, large organizations need to be compartmentalized into smaller sub-units that specialize on certain tasks. Burton et al. (2002) found that even a single misfit led to a significant loss in firm performance, measured as return on assets (see other examples of studies in Table 1.1.)

Table 1.1 Selected studies evaluating the effect of different organizational structures and/or the impact of changes in structure over time

Author(s)	Topic and sample	Key findings
Ghoshal & Nohria (1993)	The organizational design of 41 large, multi-national firms	Firms with better alignment (or fit) between their organization and the business environment had higher return on net assets and higher revenue growth
Lee, Sridhar, Henderson, & Palmatier (2015)	The effect of adopting a customer-based organizational structure in 174 firms	A customer based structure increased responsiveness and customer satisfaction, but also increased coordination costs
Hoskisson (1987)	The performance effects of adopting a multidivisional structure – longitudinal study of 62 firms	The multidivisional structure increased the rate of return for unrelated diversifiers (firms with products that are not related)
Ouchi (2006)	Implementation of a decentralized organization design in three large public school districts (Edmonton, Seattle, and Houston)	Decentralization yielded large improvements in student achievement and in organizational efficiency
Nagappan, Murphy, & Basili (2008)	The influence of project organization on software quality – examination of defects in 50 million lines of code created by programmers	The organization of the projects predicted quality with a very high degree of precision (e.g., the lower the number of different organizational units that participated on a software module, the higher the quality)
Robinson & Stocken (2013)	Centralization versus decentralization of decisions rights in 2,902 U.S. based international firms	Inappropriate decentralization of decision rights to subsidiaries reduced firm level performance (i.e. decentralization that is not warranted given e.g., the local market or need for integration within the firm)
Ater, Givati, & Rigbi (2014)	Transfer of responsibility for housing arrestees from the police to the prison authority in Israel	The reform led to an increase in the number of arrests and a decrease in crime, but arrest quality, measured by the likelihood of indictment, fell
Kuhn (2011)	Effect of delayering (removal of management layers) in 662 Swiss firms between 2000 and 2004	Delayering significantly increased firm performance
Nahm, Vonderembse, & Koufteros (2003)	The relationship between organizational structure, Lean manufacturing practices, and plant performance in 244 firms	Firms with few hierarchical layers combined with a high level of horizontal integration had higher performance
Karim (2006)	The process of configuration (re-design) of business units within 250 firms in the medical sector	Reconfiguration – i.e., adding, merging, and splitting business units – happens frequently and is perceived as beneficial

(Continued)

Table 1.1 (Continued)

Author(s)	Topic and sample	Key findings
Karim & Kaul (2015)	The effect of structural recombination on firm innovation – 71 firms in the medical sector	Structural recombination (i.e., merging internal units) had a positive effect on innovation when the units that are combined had complementary knowledge resources

The most dramatic illustrations of the value of organization design come from studies of horizontal integration. One study, published in a medical journal, investigated the outcomes over two decades for patients with a serious form of cancer (high grade bone sarcoma) (Aksnes et al., 2006). Although the same basic medical techniques were available during the time period of the study (1980–1999), the survival rate increased from 39% to 53% (the use of chemotherapy remained stable during the period, while the amputation rate decreased from 64% to 23%). The authors concluded that the improved survival rate was due to more effective use of existing medical techniques, which in turn was made possible by better organization of the hospital's cancer treatment teams. During the period, the responsibility for treating this form of cancer was centralized (transferred to one institution) and new patient databases were introduced which allowed more systematic monitoring of the activities and outcomes of the cancer treatment program. But the most significant change, according to the authors,[10] was that *the specialists involved in cancer treatment were organized into multidisciplinary teams,* where all decisions regarding diagnosis and treatment were taken by the group as a whole.

Indeed, many crises and breakdowns have been attributed to a lack of effective integration. For example, the failure to prevent the 9/11 terrorist attacks has been partly blamed on an inability to share information across different US agencies responsible for security. During the months leading up to the attacks, several agencies were receiving frequent, but fragmentary reports about threats, including reports about an imminent attack in the US by terrorists associated with Al Qaeda. However, officials employed by the various agencies often failed to share information across the different US bodies and agencies responsible for law enforcement, intelligence, and security. For example, it was known to the FBI that potential terrorists were undergoing flight training in the US, but this information was not passed on to the Federal Aviation Authorities, who issued a pilot's license to one of the terrorists. To investigate the facts and circumstances relating to the terrorist attacks, President Bush set up the 9/11 Commission. In their final report published in 2004,[11] many of the recommendations center on organizational changes required for more effective counterterrorism intelligence. The report points to "structural barriers to performing joint intelligence work" (p. 408)

10 This interpretation of the results was also emphasized in a presentation of the paper held by one of the authors, January 23, 2008.

11 *The 9/11 Commission report*. Washington, DC: National Commission on Terrorist Attacks upon the United States. Available from: www.9–11commission. gov/report/911Report.pdf

and also laments the complexity of a system of 15 different agencies in intelligence gathering and analysis (including the FBI, CIA, immigration authorities, customs service, Federal Aviation Administration, National Security Agency, etc.). One of the key recommendations made was to establish a central body, led by a National Intelligence Director, to oversee the different agencies.

At other times, however, organizational effectiveness is not caused by integration, but rather by separation of roles and processes that are incompatible. One example is how to manage innovation projects in established companies, often referred to as the "exploration versus exploitation" dilemma in management theory. The idea is that established companies need to exploit their existing capabilities to serve current customers, while exploring new products and services that may help them succeed in the future. O'Reilly and Tushman (2004) compared 35 attempts at launching breakthrough innovations by 15 business units. In particular, they examined how these innovation projects were organized.[12] In some business units, the project teams were integrated in the existing structure. In other business units, the project teams were separated out from the rest of the organization (see Figure 1.3). O'Reilly and Tushman found that 90% of the teams that were organized as a separate unit reached their goals, compared to only 25% of the teams that were integrated in the existing organization.[13] There are several possible explanations. It may require different skills and a distinct culture to develop something entirely new. It may be helpful for those who develop new products or services to be buffered from the day-to-day realities of the operations until they have a viable concept. The new product or service may also in some cases rely on a business model that competes with the current offerings of the firms, which makes it difficult to integrate the teams in the existing organization.

Table 1.2 summarizes some hypothesized effects of organization design decisions. In the table, the "direct outcomes" are the immediate effects following from organization design choices. For example, the number of layers, the number of sub-units, the size of units, etc. are direct consequences of decomposition and grouping decisions. The causal chain is somewhat longer for "intermediary" outcomes, and for "eventual outcomes" organization design choices

12 The text is a simplified description of O'Reilly & Tushman's (2004) study, which differentiated between four different ways of organizing innovation. However, the conclusion that I present is accurate.

13 However, we should note that innovation teams that were separated still reported to the same higher level manager as the heads of the units in the existing organization. In this manner, the innovation teams stayed connected to the leadership team, which ensured that their efforts were aligned with the corporate priorities.

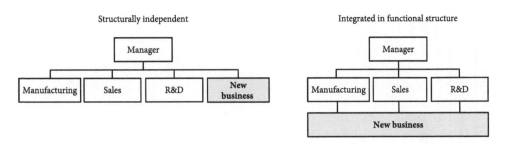

Figure 1.3 Comparison between two ways of organizing innovation efforts

Table 1.2 Traditional focus areas of organization design and some hypothesized effects

Key design activity	Description	Direct outcomes	Intermediary outcomes	Eventual outcomes
Decomposition and grouping	Sub-division of the organization into lower level elements (divisions, departments, teams, etc.) or aggregation of lower level elements (e.g., roles/jobs) into higher order units (e.g., teams, departments, divisions).	• Number of layers (the degree to which an organization has many layers of management) • Specialization/differentiation (the number of sub-units and the scope of their responsibilities) • Size of units and span of control (the number of people in each unit, and consequently the number of people reporting to each manager) • Locus of decision making (the degree to which decision-making authority is placed at a high versus low level in the organizational hierarchy) • Employee costs (cost arising from the number of employees and managers required at different levels of the organization)	• Degree of alignment with strategy (the extent to which the required organization has the capabilities, structures, and processes to realize its strategic goals) • Structural coherence (the extent to which the different units have been defined in a consistent manner in order to minimize overlaps, gaps, and goal conflicts) • Communication patterns (the extent to which people interact within versus between units) • Coordination costs (the costs associated with exchanging information and adjusting to actions of interdependent units) • Career paths (the vertical and horizontal career paths) • Role clarity (the extent to which the purpose and expectations of jobs are perceived as clear by the job holders) • Autonomy and authority (the degree to which jobs allow decision making latitude) • Inter-unit conflict (the frequency and severity of conflicts between sub-units)	• Overall performance (the organization's ability to attain its objectives and satisfy stakeholder expectations) • Innovation (the organization's ability to introduce new products, services, and processes) • Productivity (the outputs produced in relation to the inputs expended) • Customer satisfaction (customers' level of satisfaction with products, services, and support that they receive) • Quality (the number and severity of defects) • Employee satisfaction (employees' level of satisfaction with their job and their organization)

Key design activity	Description	Direct outcomes	Intermediary outcomes	Eventual outcomes
Integration	Establishment of mechanisms to facilitate vertical and horizontal coordination	• Level of vertical and horizontal integration (the degree to which there have been defined formal or informal processes crossing the main vertical organizational boundaries)	*Same as above, plus:* • Information flow and knowledge transfer (the extent to which (and the speed at which) information is actively shared across vertical and horizontal boundaries) • Resource utilization and sharing (the degree to which resources are utilized across internal boundaries) • Joint value creation (the extent to which sub-units collaborate in creating new business opportunities) • Social networks (the extent of informal ties among members of different sub-units)	

only have an indirect impact on the outcomes listed, together with many other internal and external factors. As the examples above indicate, there does exist empirical support for many of the hypothesized effects indicated in Table 1.2, but future research will undoubtedly further our understanding of the nature and strength of the linkages between different design choices and organizational outcomes.

Table 1.2 is based on the relatively narrow definition of design as the decomposition and integration of formal structures. It is also based on the traditional conception of organization design as an element of *strategy implementation* rather than *strategy formulation*, in other words, as a topic that one can attend to once the strategic goals have been set.

More recent theorizing suggests that this conceptualization may be too restrictive in some cases, in that design also influences the ability to *form* new strategies. Chandler's (1962) dictum was that "structure follows strategy" and the contingency theorists similarly operationalized structure as the *dependent variable*, whereas the environment and strategy were defined as the *independent variables* (Mintzberg, 1979). Rather than adapting the structure to the strategy, however, successful firms also take their existing structure into account when choosing which strategy to pursue. This possibility was documented in a study of US pizza restaurants reported in Yin and Zajac (2004). The results show that franchised stores were more likely to pursue complex strategies that allowed them to capitalize on their flexibility and local responsiveness as semi-independent entities, whereas company-owned stores favored simpler strategies that emphasized predictability and control.

For firms facing dynamic environments, the very distinction between strategy and structure may itself become blurred. It is rarely feasible for top managers to create longer-term strategies if the environment is undergoing rapid change. And even if it was possible to strategize from the top, Roberts (2004) pointed out that by the time a new, long-term strategy would be communicated and the organization restructured, the environment might have changed again. Management can set a broad strategic direction, but is reliant upon the decisions taken at the various levels within the organization in order to respond to on-going market developments. What management can do, however, is to create the right structure and processes to allow effective strategic decision making at lower levels of the organization. In this sense, *strategy becomes a design for an adaptive organizational structure* (Haeckel, 1999).

Design attitude

During the last few years, there have been held several conferences and workshops on design, suggesting an increased interest in the concept among both practitioners and researchers. Some of these conferences have taken a broad view – considering design as a generic approach to problem solving, relevant to all fields of management. In contrast to the prevailing "decision attitude," the goal of some key proponents, such as the group summoned by Boland and Collopy (2004), is to instill a "design attitude," inspiring and energizing new designs for products, services, and processes that are both profitable and humanly satisfying.

What implications would follow from adopting a "design attitude" in terms of how we think about the form and function of organizations? One key implication is probably that we need to consider how to conduct effective *design processes*. Traditionally, a lot of attention within organization design has been focused organizational *models*: Is a divisionalized structure better than a functional structure? Should companies adopt a market-based structure? Is a process-based structure a viable alternative to the functional organization? The development and selection of the right organization model certainly remain important issues. We need to develop better organizational models, ensure that this knowledge is disseminated to managers, and learn from the experience of implementing the models.

However, the design processes in which organizational models are developed and selected are also important. Managers face a number of challenges in such processes: How should they deal with multiple, conflicting requirements? How can they create consensus for change among different internal stakeholders? How do they ensure that the design process actually achieves its intent? An improved understanding of design processes may make it possible to provide more effective tools and methods to support managers.

The challenges faced by managers are similar to those faced by practitioners in other "design sciences," such as architecture and engineering. Whether one is designing a product, a building, or an organization, the task is similar: One must try to understand a system of multiple components, identify the requirements from different stakeholders, visualize possible solutions, and create a blueprint for how the solution can be realized (Liedtka, 2000). Although the *content* is different, the *process* of design is similar across different fields.

For product designers, sketching and modeling are important tools when they try to visualize "what might be." In organizations, visual depictions of business processes and reporting structures are often thought of mainly as tools for communicating new designs to people who have not been part of the decision process. However, these are visual tools that potentially play a much more important role:

> The problem space that a manager deals with in her mind or in her computer is dependent upon the way she represents the situation that she faces. The first step in any problem-solving

> episode is representing the problem, and to a large extent, that representation has the solution hidden within it.
>
> (Boland & Collopy, 2004, p. 9)

In addition to helping a manger frame a problem, tools also play an important social role in enabling "cognitive coordination," that is, helping to establish shared reference points among a diverse group of stakeholders in the design process (Werr et al., 1997). Sometimes, the choice of tools contributes to an unnecessary narrowing of the "problem space." Using an organization chart as the main tool in a design process may create clarity with regard to the vertical structure and reporting lines but may lead participants to ignore possibilities for improvements in terms of how units coordinate and integrate their efforts. The question is thus how we can develop effective tools to support design processes. This is an issue we shall return to repeatedly in the remaining chapters of this book.

Organizational architecture

In the literature, the term *organizational architecture* is increasingly used instead of the more traditional term *organizational structure*. The difference is not merely semantic. Organizational architecture refers to a wider set of characteristics than the term organizational structure (Gerstein, 1992). Organizational structure is usually defined as the formal reporting relationships that define roles and authority at different levels of the organization. Architecture potentially encompasses other elements, such as processes used for governance and even informal means of coordinating and organizing work (e.g., social networks and ad hoc commitments made among organizational members). The notion of architecture may also help us to see organizations, and the design process, from a different perspective. It encourages us to think about the process of building organizations, the fit between the organization and its environment, and the coherence of different design elements.

Gerstein (1992) reviewed the history of architecture and asked what lessons we could learn from physical architecture that would help us design more effective organizations. He noted, first of all, that *architecture is purposeful*. Architecture is defined as the art and science of creating structures or systems whose function fulfill an intended purpose. Similarly, one can view organizational architecture as the conceptual design of key roles, processes, and structures intended to realize the firm's strategic intent and the requirements of key stakeholders. In other words, the process of organization design must start with a fundamental understanding of the purposes to be served by the organization.

We often think about designs as applying only to unique instances, such as a product or a building (Kennedy, 2002). But organizational architectures can be adaptive and "generative" platforms, that is, allow the firm to develop and grow by generating an infinite set of processes by replicating, scaling, and reconfiguring a finite set of basic architectural elements. For example, a large manufacturing firm may create a blueprint for how to organize its plants that specifies how to design processes, roles, and operating procedures at the plants. Creating such a blueprint is a vehicle for a firm to codify its internal best practices and create a platform for knowledge sharing. But it may also help the firm expand, by reducing the time and cost that it takes to establish a new plant or re-design an existing plant. The blueprint may even be flexible enough to support a strategic move into another product area, even if it requires somewhat different machinery or manufacturing processes. In this sense, architecture is *future oriented*. An architect's building "should preferably be ahead of its time when planned so that it will be in keeping with the times as long as it stands" (Rasmussen, 1991, cited in Gerstein, 1992, pp. 14–15).

Architectures should represent *unifying and coherent structures* (McDavid, 1999). As Stephen Haeckel (1999) pointed out, a collection of decisions that make local sense are unlikely to cohere into a purposeful organizational design. Different parts of the system must "fit together." If a firm does not, at a minimum, have some common principles and priorities, local decision makers will have no common frame or standard with which decision alternatives can be compared. A manufacturing firm not only needs to ensure that each plant works effectively, but that the different plants that it operates function effectively together in a manufacturing network.

This presents us with the apparent contradiction of *designing for autonomous action*. Architectures should enable coherency by providing a *context* for individual action and decision making rather than by dictating individual behavior. Blueprints for how to organize a plant are likely to include certain mandatory elements (e.g., procedures for health, safety, and environment). But they may also contain many optional elements, intended primarily as a guide to decision making, as well as recommended practices that local plant managers are encouraged to develop further, based on the experience that they gain locally.

Axiomatic design theory

The fact that the design process is fairly generic may allow us to borrow tools and methods that are used for design in other professions. Within the engineering sciences, there is an approach called axiomatic design theory (Suh, 2001), which may be particularly suited to organization design.

As already mentioned, scholars within contingency theory have focused on how one can select an organizational structure that fits the key contingencies, including the strategy of the firm. However, the authors in this field have focused less strongly on why and how models are developed/adjusted to the unique requirements of a particular organization. The assumption has perhaps been that by first considering the firm's overall strategy, one would have enough information to select the right organizational structure. Indeed, Galbraith (2002, p. 13) stated, "Strategy establishes the goals and criteria for choosing among organizational forms." However, the strategy is rarely specific enough to allow choices to be made about alternative organizational designs, particularly at lower levels of the organization. It is not necessarily the case, either, that feasible decision alternatives even exist (Boland & Collopy, 2004). In such cases the main challenge is not to choose among pre-existing alternatives (e.g., a functional or divisional structure), but to conceive of and develop good alternatives. The high-level organizational models presented in textbooks (including the present one) are, at best, ideas that can be further developed and adapted for the particular organization that one is (re)designing. If we want to ensure the development of purposeful architectures, we need an approach that can help elucidate what the requirements are and ensure that a design is developed in a manner that maximizes the chance that the requirements will be met.

In systems theory (Ackoff & Emery, 1972), one distinguishes between the *purpose* that a system is serving (why it exists), the *functions* that it is intended to perform (what it does), and the design parameters (how it is done). Axiomatic design theory (Suh, 2001) builds on this distinction by considering the relationship between functions and design parameters (Figure 1.4).

Articulating and agreeing on a purpose for the system to be designed is fundamental in all design activities, including the design of organizations. Stephen Haeckel (1999) has called this the *reason for being* – managers must be able to explain why the organization (or a sub-unit) exists. Provided that a purpose has been defined, it will be the starting point for identifying specific functions or *functional requirements* (FRs) to the system. A function is *what* we want to achieve – a statement identifying a necessary characteristic or capability of a product (or system) for it to have value or utility for the user (or for a group of stakeholders). Ideally the FR is phrased in a solution-neutral manner (usually starting out with a verb), to avoid narrowing the space of possible solutions. For a car, a functional requirement may be "transport passengers." In organizational designs, a functional requirement can best be thought of as the purpose or desired outcomes produced by an entire organization or by a sub-unit (for example, "market and sell cars"), which in turn can be decomposed into more detailed requirements.

A *design parameter* specifies *how* we intend to satisfy a functional requirement. For a product, a design parameter may be a physical component or mechanism ("vehicle with engine"), whereas it will be an organizational sub-unit, team, or process in organizational design (for example, "sales department"). It may also be an individual role – if that role performs a unique function in the

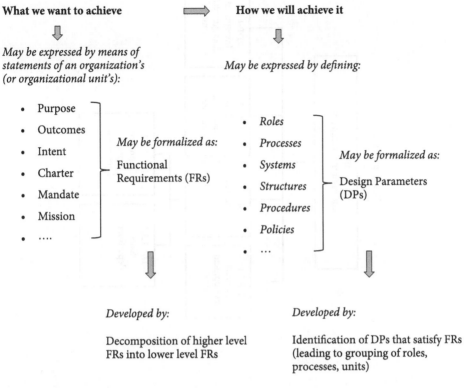

What we want to achieve ⟹ **How we will achieve it**

May be expressed by means of statements of an organization's (or organizational unit's):

May be expressed by defining:

- Purpose
- Outcomes
- Intent   *May be formalized as:*
- Charter   Functional Requirements (FRs)
- Mandate
- Mission
- ....

- *Roles*
- *Processes*
- *Systems*   *May be formalized as:*
- *Structures*   Design Parameters (DPs)
- *Procedures*
- *Policies*
- *...*

Developed by:

Decomposition of higher level FRs into lower level FRs

Developed by:

Identification of DPs that satisfy FRs (leading to grouping of roles, processes, units)

Figure 1.4 Functional requirements and design parameters and more commonly used terms to describe organizations.

organization. Design parameters are usually phrased using a noun to distinguish them from the functional requirements.

These concepts provide a refined understanding of how one may design an organization. The key proposition is that both functional requirements – and design parameters corresponding to each functional requirement – should be explicitly defined as part of the design process. As explained by Suh (2001), one starts in the "what" domain and then goes to the "how" domain. Consider the design of a life insurance company (Figure 1.5). The overall mission or strategic intent (Hamel & Prahalad, 1989) may be stated as, for example, that of "maximising profits by offering life insurance products that provide security and protection for individuals and their families." We may adopt this mission statement as our top level functional requirement. We then proceed by determining the corresponding design parameter ("Life insurance company"). We then go back to create the functional requirements at the next level. For an insurance company, there are typically four key functional requirements: First, one must develop products that customers perceive as attractive (one might add that the products should be attractive to the company as well) a key challenge is to set a price (insurance

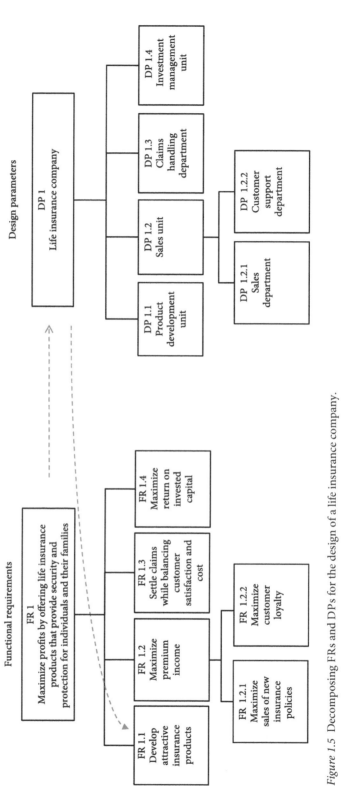

Figure 1.5 Decomposing FRs and DPs for the design of a life insurance company.

premium) that is affordable, while taking into account the insurer's risk, based on an assessment of the probability and cost of a loss. Secondly, one must maximize premium income, by maximizing sales of new insurance policies (here one might add that one should also ensure that customers don't deflect once they have bought a policy). Third, one must administer the pension plans and handle claims. Finally, one must maximize the return on invested capital. (A key source of income for insurance companies is the profits earned from investments funded by the income from the sales of insurance policies.) Each of these requirements is satisfied by the definition of an organizational unit.[14] This process of decomposing proceeds layer by layer until one has provided enough information to implement the design.

The design parameters listed in Figure 1.5 represent the structure of a traditional insurance company. However, other design options exist. One key factor is the extent to which an insurance company is vertically integrated (i.e., the extent to which it controls lower-level processes involved in the development and delivery of its products and services). There are insurance companies that do not have any internal sales units and that instead rely on intermediaries to distribute their products. There are even insurance companies that outsource the investment management process to competitors deemed as having superior capabilities in this area.

It's important to note that although design parameters, in principle, are formulated to satisfy functional requirements, the relationship is to some extent reciprocal in the sense that high level design parameters will also have an influence on lower level functional requirements. For example, if an insurance company defines a sales unit as a DP, it may at a lower level identify "Manage sales process" as an FR, whereas this will not be a relevant FR for a company that has chosen an intermediary channel to sell and distribute products. (Such a company may instead identify "Manage intermediaries" as a lower level functional requirement.)

The *design hierarchy* created by decomposition is somewhat different from the term *hierarchical structure*. As Thompson (1967) himself pointed out, it is rather unfortunate that the term hierarchy is associated only with "highness" and "lowness" related to authority relationships. Although the chosen design will be translated into an organizational structure, which also represents a hierarchy of authority, axiomatic theory is primarily about defining the *hierarchy of functionality* (Haeckel, 1999). Each level in a design hierarchy is not only higher than the level below, but also represents a more inclusive clustering, one that combines and integrates the functions of lower level units.

There are several advantages to using these principles derived from axiomatic theory. By defining functional requirements, one orients the process toward objectives and desired outcomes. Second, by gradually decomposing both FRs and DPs, one creates a design

14 Minimization of cost is another possible functional requirement. In this case, it applies to all of the design parameters and may thus instead be treated separately, as *a constraint* (see Suh, 2001, and discussion below).

15 The ability to link higher and lower level objectives is an important feature in the axiomatic approach. A key shortcoming of many "mission statements" is that they remain isolated, high level statements that rarely are operationalized. In contrast, a design hierarchy developed according to the axiomatic approach is not terminated before one has developed a design that can be realized.

In the literature, it is common to distinguish between two types of design. The first is strategic design – top-down processes aimed at aligning the overall structure with the strategy, and usually focused only on defining the main units, key executive roles, and their reporting relationships. Operational design, on the other hand, is the more frequent adjustments made to roles and structures within sub-units, often driven by process improvement initiatives with targets related to quality or cost. This distinction is also relevant here. Operational design is simply the specification of lower level FRs and DPs.

hierarchy that links higher level objectives to lower level roles and processes.[15] Third, this approach should facilitate the creation of coherent designs if one ensures that lower level FRs collectively satisfy the FR at the higher level. Finally, by mapping the FRs against the DPs in a so-called design matrix (as illustrated in Table 1.3) one may evaluate the correspondence between FRs and DPs more systematically. The most obvious requirement is that there should exist DPs to satisfy every FR. The approach also encourages an analysis of dependencies among the different FRs and DPs to control the total number of FRs and ensure that the achievement of one FR does not compromise the achievement of another (a topic which will be discussed in more detail in the next chapter).

By abstracting key features from a specific design, the tools used in axiomatic design should facilitate effective communication between practitioners, and allow comparisons across organizations. For example, by mapping different insurance companies by means of a matrix as shown in Table 1.3, one would quickly be able to identify the key features of the design chosen by the different companies (of course, provided that the information the matrices contain has been accurately recorded).

In contrast, the PowerPoint presentations that are used in most organizations to describe structures and processes often fail to convey the underlying logic of the designs being presented. Different individuals may use a slightly different format for describing the same organizational characteristics (perhaps as a result of the relative ease by which graphical symbols can be created with today's software). Many presentations do not explicitly list the design criteria (why a given design was chosen), what the functional requirements of the organization are (what it is supposed to do or what goals it is supposed to achieve), let alone how functional requirements map to the design parameters. Without such information it is difficult to systematically share knowledge and compare organizational models. In contrast, the mapping tools used in axiomatic design provide a standard "vocabulary and grammar" for describing organizational models.

One will rarely have complete freedom in defining the design parameters. There will usually be a number of both internal and external constraints that reduce the number of design options that are available. Internal stakeholders, such as worker unions, may oppose some of the options that one is considering. As for external constraints, there may be laws and regulations for the industry that also have implications for organizational choices. For example, the financial services industry in most countries is already highly regulated, but following the finance crisis in 2007–2008, even stronger regulation was introduced. There is an international body – the Basel Committee on Banking Supervision – which develops guidelines and supervisory standards for banks that member states may adopt in statutory form. (In Europe, similar guidelines for insurance companies are developed as part of the solvency initiative.) Some of

Table 1.3 Design matrix that maps functional requirements against design parameters

Functional requirements	Design parameters			
	Product development unit	*Sales unit*	*Pensions and claims settlement unit*	*Investment management unit*
Develop attractive insurance products	X			
Maximize premium income		X		
Administer client accounts and settlements			X	
Maximize return on managed funds				X

the guidelines being developed affect organization design directly, for example, by specifying the roles, processes, and structure of the risk management function in financial institutions.

"Layers" of design parameters

We mentioned that roles, units, and processes are examples of organizational design parameters.[16] This topic deserves some more deliberation, as it goes to the heart of how we define organization design. The term was traditionally defined rather narrowly, as the formal and semi-formal means used to divide labor and integrate the work of different roles and sub-units. More recently, the tendency is to employ very wide definitions of organization design, and some practitioners and authors now include informal and emergent aspects of organizations, such as corporate culture, or individual level characteristics, such as attitudes and skills.

Yet as Mintzberg (1979) stated, design assumes discretion, that is, an ability to alter a system. This means that our definitional framework should only include parameters that a manager actually can manipulate. At the same time, it should be broad enough to include all of the relevant design parameters that are at a manager's disposal. Moreover, recognizing that design activities may take place at many levels – from individual roles to the overall structure of large organizations – we should try to avoid restricting our definition to design parameters that are only applicable at one particular level.

Given these considerations, we would suggest that organizational design parameters can be conceptualized as five different "layers" (Table 1.4). The first layer is the *governance model*, which defines the formal roles, decision rights, and accountabilities. The second layer is the *operating model*, which decomposes the core activities of the organization into units and processes. The third layer is the *resource*

16 In axiomatic design theory, there is no formal restriction with regards to elements that may be considered a design parameter as long as they fulfil a function and can be manipulated by the designer. In the examples provided by Suh (2001) design parameters include both physical components and the effects produced by those components.

Table 1.4 Layers of organizational design parameters

Design parameter	Examples
Governance model	• Formal reporting structure • Decision rights (decision making authority of different levels/roles) and accountabilities • Decision bodies (management teams, steering groups, technology boards, etc.)
Operating model	• Work units and interfaces • Key processes
Resource model	• Designation of units as cost, revenue, or profit centre • Principles for internal transactions (e.g., whether cost or market price is to be used) • How a sub-unit is to be funded
Contracting model	• Designation of units as either (internal) customer or (internal) supplier • Principles and processes to be used to establish and fulfil commitments toward other units
Social network model	• Network forums • Mentoring program • Knowledge management system

model, which defines the principles and processes used to fund units and allocate resources. The fourth is the *contracting model*, which specifies how a role or unit will interact with other roles or units to establish agreements and fulfill commitments. Finally, we also include a layer called the *social network model*, to cover design parameters that are chosen to deliberately shape the social network and create ties between individuals, for example, in order to facilitate efficient knowledge sharing and coordination across two formally defined units. Together with the corresponding functional requirements, these five layers constitute an "organizational architecture," that is, a complete design of an organization.

These design parameters are relevant across hierarchical levels. For example, governance issues such as decision rights may be defined for an individual role or for a top management team. Key processes and interfaces may be defined for both a small sub-unit and a large division, and so on. Moreover, this framework is not only relevant for the design of roles and units when considered as elements in a vertical structure, but also for the definition of *cross-unit*, horizontal processes. (In Chapter 7 we shall use the exact same categorization in considering different types of interdependencies that emerge between different roles and units in an organization.)

Design oriented research

A number of authors have recently developed proposals for how to bridge the gap between theory and practice in organizational studies and in management research more generally. There is generally broad agreement that business schools need to focus more strongly on producing managerially relevant research; on the other hand, there is also some uncertainty about the right approach to achieve this goal. Some scholars are concerned that the quest for relevance will reduce academic rigor, with the risk of producing findings that are incorrect, or promoting prescriptions that do not contribute to increased business performance (e.g., Markides, 2007). Vermeulen (2005) has proposed, however, that this challenge may be handled by asking research questions that are important to managers but investigate the questions by using conventional research methods.

Two Dutch professors, van Aken and Romme (2009), have described in more detail how such a research paradigm can be developed. They call their approach "design oriented" research. The purpose is to build a *solutions-oriented* science of management and thereby support design processes that practitioners engage in. For organization design, this means improving how managers design organizations to increase performance or attain specified goals. An important aspect of design oriented research is to formulate and test *design propositions* (also called design rules). Design propositions are similar to descriptive, scientific hypotheses in terms of logical structure. However, unlike scientific hypotheses, which are descriptive, design propositions are prescriptive, that is, they contain rules for *how to achieve a given goal in a given situation* (see Table 1.5 for an example).

The principles used in design oriented research – together with the tools of axiomatic design – provide a framework for how practitioners (particularly consultants) could structure their methodologies. By expressing a methodology in the form of design propositions, one would facilitate a more cumulative knowledge building process,

Table 1.5 Comparison between science and design mode of inquiry

	Science mode	Design mode
Purpose	Produce descriptive (general and objective) knowledge supported by data about cause-and-effect relationships	Guide action to change systems and produce *pragmatically valid* knowledge (knowledge that is actionable and open to validation/disconfirmation)
General form	"If X, then Y" Or: "X is positively or negatively related to Y"	"In Situation S, in order to achieve A, do B"
Example	The best performing organizations are those that are structured in a manner that maximizes "fit" with key contingencies	In developing and selecting a design, to ensure that the structure will maximize performance: • Identify key contingencies (external and internal) • Translate these into *functional requirements* • Identify design parameters that satisfy the functional requirements

which will contribute to more effective prescriptive knowledge. It is essentially about using the real world as a laboratory. Organization re-design projects are the experiments, whose outcomes are used to test and refine our design propositions, which in turn enable improvements in the design process. At the same time, the design propositions provide an interface to academic research (Romme, 2003). Design propositions should not only be grounded in managerial experience but reflect relevant academic knowledge. Scholars also have an important role to play in empirically validating the outcomes from applying the design propositions.

This book adopts this approach by identifying a set of design propositions in each chapter. The design propositions serve three purposes. First, they capture the key points in each chapter. Secondly, the intention has been to formulate the propositions at a level of specificity that will allow a manager or consultant to use them as a basis for design interventions. Finally, the intention has also been to formulate the propositions in a falsifiable manner, to allow others to build on this work by testing and refining the propositions. It is hoped that the majority of the propositions will survive such testing by allowing organizational designers to produce the intended consequences. But it is also to be expected that some of the propositions will need to be revised, that new propositions will need to be added, and that a few may be disconfirmed altogether. A set of research questions is also identified; these summarize important issues that should be examined more closely in order to further our understanding of organization design.

Conclusion

In designing organizations, managers determine how work is to be performed inside an organization by defining roles, processes, and formal authority relationships. In the literature, four key concepts used to explain organization design are hierarchical composition, task uncertainty, coordination cost, and strategy and structure alignment (the latter being a key element in contingency theory).

Empirical research confirms the value of effective designs, and documents the risks associated with inappropriate designs. Yet the field of organization design must also confront some challenges. Many leading business "gurus" have dismissed the value of organization design. Business schools have placed little emphasis on organization design in their curriculums, and research within organization theory has been neglecting organization design issues. Many leading scholars today concede that academic research in the field has failed to make an influential contribution to practice. (The main exception is organizational economics, which has influenced choices made by organizations in the area of corporate governance.)

These challenges have created a debate about how the field can be revitalized. Six proposed responses to this challenge are discussed in this chapter. The first is to reaffirm the value of design – as defined in the classic texts in the field – by demonstrating its effects on key organizational outcomes. Secondly, we discussed that a different orientation, a "design attitude," may be needed in terms of how we approach problem solving processes in business, including those dealing with organization design issues. Furthermore, in line with recent work in the field, the chapter proposes using *architecture* as the key concept. This implies that the mission of the organization design discipline should be to help leaders develop organizational architectures that are *purposeful* and *future oriented*, and which balance the need for *autonomous action* with the need for *system coherency*. To create purposeful architectures, it is necessary to link design parameters to functional requirements. It was shown, utilizing an example of a life insurance company, how this may be done by utilizing *axiomatic design principles*, originally developed for the engineering sciences. The chapter introduced five layers of organizational design parameters: The governance model, the operating model, the resource model, the contracting model, and the social network model. Finally, to create a more effective interface between research and practice, Romme (2003) recommended that one adopt a research paradigm focused on developing prescriptive knowledge based on the formulation of *design propositions* that can be tested by practitioners in the field.

Design propositions

Objective	*Create rigorous yet pragmatically valid knowledge about organization design*
1.1	Re-orient design inquiry toward the goal of identifying architectures that are purposeful, future oriented, unifying and coherent, yet allow autonomous action
1.2	Adopt the design matrix as a tool to standardize the description of organization design features
1.3	Formulate prescriptive knowledge in the form of Design Propositions (actionable and testable hypotheses about interventions to achieve specific goals)
Objective	*Create organizational architectures that enable the attainment of strategic goals*
1.4	Translate the purpose and goals of the organization into explicit functional requirements
1.5	Define design parameters corresponding to each functional requirement
1.6	Decompose the functional requirements and design parameters (by iterating between FRs and DPs) until a realizable design has been defined

Review questions

1 How does organization design differ from the traditional conception of organization theory?
2 What does the concept of hierarchical decomposition entail?
3 What is the relationship between strategy and organizational structure?
4 What are some key assumptions in the information processing view of organization design?
5 How do organization design choices influence organizational effectiveness?
6 What are the characteristics of (good) architecture that suggest how we can design more effective organizations?
7 What are the five "layers" of design parameters?
8 How would you formulate the key functional requirements for a university, or a hospital? What would be the design parameters?
9 The chapter reviews the advantages of the axiomatic design approach. What may be some limitations of this approach?
10 The chapter reviews some of the advantages of adopting a "design attitude." What are the limitations of a design attitude? Under what circumstances should designers instead adopt a "decision attitude"?
11 Can effective organization design be a source of competitive advantage? How?

Research questions

1 How does decomposition (or division of labor) affect organizational functioning, for example, the way problems are interpreted and how learning occurs (cf. Jacobides, 2006)?
2 How can we identify the causal paths linking organizational design choices, intermediary outcomes, and eventual outcomes (e.g., financial performance)?
3 What are the strengths and limitations of axiomatic design theory, when applied to social systems?
4 How can we improve the *practice* of organization design?
5 How can we develop and test prescriptive theory that is usable by practitioners?
6 What are the best methods for teaching organization design concepts and methods?

References

Ackoff, R.L. & Emery, F. E. (1972). *On Purposeful Systems*. Chicago: Aldine-Atherton.

Aksnes, L. H. et al. (2006). Management of high-grade bone sarcomas over two decades: The Norwegian Radium Hospital experience. *Acta Oncologica, 45*, 1, 38–46.

Ater, I., Givati, Y., & Rigbi, O. (2014). Organizational structure, police activity and crime. *Journal of Public Economics*, 115, 62–71.

Baldwin, C. Y. & Clark, K. B. (2000). *Design Rules – Vol. 1: The Power of Modularity*. Cambridge, MA: MIT Press.

Bettis, R. (1991). Strategic management and the straightjacket: An editorial essay. *Organization Science*, 2, 315–319.

Boland, R. J. & Collopy, F. (2004). Design matters for management. In R. J. Boland & F. Collopy, *Managing as Designing*. Stanford: Stanford Business Books.

Burton, R. M., Lauridsen, J., & Obel, B. (2002). Return on assets loss from situational and contingency misfits. *Management Science*, 48, 11, 1461–1485.

Campbell, A. (2012). Can we make organisations more collaborative? *360° The Ashridge Journal*, Spring, 50–53. Available from: www.ashridge.org.uk/insights/360-the-ashridge-journal/previous-editions-of-360/

Chandler, A. (1962). *Strategy and Structure: Chapters in the History of the Industrial Enterprise*. Cambridge, MA: MIT Press.

Daft, R. L. & Lengel, R. H. (1984). Information richness: A new approach to managerial information processing and organizational design. *Research in Organizational Behavior*, 6, 191–234.

Davis, J. H., Schoorman, F. D., & Donaldson, L. (1997). Toward a stewardship theory of management. *Academy of Management Review*, 22, 20–47.

Donaldson, L. (2001). *The Contingency Theory of Organisations*. Thousand Oaks, CA: Sage.

Donaldson, L. (1995). *Anti-American Theories of Organization*. Cambridge: Cambridge University Press.

Egeberg, M. (1989). Effekter av organisasjonsendring i forvaltningen ["The effects of reorganizations in government department and agencies," not translated]. In Egeberg, M. (Ed.): *Institusjonspolitikk og forvaltningsutvikling. Bidrag til en anvendt statsvitenskap*. Oslo: Tano.

Felin, T. & Foss, N. J. (2009). Social reality, the boundaries of self-fulfilling prophecy, and economics. *Organization Science*, 20, 3, 654–668.

Foss, N.J. (2003). Selective intervention and internal hybrids: Interpreting and learning from the rise and decline of the spaghetti organization. *Organization Science*, 4, 331–349.

Galbraith, J. (2002). *Designing Organizations: An Executive Guide to Strategy, Structure, and Process*. San Francisco: Jossey-Bass.

Galbraith, J. R. (1974). Organization design: An information processing view. *Interfaces*, 4, 3, 28–36.

Gerstein, M. S. (1992). From machine bureaucracies to networked organizations: An architectural journey. In D. A. Nadler, M. S. Gerstein, R. B. Shaw, and associates, *Organizational Architecture: Designs for Changing Organizations*. San Francisco: Jossey-Bass.

Ghoshal, S. (2005). Bad management theories are destroying good management practices. *Academy of Management Learning and Education*, *4*, 1, 75–91.

Ghoshal, S. & Nohria, N. (1993). Horses for courses: Organizational forms for multinational corporations. *Sloan Management Review*, *34*, 2, 23–35.

Gulick, L. & Urwick, L. (eds.) (1937). *Papers on the Science of Administration*. New York: Institute of Public Administration.

Haeckel, S. H. (1999). *Adaptive Enterprise: Creating and Leading Sense-and-respond Organizations*. Boston: Harvard Business School Press.

Hamel, G. & Prahalad, C.K. (1989). Strategic intent. *Harvard Business Review*, *67*, May/June, 63–76.

Hammer, M. (2004). Deep change. *Harvard Business Review* 82, 4, 84–93.

Hammer, M. (2001). *The Agenda: What Every Business Must Do To Dominate the Decade*. New York: Crown Business.

Hansen, M. (2009). *Collaboration*. Boston: Harvard Business School Press.

Heath, C. & Staudenmayer, N. (2000). Coordination neglect: How lay theories of organizing complicate coordination in organizations. *Research in Organizational Behavior*, *22*, 53–191.

Hoskisson, R. E. (1987). Multidivisional structure and performance: The contingency of diversification strategy. *Academy of Management Journal*, *30*, 4, 625–644.

Jacobides, M. G. (2006). The architecture and design of organizational capabilities. *Industrial and Corporate Change*, *15*, 1, 151–171.

Jensen, M. C. (1983). Organization theory and methodology. *Accounting Review*, *56*, 319–338.

Karim, S. (2006). Modularity in organizational structure: The reconfiguration of internally developed and acquired business units. *Strategic Management Journal*, *27*, 9, 799–823.

Karim, S. & Kaul, A. (2015). Structural recombination and innovation: Unlocking intraorganizational knowledge synergy through structural change. *Organization Science*, *26*, 2, 439–455.

Kennedy, M. (2002). Management Decisions versus Design. Paper presented at the Frontiers of Management conference, Weatherhead School of Management, Case Western University, June 14–15.

Kleinbaum, A. M. (2008). The Social Structure of Organization: Coordination in a Large, Multi-Business Firm. Harvard University, Doctoral dissertation, available at SSRN: https://ssrn.com/abstract=1356704

Kuhn, D. (2011). Delayering and Firm Performance: Evidence from Swiss Firm-level Data. Working paper 2011/02 D–134, University of Basel. Retrieved from https://ideas.repec.org/p/bsl/wpaper/2011-02.html

Lawrence, P. R. & Lorsch, J. W. (1969). *Organization and Environment*. Boston, MA: Harvard Business School Press.

Leavitt, H. J. (2005). *Top Down: Why Hierarchies are Here to Stay and How to Manage Them More Effectively.* Boston, MA: Harvard Business School Press.

Lee, J.-Y., Sridhar, S., Henderson, C. M., & Palmatier, R. W. (2015). Effect of customer-centric structure on long-term financial performance. *Marketing Science, 34,* 2, 250–268.

Liedtka, J. (2000). In defense of strategy as design. *California Management Review, 42,* 8–30.

Markides, C. (2007). In search of ambidextrous professors. *Academy of Management Journal, 50,* 4, 762–768.

McDavid, D. W. (1999). A standard for architecture description. *IBM Systems Journal, 38,* 1, 12–31.

Miller, D., Greenwood, R., & Prakash, R. (2009). What happened to organization theory? *Journal of Management Inquiry, 18,* 4, 273–279.

Mintzberg, H. (1979). *The Structuring of Organizations.* Englewood Cliffs, NJ: Prentice-Hall.

Nadler, D. & Tushman, M. (1997). *Competing by Design: The Power of Organizational Architecture.* New York: Oxford University Press.

Nagappan, N., Murphy, B., & Basili, V. (2008). The influence of organizational structure on software quality: an empirical case study. Proceedings of the 30th International Conference on Software Engineering. Leipzig, Germany.

Nahm, A. Y., Vonderembse, M. A., & Koufteros, X. A. (2003). The impact of organizational structure on time-based manufacturing and plant performance. *Journal of Operations Management, 21,* 281–306.

O'Reilly, C. A. & Tushman, M. L. (2004). The ambidextrous organisation. *Harvard Business Review, 82,* 4, 74–81.

Ouchi, W. G. (2006). Power to the principals: Decentralization in three large school districts. *Organization Science, 17,* 2, 298–307.

Peters, T. (2006). *Re-imagine.* New York: DK Publishing.

Pfeffer, J. (1997). *New Directions for Organization Theory: Problems and Prospects.* New York: Oxford University Press.

Roberts, J. (2004). The *Modern Firm. Organizational Design for Performance and Growth.* New York: Oxford University Press.

Robinson, L. A. & Stocken, P. C. (2013). Location of decision rights within multinational firms. *Journal of Accounting Research, 51,* 5, 1261–1297.

Romme, G. L. A. (2003). Making a difference: Organization as design. *Organization Science, 14,* 5, 558–573.

Rumelt, R. P. (1974). *Strategy, Structure, and Economic Performance.* Cambridge, MA: Harvard University Press.

Rynes, S. L., Colbert, A. E., & Brown, K. G. (2002). HR Professionals' beliefs about effective human resource practices: correspondence between research and practice. *Human Resource Management, 41*(2), 149–174.

Sanchez, R. (1995). Strategic flexibility in product competition. *Strategic Management Journal, 16,* 135–159.

Simon, H. A. (1996). *The Sciences of the Artificial*, 3rd edition. Cambridge, MA: MIT Press.

Smith, A. (1776/1977). *An Inquiry Into the Nature and Causes of the Wealth of Nations*. Chicago: University of Chicago Press.

Suh, N. P. (2001). *Axiomatic Design: Advances and Applications*. Oxford: Oxford University Press.

Thompson, J. (1967). *Organizations in Action*. New York: McGraw-Hill.

Tushman, M. L. & Nadler, D. A. (1978). Information processing as an integrating concept in organizational design. *The Academy of Management Review, 3*(3), 613–624.

Van Aken, J. E. & Romme, A. G. L. (2009). Reinventing the future: Adding design science to the repertoire of organization and management studies. *Organization Management Journal, 6*, 5–12.

Ven, A. H. Van De, Delbecq, A. L., & Koenig, R. (1976). Determinants of coordination modes within organizations. *American Sociological Review, 41*, 2, 322.

Vermeulen, F. (2005). On rigor and relevance: Fostering dialectic progress in management research. *Academy of Management Journal, 48*, 978–982.

Werr, A., Stjernberg, T., & Docherty, P. (1997) The functions of methods of change in management consulting. *Journal of Organizational Change Management, 10*, 4, 288–307.

Williamson, O. E. (1981). The economics of organization: The transaction cost approach. *American Journal of Sociology*, 87, 548–577.

Wong, S., DeSanctis, G., & Staudenmayer, N. (2007). The relationship between task interdependency and role stress: A revisit of the job demands-control model. *Journal of Management Studies, 44*, 2, 284–303.

Worren, N., Moore, K., & Elliott, R. (2002). When theories become tools: Toward a framework for pragmatic validity. *Human Relations, 55*, 10, 1227–1249.

Yin, X. & Zajac, E. J. (2004). The strategy/governance structure fit relationship: Theory and evidence in franchising arrangements. *Strategic Management Journal, 25*, 365–383.

2 Organizational complexity

Chapter overview

Background	• Complexity is recognized by economists and management scholars as a key factor limiting the growth and profitability of large firms.
	• More recent studies have exposed the negative effects of internal complexity on quality and productivity, as well as employee well-being.
	• Indicators suggest that the level of complexity continues to increase in many organizations.
Challenges	• Managers may overlook factors that lead to the gradual build-up of complexity over time.
	• Some theorists view *internal* complexity as an inevitable result of *external* complexity, discounting the possibility of organizational simplification.
	• The concept is poorly defined, and more rigorous methods to measure and manage complexity are lacking.
Key questions	• How can we define the concept of organizational complexity?
	• How can we develop a proactive agenda for managing and reducing organizational complexity?
Proposed approach	• Adopt a clear definitional framework to allow —identification, measurement, and analysis of complexity.
	• Identify the overall organizational strategy to manage, reduce, or prevent complexity.
	• Propose three design criteria for organizational simplification.

Introduction

A multinational supplier of medical equipment chose to reorganize from a product-based to a process-based organization. The key purpose was to increase process orientation by implementing a structure more aligned with its value chain. Whereas the previous organization consisted of three main divisions, each responsible for one product, the new structure comprised four global business areas: Product development, Operations (i.e., manufacturing), Marketing, and Sales. The business area called Operations was further sub-divided into two parts, one consisting of production plants located in different countries, and another with common staff and support units (Supply Chain, HR, Finance, etc.). The new organizational structure contained several intricate reporting relationships. For example, the quality manager for a particular production plant would take part in the leadership team meetings at the plant, but would no longer report to the director of the plant, but to a manager in the so-called Supply Chain unit, who would typically be located in a different country. To explain the new structure, the company had distributed thick booklets with dozens of organization charts. Yet there were indications that some managers were confused. In the booklet, none of the charts described how the new reporting relationships would match up with the processes. In interviews that were held one and a half years after the change, managers were asked whether the new structure had actually contributed to increased process orientation. One senior marketing manager remarked:

> We introduced a new structure 1.5 years ago, we went from a divisional (product-based) structure to a process-based structure . . . but roles and responsibilities are still not clear . . . we spend way too much time in internal coordination between the units . . . we're still working in silos . . . then there are overlaps, for example, we have split marketing and sales into two functions . . . is it the sales director or the marketing director that should decide?

This example raises several important questions. Why do managers sometimes select organizational models that seem to increase, rather than decrease, complexity? What is the impact of complexity on performance? How does it affect the work of individual employees? Can we manage, reduce, or even avoid complexity? These are the issues we will discuss in this chapter. We start by considering how the concept can be defined.

Simplicity versus complexity

In classical economics, one expected *scale economies* to provide important advantages to large firms. Larger scale means, among things, that a firm can achieve cost advantages: Higher production volume means that major investments and overhead costs can be spread over more units, leading to lower average costs per unit (Barney, 1996). Larger firms may also gain market power and thus enjoy higher profitability due to reduced competition in the industry. However, economists also recognize that there are important *diseconomies of scale*, which leads to an increase of costs when firms grow too large. Economists include complexity among "managerial diseconomies," that is, factors that impede effective control and operation of firms that become too large. One of the most well-known proponents of this view is the 2009 Nobel Prize winner in economical sciences, Oliver Williamson, who developed the transaction cost approach. Transaction costs are the costs related to planning and monitoring task completion in an organization, including the negotiation of agreements and the handling of disputes with internal and external parties. Williamson argued that transaction costs generally increase with size, mainly due to growing bureaucracy. As stated in Canbäck et al. (2006), "Problems are solved by adding structure and the firm reaches a point at which the added structure costs more than the problems solved" (p. 34).

Economists have generally not defined complexity or related terms with any great precision, but a possible definition can be found in organization theory. Organizational theorists traditionally viewed complexity as the increasing *differentiation* or variety brought about by increasing size. In empirical studies of complexity, one would thus count the number of elements in an organization, such as the number of different products, technologies, or processes, or, in terms of organization design variables, the number of subunits and hierarchical levels (Burton & Forsyth, 1986; see also Blau & McKinley, 1979; Anderson, 1999; Ashmos et al., 2000).

More recently, another definition, which we will adopt in this book, has been proposed by scholars working in engineering and technology management. This definition places a stronger emphasis on *how the elements of the system are related to each other* – in other words, on interdependencies (Suh, 2001; Baldwin & Clark, 2000). This approach, originally developed by Simon (1962), allows for the possibility that the degree of complexity may vary in systems of equal size.

To see how this definition may help in conceptualizing complexity, imagine a white goods company with three product lines:[1] Dishwashers, washing machines, and vacuum cleaners, which are sold to customers – the purchasing departments of retailers with several stores – in three different geographic markets: North, West, and South (Figure 2.1a). The company hires three sales representatives, one for each regional market. The sales representative has a number of responsibilities, such as identifying sales leads, preparing proposals, negotiating contracts, ensuring product delivery, and monitoring customer satisfaction. For simplicity, let us assume that

1 I here extend on an example borrowed from Ethiraj and Levinthal (2009).

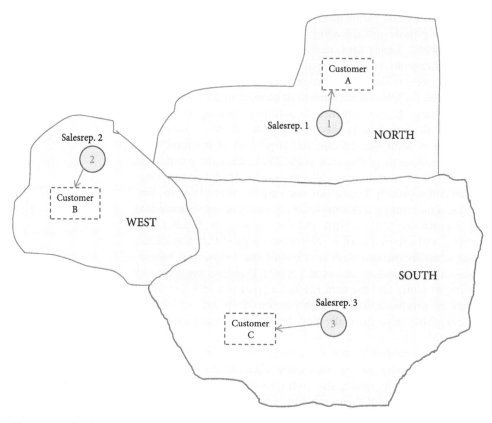

Figure 2.1a Simple organization.

the customers in the three regions don't overlap (each customer is only represented in one region), that the customers may potentially buy all three products, and that the manufacturer has the necessary capacity to meet customer demand (i.e., there is no need to prioritize between customers in the three regions). In this case we have what we can call a *simple organization:* The performance of one unit (or, in this case, a sales representative) is largely unrelated to the efforts of other units (or, in this case, other sales representatives). Each customer representatives decides which customers to target within their respective regions, which products to offer them, and how to negotiate terms and conditions.

However, a different situation emerges if management decides to organize sales by product rather than by geography. In other words, the three sales representatives now work across the three regions. The customers will have three sales representatives from the same manufacturer visiting them: The first offering dishwashers, the second washing machines, and the third vacuum cleaners (Figure 2.1b). The work processes will now be interdependent: For example, it is necessary for each sales representative to check with the others before

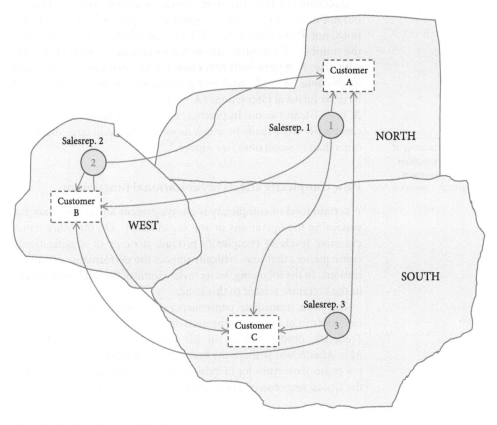

Figure 2.1b Complex organization.

changing sales terms and conditions (if they intend to represent their company in a consistent manner). The new structure may also create goal conflicts between the three representatives. If the client has limited retail space or a limited budget to spend on home care products, the efforts of sales representative 1, selling dishwashers, may be hampered if sales representative 2 has already secured a sale for washing machines to the same customer. (However, the interdependencies may also lead to positive performance effects, for example, when an existing relationship with a client who has bought vacuum cleaners leads to a sale of washing machines and dishwashers later on.) The decision to re-structure the company creates a *complex organization*: Multiple inter-dependencies emerge between roles or units. The main effect of the interdependencies is that actions and decisions made by one role or unit potentially affect the performance of other units. In general, a product-based structure is not necessarily inferior to a geographical organization, but in this particular case, it leads to higher coordination costs.[2] It may also lead to goal conflicts, as there is a risk that the efforts that each sales representative makes to achieve his or her goals may negatively impact the other two sales representatives.[3]

2 The concept of coordination costs is discussed in more detail in Chapter 5.

3 One could imagine other scenarios, where the effect would have been the opposite. For example, a product-based organization might lead to a lower degree of complexity than a geographical organization if customers operate across different geographies yet maintain a centralized purchasing office.

According to this reasoning, a large organization is *complicated* but not necessarily *complex*: Complexity is primarily about interactions, not about size (Suh, 2005). On the other hand, it is true that the number of potential interdependencies increases dramatically with size: A system with two elements has two potential bilateral interactions (A → B and B ← A); a system with three elements will have six bilateral interactions (A → B, A → C, B → A, B → C, C → A, C → B), and so on. In practice, then, the challenge of managing complexity will usually be much more significant in large organizations than in small ones (see Figure 2.2).[4]

4 The total number of potential interactions between n structural elements of a system is n(n–1).

How complexity affects organizational functioning

A certain level of complexity is always present and is necessary for sustaining the operations of any organization. On the other hand, excessive levels of complexity produce a range of organizational consequences that may critically impact the performance of organizations. In the following, let us review some of the studies discussed in the literature related to this issue.

The most immediate consequences of complexity are *increased time and cost* of completing projects or performing business processes. Frederick Brooks (1975), in his classic work on the *Mythical Man-Month,* was perhaps the first to point out that complexity was a key cause of overruns for IT projects. When schedule slippage occurs, the typical response of a project manager is to add more manpower.

Number of system elements	Number of potential interdependencies	Increase from adding one system element
2	2	
3	6	4
4	12	6
5	20	8
6	30	10

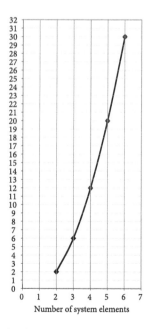

Figure 2.2 The number of potential bilateral interdependencies as a result of increases in the number of system elements.

Yet Brooks observed that *adding manpower to a late project made it later*. The explanation is straightforward: Project managers forget the existence of interdependencies between software engineers when estimating the required work effort – software engineers spend a lot of time communicating with each other in order to coordinate their work and resolve issues that relate to different components or modules of the software system. Adding more manpower leads to a further increase in coordination cost, which may sometimes offset the effect of the added capacity. (The increase in coordination cost will depend on the size of the project as well as the degree of interdependency between the different modules that the software engineers are configuring.) For example, adding two new software engineers to a project of four engineers introduces 18 new potential interfaces (four engineers have 12 possible interdependencies; six engineers have 30 possible interdependencies) (cf. Figure 2.2).

Whereas Brook's work was based largely on anecdotal evidence, there are also empirical studies that examine the relationship between organizational complexity and productivity. One example is the research reported in Hihn et al. (1990), who considered the relationship between the structure and performance of software projects. Complexity was measured by indices that reflected the number of interfaces that the project team would need to handle. Complexity was rated as low if the software was developed within one unit of the organization, and as high if it involved several units of the firm or external partners. As expected, productivity was lower for projects with a complex structure.[5] Importantly, it was also found that the negative effect of volatility (e.g., changes in requirements during the project) was less serious for the projects with a simple structure than for projects with complex structures. In other words, the project teams with a simple structure seemed to have a better ability to respond to change.

Carillo and Kopelman (1991) examined the relationship between organizational structure and productivity in 234 branches of a US bank. The structural variables included size, the number of hierarchical levels in each branch, and the ratio of staff versus production workers. The results indicated that there was a negative relationship between size and productivity, and between the number of hierarchical levels and productivity. The smaller branches had approximately 31% greater efficiency than the larger ones, and the branches with one hierarchical level were approximately 44% more productive than branches with five levels.

Complexity also affects the propensity to commit errors, which in turn influences both quality and the risk of accidents. A common error is simply to omit one step in a process – a worker in a production facility may forget to fasten a bolt or a nurse may drop administering a pill. Errors might also occur because people misinterpret instructions or procedures, or apply the wrong procedure. Some studies show that the defect rates in production processes are strongly related to *the number of process steps* executed (Hinckley,

5 In empirical studies of the effects of organizational complexity, it is important to control for other factors that may lead to performance differences, such as the size and complexity of the task itself. In the Hihn et al (1990) study, the productivity data were adjusted based on differences in the project tasks and the experience level of the project team members.

2003). The same conclusion was reached by researchers looking at errors in hospitals, who found that the likelihood of an adverse event increased by 6% *for each day* a patient spent in a hospital (Andrews et al., 1997). The key implication of these studies is that simplifying production processes may be the single most effective means of reducing defect rates.

Yet the most serious consequences are not related to errors related to individual steps in a process, but to the more systemic risk that is created in highly interlinked systems (both technological and organizational). Today, unanticipated *interactions among components* is the most frequent source of serious accidents (Perrow, 1984). Each component of a system may be safe when viewed in isolation; however, with increasing complexity it becomes difficult both to identify risk sources and to mitigate risk when it is detected: Complex interdependencies essentially mean that a failure of one component can quickly propagate through the system in unexpected ways.

> In October 1996, Aeroperú Flight 603 crashed into the Pacific Ocean, killing nine crew members and sixty-one passengers. The aircraft investigation revealed that the cause of the accident was a piece of masking tape accidentally left over the so-called static ports (air intakes) by cleaning personnel. The blocked static ports led the basic flight instruments to relay false airspeed, altitude and vertical speed data, which created complete confusion in the cockpit, as the pilots believed they were flying at a safe altitude, when in fact they were approaching sea level. The trial following the accident identified both defective design by The Boeing Company, the aircraft's manufacturer, and negligent maintenance procedures as contributing to the accident.[6]

6 Source: http://en.wikipedia.org/wiki/Aeroper%C3%BA_Flight_603

The Aeroperú accident raises the question of how such a minor error – a failure to remove a masking tape during cleaning – could have such catastrophic consequences. It is clearly related to the complexity of the airplane itself from a technical point of view. But the technological complexity may in turn reflect the organization of the manufacturer. It is likely that the design of the static ports and the design of the flight instruments were done in two separate sub-teams of Boeing's development organization. Hence a contributing cause may be a difficulty of interchanging information among sub-teams of the development project.

Another symptom of complexity is a lack of clear goals. This phenomenon has been the subject of several studies among public management scholars.[7] Chun and Rainey (2005) examined the existence of *goal ambiguity* in US federal agencies and relationship with employees' ratings of organizational effectiveness. They defined ambiguity as the extent to which an organizational goal or a set of

7 However, the level of goal ambiguity is not necessarily higher in public than in private sector organizations.

goals allows leeway for interpretation. But they also distinguished between different facets of ambiguity. For example, ambiguity may be related to the interpretive leeway in understanding or explaining the actual mission, in selecting specific actions to accomplish the mission, in evaluating the progress toward accomplishing the mission, or in prioritizing among multiple goals that the unit has been given. As hypothesized, they found that goal ambiguity was negatively correlated to ratings of organizational effectiveness.

In some organizations, employees do not even agree about how the boundaries in the organization are drawn. In a study of 43 teams in a large multinational company, Mortensen (2004) found that people in only 13 of the 43 teams agreed who the members of their team were. Teams that exhibited such *boundary disagreement* reported significantly lower performance than those experiencing no boundary disagreement. Interestingly, it was found that the team members were confident of their own understanding when asked to name team members, and were unaware of their own ignorance and of the existence of boundary disagreement among teammates. Mortensen (2004) explains that people have differing frames of reference on which they base their evaluation of a typical team member.

Ambiguity regarding missions or boundaries at the team or organizational level may create *role ambiguity* at the individual level (Pandey & Wright, 2006). In a study in an insurance company, Posner and Butterfield (1978) found that role ambiguity was negatively related to job satisfaction among employees. An independent measure of effectiveness showed that members in high-performing offices had greater role clarity than members in low-performing offices. One might expect roles at higher levels to be more ambiguous as they typically involve tasks with more uncertainty than roles at lower levels in the organization. But interestingly, the results showed that *role clarity was higher at higher organizational levels*. This finding may be interpreted in several ways. At higher organizational levels, there may exist more objective, outcome-based measures that can be used to define individual roles (e.g., a senior executive can be made directly accountable for unit profitability). But it may also indicate that higher-level managers in this firm ignored the need for proper definition of jobs at lower levels of the organization.

Researchers have studied soldiers working in situations where the mission is unclear and where success is a remote possibility. For example, the soldiers that were deployed as part of the US operation in Somalia in 1992 arrived there motivated and committed, but as the operation wore on, many became demoralized and disengaged due to shifts in the overall mission and vague rules of engagement, which made it difficult for the soldiers to protect civilians (Britt, 2003). As pointed out by Britt (2003), there is a common misconception that job engagement is a personality trait and that motivated people will throw themselves with equal enthusiasm into pretty much any job. Yet the research actually shows that that those employees that are the most highly engaged in their work report the lowest levels of job satisfaction when roles are ambiguous (ibid.).

In a study conducted with 125 middle managers, a combination of high amounts of interdependency and role ambiguity (i.e., ambiguity caused by unclear or hidden interdependencies toward other units or individuals) was identified as a key source of stress. Managers confronted with such a challenge may be dependent on others for resources or support in order to perform their tasks, yet be unsure about with whom or about what they are supposed to coordinate (Wong et al., 2007). On the other hand, the study also concluded that some managers were able to handle a great number of interdependencies, as long as there was sufficient clarity with regard to goals and structure.

Organizational complexity may also make it more difficult to monitor that employees comply with ethical standards. Fleming and Zyglidopoulus (2008) argued that organizational complexity in some cases has amplified the severity and pervasiveness of fraudulent practices, including the large-scale corruption that occurred in cases such as Enron, Arthur Andersen, WorldCom, and Barings Bank. A "fog of complexity" makes deception difficult to understand and control, because activities are conducted out of the boundaries of normal managerial control. Moreover, they hypothesize that complexity will make it more likely that deviances from acceptable business practices gain momentum and escalate into organizational phenomena: "A lie told in the past by individuals can spread into the future by making any effort for honest reporting misleading at best" (p. 16).

Complexity also has important implications for strategic decision makers. One would expect, for example, that it becomes harder to forecast future results the more complex a business is. There is no study on this issue employing the same definition as we introduced above, but if we accept size as a proxy for internal complexity, we may use a study described in Meyer (2002) that was conducted in a global pharmaceutical firm. This study plotted the accuracy of revenue forecasts for various country subsidiaries of the firm as a function of their size. The measure of size was prior year sales, while the measure of forecast accuracy was the percentage deviation of actual from projected sales in the current year. The data showed that forecast accuracy declined sharply with size. According to Suh (2001), complexity essentially *increases overall uncertainty* by decreasing the probability that a given strategic decision will have the intended effect. This may explain why it was more difficult to produce reliable forecasts in larger than in small units.

Rising complexity

The existence of diseconomies of scale, such as factors leading to a high internal complexity of large firms, has been acknowledged by economists since the 1920s (Canbäck et al., 2006). What is more problematical, however, is that the overall level of complexity seems to be increasing, independent of firm size. Unfortunately, there are no studies that track the same indicator of complexity over a significant amount of time. The studies that have been conducted employ different definitions and methodologies. This means that we have an incomplete picture of the degree of complexity and its evolution over time. Nevertheless, when piecing together the findings from different studies, a fairly clear trend emerges.

The design of organizations has changed considerably during the last two or three decades. A number of studies have documented the introduction of cross-functional, horizontal processes, and the increasing prevalence of project-based work. This trend started in the 1990s, when Whittington et al. (1999) found a significant increase in "horizontal linkages" in a study conducted in European companies between 1992 and 1996. They also found evidence of delayering, that is, that organizations were removing management levels. Some have argued that old hierarchies have been dismantled; it is probably more appropriate to say that hierarchy is being complemented by the use of flexible and dynamic organizational arrangements, such as temporary project teams and cross functional business processes.

Organizations have also become much more "coordination intensive," a development that has been spurred by the introduction of new communication technologies (Malone, 2004). Some indirect evidence for this trend can be found by looking at the usage of communication technologies and the frequency of meetings in organizations. Information technologies, such as e-mail, have made it possible to coordinate by communicating with far more people, more quickly, at a much lower cost than before. On average, employees now spend 28% of their work time reading and answering e-mail messages (Chui et al., 2012). The total volume of e-mail traffic increases about 3% per year (The Radicati Group, 2016). Another relevant indicator of the amount of coordination is corporate meeting activity. There are no studies of corporate meeting activity that has been repeated over a longer period of time, but we can combine data from various studies conducted at different points in time. The trend from these seems very clear: Both the frequency and duration of meetings have increased markedly. A conservative estimate is that managers currently spend 50% of their time in meetings, on average. For senior executives the estimate is even higher – up to 70%. This can be compared to a study conducted in the 1960s, which showed that managers only spent 3.5 hours per week in planned meetings (somewhat more time was spent on unplanned meetings) (Romano & Nunamaker, 2001).

By and large, the effect of these changes may be positive: Delayering may reduce costs, improve accountability and decentralize decision making, and improve the speed of decision making and the quality of communication (as there are fewer levels across which one needs to share information). The increase in horizontal linkages between units may lead to increased integration and thereby reduce the effect of organizational "silos." The greater reliance on teams and project-based work may contribute to increased speed and flexibility.

Although the overall effect may be positive, many observers have noted that these changes have also led to increasing complexity, which is placing new demands on managers and employees. Many large organizations are suffering from "collaboration overload." Employees may participate in multiple teams or projects and must often balance competing priorities. Employees are also expected to share knowledge and be responsive to requests for information from others. In some organizations, internal experts and senior managers spend as much as 95% of their time on the phone, on e-mail, or in meetings (face to face or virtual) (Cross & Gray, 2013).

There is now ample evidence that this issue is becoming a concern for business leaders. It was first identified in a PwC survey in 2006, which included responses from 1,400 CEOs globally (PriceWaterhouseCoopers, 2006). Overall, more than three-quarters of the CEOs stated that complexity had increased during the preceding three years (that is, during the 2003–2006 period) (see Figure 2.3). But they believed that complexity could be reduced by improving the internal organization. No less than 97% of the respondents indicated that they were engaged in at least one improvement program to reduce internal complexity. "Organizational structure" was rated the second most common focus area for these improvement programs, after "Information technology."

"What is the level of complexity in your organization today compared to three years ago?"

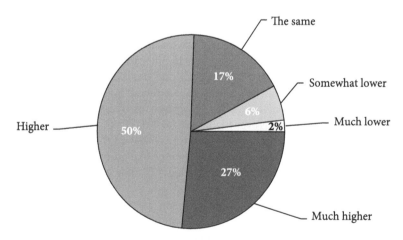

Figure 2.3 Excerpt from PwC's Global CEO study conducted in 2006.
(Source: Based on data reported in PriceWaterhouseCoopers, 2006).

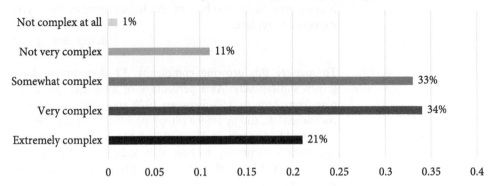

Figure 2.4 Excerpt from the Economist Intelligence Unit's 2015 report.
(Source: Economist Intelligence Unit, 2015).

The trend has been confirmed in a more recent study conducted by IBM (2010) and in two studies conducted by the Economist Intelligence Unit (2011; 2015). In the IBM study, the participants indicated that they expected the level of complexity to continue to increase. The Economist Intelligence Unit surveys included items about the role of internal, organizational factors. In the 2011 survey, 57% of the respondents agreed that their organizational structure contributed to an increase in the complexity in their firm. In the 2015 survey, over half of the respondents characterized the structure of their firms as either very or extremely complex (Figure 2.4). The respondents were also asked about the consequences of organizational complexity. Frequently mentioned consequences included conflicting priorities, slow decision making, and excessive time used on internal coordination.

The same trends are evident in studies considering other functional areas. In the IT area, a key topic of debate has been the high complexity in IT infrastructure and applications platforms. During the last couple of decades, an important priority for many IT leaders has been to simplify the work for the IT function, by reducing the number of applications and standardizing around large ERP (Enterprise Resource Planning) systems. These efforts have paid off for some firms. A study of 623 large US firms concluded that ERP installations had led to improved productivity and performance, particularly for those combining ERP with CRM (customer relationship management) and SCM (supply chain management) systems (Aral, Brynjolfsson, & Wu, 2006). However, other experts have warned that the implementation of ERP systems in some cases has increased, rather than decreased, complexity:

> Companies ended up having several instances of the same ERP systems or a variety of different ERP systems altogether, further

complicating their IT landscape. In the end, ERP systems became just another subset of the legacy systems they were supposed to replace.

(Rettig, 2007, p. 23)

To manage this growing complexity, IT departments have grown substantially: As a percentage of total investment, IT rose from 2.6% to 3.5% between 1970 and 1980. By 1990 IT consumed 9%, and by 1999 a whopping 22% of total investment went to IT. Growth in IT spending has fallen off, but it is nonetheless surprising to hear that today's IT departments spend 70% to 80% of their budgets just trying to keep existing systems running.

(Rettig, 2007, p. 21)

There is also a growing interest in the implications of complexity for supply chain management. Product proliferation has been identified as a key driver of complexity in the supply chain. One study estimated that 1.7 product models are being introduced for every product being discontinued (Hoole, 2006). An additional factor is outsourcing: Activities that were previously been conducted within the organization – such as manufacturing, distribution, accounting, and IT – are increasingly performed by external suppliers. In some cases work is being "offshored" to suppliers in low-cost locations, and it has been estimated that there are 3,500 outsourcing providers in India alone. Although modern supply chain management methods have led to increased quality, speed, and flexibility, some authors (e.g., Blecker & Kersten, 2006) argue that it has simultaneously led to dramatically increased complexity. In particular, scholars associated with Cranfield University in the UK have questioned the introduction of "Lean" practices and argued that these practices sometimes increase vulnerability of the supply chain (Peck, 2005). The main focus of Lean is increasing efficiency. The tight coupling between the activities in a Lean process (such as the elimination of inventory in the system to "buffer" any interruptions) means that operational difficulties at a single supplier can impact every other organization in the supply network.

The 2007–2008 financial crisis was also partly attributed to rising complexity, both within individual firms and in the finance industry as a whole. Ben Bernanke, the chairman of the US Federal Reserve Board, emphasized in a speech that the complexity of credit card plans and mortgage products in some cases served to disguise unfair and deceptive practices, and made it difficult for even the most diligent consumers to evaluate the features of different products and make appropriate choices (Bernanke, 2009).

Many observers have commented upon the interconnected nature of the financial system, where a failure of individual components may destroy the whole. As stated by the deputy governor of the Bank of France, Jean-Pierre Landau (2009, p. 1): "Transmissions of shocks occur through networks (. . .) this potentially creates numerous feedback loops and amplification effects." New techniques for managing financial risk made it possible to spread the risk more broadly, but also meant that the network of counterparties expanded in scale and complexity, which in turn led to a loss of information, making it hard to assess the real risk profile of the underlying assets.

Herring and Carmassi (2010) linked these challenges to organization design in their analysis of international financial conglomerates. They concluded that the complexity of the corporate structures of the conglomerates itself was a source of significant systemic risk, which also impeded timely regulatory intervention and disposition. They concluded that rather than being "too big to fail," as it is commonly said, the large financial institutions have become "too complex to fail."

Why is complexity allowed to grow?

The findings and viewpoints reviewed so far are rather uncontroversial: There is a broad consensus among both scholars and practitioners that complexity has been increasing. Few people would disagree with the assertion that complexity has potential negative effects, and few people would deliberately seek to increase complexity. So the paradox we have to address is why complexity is still increasing in many organizations.

One possible explanation would be that the level of internal complexity in an organization largely reflects the increasing level of *external* complexity. The proponents of this view often refer to Ashby (1956), who formulated the law of *requisite variety*. This law states that the variety within a system must be at least as great as the environmental variety against which it is attempting to regulate itself. As Galbraith (2000, p. 2) stated: "A company's organisation must be as complex as its business (. . .) If the business is simple, the organisation can be simple."

Without doubt, a firm's environment is an important driver of internal complexity. There are examples in practically all industries of external changes that force companies to introduce more complex internal structures. The introduction of a new regulatory framework (e.g., the Sarbanes-Oxley act for corporate governance, or the Basel II or Solvency II conventions) force firms to implement new (and potentially very complex) audit and governance processes. More differentiated customer needs may lead manufacturing companies to offer a higher number of new product models, which increases internal complexity (as it leads to the introduction of new manufacturing processes and the establishment of roles and units responsible for the each of the new products, etc.). Similarly, extending operations into new territories (particularly foreign countries) introduces complexity in several ways, for example, by requiring the company to modify products or add product variants, establish additional organizational units (e.g., country subsidiaries), and adapt to a new set of laws and regulations.

However, the fact that organizations in the same industry are subject to the same environmental forces does not necessarily mean that they respond by adopting identical structures. As pointed out by Gresov and Drazin (1997), environmental contingencies dictate the functions, and not the structure of an organization (cf. the distinction between functions/functional requirements and structure/design parameters discussed in Chapter 1). Today, for example, many telecom firms experience that basic voice/data network services are being commoditized, and that future survival depends on the ability to develop new services to both consumers and businesses, related to (among other things) mobile banking, social networking, or connected devices (Internet of Things – IoT). Responding to this challenge is not optional. But managers of telecom firms have many choices with regard to *how* they may respond, and even more with regard to how specific initiatives are to be organized. They may decide to maintain a focus on traditional telecom operations, and outsource the development of new services, or they may partner with other firms that have this capability. If they decide to develop new services internally, they may give the responsibility to the existing business units, establish a strategic initiative across the units, or establish a new business unit focused on developing new offerings. The level of organizational complexity in their organizations will partly be a result of which option that is selected (and of how it is implemented).

This line of reasoning is consistent with Child's (1972) concept of "strategic choice." At the time of his article, there was a tendency among contingency theorists to view the relationship between external demands (or contingencies) and internal organizational structure as deterministic; but Child argued that the organizational structure is influenced by managerial choices. Consequently, the increase in complexity cannot be attributed solely to external factors. The basic proposition of the transaction cost approach was that diseconomies of scale increase with increasing size. But Williamson (1975) also pointed out that there are factors that may moderate the (predicted negative) relationship between firm size and performance. Two important moderating factors that he mentioned were appropriate organization of activities within the firm and effective governance practices. The role of these moderating factors was confirmed in the study reported in Canbäck et al. (2006). There is also some indirect support for this hypothesis in the studies that consider the relationship between firm size and performance: Some of these studies show that smaller firms outperform larger firms (Dhawan, 2001) while others show that larger firms outperform smaller firms (Schmalensee, 1989). It is important to note that these studies simply correlate financial performance with size – they do not measure the level of complexity directly. Nevertheless, the inconclusive results suggest that some managers are able to keep the level of complexity in check even as the firm grows.

If we accept that managerial choices play a role, it is important to explain why managers sometimes make suboptimal decisions. We also need to understand why the overall level of internal complexity seems to be increasing for firms in many industries. We do not have definitive answers to these questions, but we may encounter some likely explanations by considering the nature of decision-making processes within firms. It is also useful to consider the methods that are available to managers and the impact of new management concepts and organizational forms.

It is well established that decision makers simplify the structure of intractable problems in order to select a course of action (e.g., Schwenk, 1984). When considering alternative options for organizing a firm, managers may thus fail to see the real implications of alternative models, and inadvertently select organizational models that increase rather than decrease complexity.

There are various cognitive biases that may play a role. One bias identified by Heath and Staudenmayer (2000) is "partition focus," that is, the tendency for people to partition a task prematurely, resulting in subsequent integration problems. For example, when faced with a new project, software managers tend to immediately divide the effort into five or six pieces, and assign each piece to a development team. Once allocated a responsibility, software engineers (as other workers) often display another limitation – which Heath and Staudenmayer call "component focus": More effort is devoted to completing one's own piece of work than on understanding how the piece fits into the overall system. Only in later stages of the project is it discovered that there are significant interdependencies between the pieces, which cannot be resolved without intensive communication between the various teams in the project.

Another possible explanation is a phenomenon called "the tyranny of small decisions" (Haraldsson et al., 2008). Managers in organizations make local, independent decisions, which are relatively insignificant when seen separately, but which create complexity in a cumulative manner over time. Decisions about local issues often occur "under the radar" of senior executives. In some firms, senior executives are primarily concerned about the composition of their own leadership team and the performance of their direct reports, and rarely question the way units are designed one or more levels down in the organization, unless they receive reports of dysfunctional practices or problems. This means that sub-unit managers have relatively ample latitude in defining roles and responsibilities within their own units. Thus the actual design of large organizations is the result of hundreds of small compromises and adjustments that are made to resolve local issues.

It is also likely that the adoption of new management concepts and organizational forms has contributed to the increase in complexity.

The traditional functional organization – with different functions for sales, manufacturing, service and so on – was a frequent target of criticism during the 1980s and 1990s. It became clear that the internal functions frequently represented isolated "silos" that in fact aggravated people's pre-existing "component focus." Important new organizational concepts were introduced to counter this tendency, such as the idea of end-to-end processes and cross-functional teams. However, at times, new roles and structures are simply added *on top of* the existing formal organization. For example, in an attempt to create greater process orientation, companies have typically created roles for managers as the "process owners" of end-to-end processes. However, this creates an immediate challenge in terms of accountability, as two dimensions of managers are now responsible for process performance (the process owners and the respective functional managers).[8] A national railway company went one step further by introducing – in addition to the two dimensions of functions and processes – a *third* dimension of "process coordinators," who were supposed to facilitate coordination between functional managers and process owners. As Heath and Staudenmayer (2000) observed, coordination problems are frequently repaired by introducing even more coordination mechanisms. The challenge of integrating the "process dimension" into the organization's systems of roles and accountabilities has until recently received little attention by the proponents of process improvement techniques such as agile, Lean, and Six Sigma.

8 In a study reported in Pritchard and Armistead (1999), "confusion or ambiguity between functions and processes" was ranked as one of the greatest difficulties in implementing process-based organizations.

Developing a new agenda for managing and re-designing complex organizations

The evidence pointing to negative implications of complexity and the indications that complexity is increasing raise the question of how one can respond in a more effective manner. How can organizations be designed in a manner that minimizes complexity, or that prevents the build-up of complexity? The following section discusses two possible ways in which to confront this challenge. The first is related to the need for a clear definition of the concept itself. Secondly, we consider the organizational strategies that leaders may adopt to manage complexity.

Definitional framework

In the PwC study cited above, only 4% of CEOs indicated that they were able to measure the internal complexity in their firms. At the most fundamental level, we cannot expect to be able to reduce complexity unless we have a method that lets us identify, document, and ideally, measure it. In Chapter 1, we introduced the difference between functional requirements and design parameters. This distinction makes it possible to conceptualize complexity by viewing it from two different angles. The first is based on axiomatic design theory

(Suh, 2005), and considers the relationship between functional requirements and design parameters. The second considers the relationships among design parameters (Eppinger, 2001).

A simple example, drawn from political philosophy, may serve as an illustration. The French philosopher Montesquieu was the first to outline the three basic functions of government: Legislate (create laws), Enforce (implement and enforce laws), and Provide for Justice (interpret and apply law and resolve disputes). These are essentially functional requirements for the design of governments. The functions are performed by three different systems: The judicial system (the courts), the elected legislature (i.e., the parliament, or the congress in the US), and the executive branch of government (state institutions including law enforcement agencies). Montesquieu's real innovation, however, was in pointing out that effective government required *separation of powers*. The influence of any one power should not be able to exceed that of the other two, either singly or in combination. In Table 2.1 these relationships have been mapped in a design matrix (cf. Chapter 1).[9]

Modern political systems vary in their degree of separation. For example, in parliamentary systems, the prime minister and the cabinet are drawn from the parliament, and the members of parliament often select the leaders of the executive branch of the government. According to Saunders (2006) a full separation of powers would imply, for example, that members of the executive should be independently selected. Nevertheless, all democratic systems maintain some degree of separation and it is interesting to note that a lack of separation, or what Suh (2001; 2005) calls *coupling* between functional requirements, is usually associated with ineffective or dysfunctional government. For example, in some countries, corruption and interference from politicians or governmental officials threaten judicial independence. Given our definition here, such governments would represent a more *complex* design. There are two or more design parameters affecting the same functional requirement ("Provide for Justice"). The judicial branch cannot work independently to fulfill its mission. In countries governed by despotic leaders, the legislative, judiciary, and executive powers are all in the same

9 The example is inspired by a teaching note written by Le Mée (2000).

Table 2.1 Design matrix illustrating the design intent for a democratic government

Functional requirements	Design parameters		
	Elected legislature	Judicial system	State institutions
Legislate	X		
Provide for Justice		X	
Enforce			X

hands. Although there is only one design parameter in this case (i.e., the despotic leader), this is also an example of a coupled design, because one design parameter affects three functional requirements and hence the functional requirements cannot be satisfied independently (Suh, 2001; 2005).

Montesquieu also noted, however, that the three systems of government were dependent upon each other. A judge relies on the laws made by elected politicians in order to impose a sentence. The executive branch of the government also relies on the laws written by the legislators as well as the interpretation of the law made by the courts in order to carry out their mandate (see Figure 2.5). These dependencies are related, but not equivalent, to the interdependencies between functional requirements described above, as they concern what we in organization design terminology would call *process dependencies:* One unit (or individual role in an organization) is reliant upon decisions, information, or deliverables produced in another unit (or by another individual) in order to perform its activities. From this perspective, complexity can be defined as the existence of process interdependencies or, more generally, interdependencies *between design parameters*. They can be represented by means of a design structure matrix (DSM) as shown in Figure 2.5. (The DSM is described in more detail in Chapter 5. Unlike the design matrix (Table 2.1), it does not display the relationship between design parameters and functional requirements, but shows the relationships between the design parameters.) In this case, the interdependencies fall below the diagonal (the matrix is "lower triangular"). A lower triangular DSM usually implies that design parameters must be set in a sequence (or be performed sequentially, if they represent steps in a work process). In a society, for example, laws must be passed before they can be used by a court to produce a sentence. In a completely uncoupled design (i.e., a matrix with no interdependencies), parallel processing would be possible. Nevertheless, lower

		Design parameters		
		1	2	3
#	Design parameters	Elected legislature	Judicial system	State institutions
1	Elected legislature			
2	Judicial system	X		
3	State institutions	X	X	

Figure 2.5 Design structure matrix (DSM) showing process interdependencies between the three branches of government in a democratic society.

triangular matrices are still preferable to matrices with entries above the diagonal. Entries above the diagonal result in higher complexity as they may imply cyclical dependency relations, i.e., that processes require iteration back and forth before they can be completed.

The same principles may be used to analyze private corporations. The CEO of a corporation corresponds to the head of government, the shareholder meeting to parliament, and the company board to the members of cabinet (Benz & Frey, 2007). These bodies carry out separate functions, and their role and composition are regulated by law in many countries. Indeed, the principle of separation of power is central in some theoretical frameworks used to analyze corporate governance issues, most notably in *agency theory* (Jensen, 1983). Agency theory is concerned with the so-called principal-agent problem, which refers to relationships where one party (the principal) delegates work to another (the agent) who performs the work. The key concern is conflict of interests between the principal and the agent. For example, a company owner will be motivated to increase shareholder value, whereas a CEO will be motivated to maximize his or her own remuneration, power, or status. Agency theory specifies various mechanisms to ensure that the agent does not deviate from the preferences of the principal in his or her execution of the task. Proponents of agency theory have introduced specific proposals for changes in order to increase monitoring and control of management, such as splitting the role of the chairman and the CEO, increasing the number of independent directors on company boards, and separating the auditing function from the executive; for example, by requiring the members of audit committees to be independent directors.

As pointed out by Jensen (1983), agency theory essentially formalizes principles that have evolved from long experience and thus have proved to have survival value. A widely practiced principle is to separate operations responsibility from accounting responsibility. In most companies, the person who receives cash will not be the same as the one who keeps the record of the transaction, nor will the same person be able to both authorize and receive payments.

Benz and Frey (2007) argue, however, that the principle of separation of power is still applied much less strictly in private corporations than in public institutions. As an example, following the Sarbanes-Oxley Act, it is now an internal audit committee, rather than the CEO or a member of the executive team, which selects the external auditor. The members of the audit committee are selected by the board, but the board may be influenced by CEO preferences. Benz and Frey (2007) propose that the independence of the auditing process could be further improved by instead allowing the shareholders to elect the members of the audit committee. They argue that the independence of a committee depends on it having been "freely chosen by the people who have an interest in it being independent – in this case, the shareholders" (p. 95).

Achieving simplification: design criteria

The principles discussed in this chapter lead to three design criteria. These design criteria are relevant for all organizations that seek to reduce complexity (In addition to these *generic* criteria, in Chapter 8, we discuss design criteria that are developed specifically for the organization that one is (re-)designing.)

1. Minimize coupling between functional requirements

This criterion is based on Suh's *independence axiom* (1990; 2001; 2005). As we have seen, functional requirements (FRs) are the description of the outcomes that the organization needs to produce (the FRs thus describe the organization's "functionality"). The criterion implies that we must first define the functional requirements, and then design the organization (specified as design parameters (DPs)) such that each of the FRs can be satisfied without negatively affecting the other FRs (i.e. the FRs are independent).

To evaluate the relationships between the functional requirements, one can make pairwise comparisons (FR_1 against FR_2, FR_2 against FR_1, and so on).[10] If we assume that one has identified two functional requirements with two corresponding design parameters, the generic form of the question may be formulated as follows:

> 1. When DP_1 implements measures to maximize FR_1, what effect does this typically have on the ability of DP_2 to maximize FR_2?

and:

> 2. When DP_2 implements measures to maximize FR_2, what effect does this typically have on the ability of DP_1 to maximize FR_1?

If one finds that efforts aimed at achieving one FR negatively affect the ability to achieve another FR, one has an instance of coupling (or "functional conflict").

There is no standard approach to remove coupling, and it will often require creativity to find a solution that decouples the FRs (Figure 2.6). At times, it will be necessary to re-design the overall organizational structure. As an example, in the case of the white goods manufacturer described at the beginning of the chapter, the goal conflicts between the sales representatives (when organized according to products) may be minimized by reverting to the geographical organizational

10 A methodology for assessing coupling is described in more detail in Worren (2018).

structure. Where there is coupling between FRs related to the activities performed by a sub-unit or an individual role, one can usually keep the overall organizational model, but must *separate* roles or sub-units, that is, ensure that the functional requirements that are in conflict are assigned to different roles or sub-units (depending on the level of analysis). Both empirical research and computer simulations confirm that it is possible to perform conflicting or incompatible activities in an organization (without a loss of productivity) as long as they are not carried out by the same sub-unit (Huckman & Zinner, 2008, pp. 188–189; Ethiraj & Levinthal, 2009).

Figure 2.6 Simplification according to axiomatic design – decoupling of functional requirements that are in conflict.

2. *Minimize coordination costs*

This criterion is based on Thompson (1967) (see Chapter 1) and the more recent work carried out by Tushman and Nadler (1978) and Eppinger and Browning (2016). These authors view organizations as information processing systems (cf. Chapter 1) and consider the cost of interchanging information and achieving coordination across sub-units. To minimize coordination costs, we need to consider the formal structure of the organization in relation to the work processes, and find the grouping of roles and sub-units that best matches the work process interdependencies (Figure 2.7). (In Chapter 5 we describe how one can use the design structure matrix (DSM) to analyze interdependencies between DPs and find an appropriate grouping of roles or sub-units.).

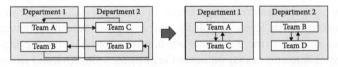

Figure 2.7 Simplification according to an information processing perspective – alignment of formal boundaries with work process interdependencies.

In some cases, one will have more than one alternative that satisfies these two criteria (as well as the firm-specific design criteria that may have been identified – cf. Chapter 8). In these situations, there is a third criterion that should be used to select the best alternative.

3. Among two or more viable options, select the one that has the highest probability of being implemented[11]

This criterion is based on Suh's (1990; 2001) information axiom. It implies that we need to consider the complexity of the proposed organizational model(s) relative to the maturity of the organization. A proposed organizational model may be adequate from a purely functional point of view, yet the current organization may be incapable of implementing it. The key consideration here is thus whether the organization has the necessary capability to implement the proposed design (or work according to the principles implied by the design, once implemented). For example, one of the proposals on the table may require significant improvements in the effectiveness of internal work processes or radical changes in the way different units relate to each other. Some organizations will have the resources and skills to implement such changes, while others will not. Another consideration is the degree of political support. Naturally, it is easier to implement an organizational model that has support among a critical mass of managers, employees, and other stakeholders (see Chapter 8).

11 As stated, this criterion is derived from Suh's (2001) *information axiom*, but has been re-interpreted to fit an organizational context.

Discussion

Two definitions of complexity have been described: The first defines complexity as interdependency (coupling) between functional requirements and design parameters. According to this definition, a complex organization is one where two or more design parameters (e.g., sub-units) are addressing the same functional requirement. A design matrix (Suh, 2001; 2005) was used to illustrate the existence of coupling. Coupling means that attempts at achieving a particular FR may impact the ability to achieve one or more other FRs. In organizations, coupling increases uncertainty (it becomes less clear for decision makers which levers to pull to achieve a given outcome), reduces accountability (more than one sub-unit is responsible for achieving a given outcome, or may influence the outcome indirectly), and creates goal conflicts (achievement of one sub-unit's goals may compromise the ability of another sub-unit to achieve its goals). The overall effect of high complexity is a *decreased probability that the organization will be able to achieve all of the goals that it is pursuing* (Suh, 2005).[12]

12 As a consequence, one would thus expect that the degree of complexity is related to the level of strategic risk as perceived by decision makers: The more complex the organization, the higher the risk associated with the achievement of functional requirements.

The second definition states that complexity is due to interdependencies between design parameters; this was illustrated by means of a design structure matrix (DSM) (Eppinger, 2001). A complex organization according to this definition is one with many cross-unit interdependencies that requires frequent coordination and information exchange. Process interdependencies create coordination costs (because two or more sub-units need to coordinate and adjust to each other's plans or actions) and reduce organizational flexibility (because changes cannot be made independently in one sub-unit, without affecting the work performed by other units).

We may add that it is not only the existence of an interdependency that counts, but also our degree of knowledge of the existence of the interdependency, and the relative uncertainty and predictability of the interdependency. In today's more fluid organizations, it may not always be clear with whom a manager should interface with in order to complete a task. This has given rise to what is called *hidden interdependencies* (Wong, DeSanctis, & Staudenmayer, 2007). A lack of knowledge of interdependencies may thus in itself be a source of complexity.

An important implication of this definitional framework is that it points to the possibility of creating analytical tools to support organization design processes. The most frequently used tool, the organization chart, only displays one dimension of the organization – the formal reporting structure – and often conceals the inherent complexity of a design. An organization chart shows (at best) the design parameters of a current or future organization, but not how the design parameters interact or how they address functional requirements. It is therefore difficult to use organization charts as a means for comparing and evaluating different design options that are developed as part of a re-design process. The design matrix and design structure matrix (DSM) are alternative tools that can be considered. They can be used to extract the key features of an organization design and may thus allow systematic comparison and evaluation of design options.

One should perhaps distinguish between two types of measures that organizations can use to gauge the level of complexity. The first is "direct" measures reflecting the structural designs. One could use the design matrix and design structure matrix (DSM) to map an organization (or parts of it). (The level of interdependence, as well as the total number of interdependencies, are factors that can be quantified in such a mapping.) Secondly, one could use indicators that reflect the various consequences that complexity may have. Both objective, work process data (e.g., cycle time, cost, quality), and perceptual measures (e.g., employee surveys that include items regarding job design, goals, and structure, etc.) may be used for this purpose.

Organizational strategies

There are basically three generic strategies that one can adopt in the face of increasing complexity (Serdarasan, 2013) (Figure 2.8). An important premise is that one is able to distinguish between

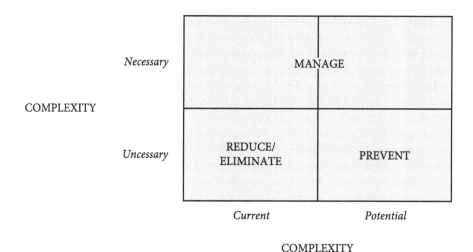

COMPLEXITY

Necessary   MANAGE

Uncessary   REDUCE/   PREVENT
               ELIMINATE

          Current   *Potential*

COMPLEXITY

Figure 2.8 Strategies for dealing with organizational complexity.
(Source: Serdarasan, 2013).

necessary and unnecessary complexity. Although there is no objective way to make this distinction, we can, in principle, define necessary complexity as the level of complexity necessary to perform the functions of a system, and unnecessary complexity as complexity that does not provide additional value to the system (the organization), or that can be avoided with little or no loss in the functions performed.

Above we described how companies sometimes adapt their structure in response to external changes. Managerial choices in such cases influence both the level of *necessary* and the level of *unnecessary* complexity. If customer needs are changing, or becoming more differentiated, the response may be to increase the frequency of product upgrades or develop entirely new products. Some increase in internal complexity may be an unavoidable result of such changes. At the same time, such a move may also lead to an increase in unnecessary (i.e., avoidable) complexity. The introduction of new product offerings may result in duplication of business processes, the introduction of new product components (where standard parts could have been utilized), incompatible infrastructure components (e.g., two or more IT systems), and the establishment of organizational roles and units with conflicting goals and KPIs (Key Performance Indicators). Similarly, the adoption of a new regulatory framework may be necessary, and also lead to important benefits for individual companies, such as improvements in internal control and audit processes (Wagner & Dittmar, 2006). But it may also result in unnecessary complexity: At times, the adoption of new governance processes lead to the establishment of multiple internal governance bodies and a multiplication of the steps that need to be performed in order to authorize a business decision. The end result may be to increase costs and slow down strategic decision making.

It is an important research question to identify what level of complexity a given type of organization can sustain, and what level of complexity is likely to be dysfunctional and hurt performance. However, even if more objective methods are developed to assess the level of complexity, in the end it is the key stakeholders in the organization who themselves must identify complexity as an issue. So it may be appropriate to say that it is when stakeholders *perceive* organizational complexity to be too high, that actions should be initiated to improve the situation. It is possible that outsiders at times perceive the level of complexity differently from managers inside the organization; something that appears chaotic to an outsider may in fact have an orderly structure (cf. Abrahamson, 2002). On the other hand, insiders may also be blinded by being immersed in the culture and mental models of their organization; the tools and methods that we have described here have an important role in sensitizing managers to the complexity that actually exists, and hopefully, in spurring them to do something about it.

Provided that one has arrived at a consensus about the acceptable level of complexity, there are two strategies that can be employed to deal with internal complexity that is deemed unnecessary. In the short term, one should try to reduce the level of unnecessary complexity. For example, a firm may be able to reduce organizational complexity by standardizing business processes, minimizing the number of individual roles performing the same job, and eliminating conflicting goals and KPIs.

The key strategy to deal with *necessary* complexity is to manage it. Large firms consist of multiple operating units, utilize many different production processes, employ diverse technologies, and rely on a global network of suppliers. They may also be characterized by highly layered hierarchies and intricate governance processes. If the firms' leaders believe that the level of complexity is necessary to sustain its operations, they should attempt to reduce the impact of the complexity on the organization's performance. For example, to avoid confusion among employees, managers may make an effort to explain how the organization is structured and clearly communicate how the key processes are performed, and how roles and responsibilities have been allocated. The firm may also help employees develop the skills required to work in a complex organization. For example, by improving communication and negotiation skills, employees may be better able to handle issues that arise in cross-unit or cross-functional teams.

Although periodic re-design may be required in order to reduce or eliminate complexity, the ideal strategy is to prevent the build-up of complexity, by selecting designs that minimize complexity in the first place, so that one avoids the need for frequent fixes or restructuring exercises. Ideally, one should not only select the design option that is optimal today – but one that also ensures that the level of complexity will be manageable in the future. The organizational model that is selected should be robust enough to accommodate changes that may occur in products, markets, or internal processes. Of course, this is easier said than done. There are organizations that alter their structure almost every year and change back and forth between organizational models based on product or geography, or between centralized and decentralized structures. But one may succeed in creating more robust designs by making a conscious effort to evaluate the inherent complexity of any proposal aimed at changing the organization and by selecting a design that minimizes (unnecessary) complexity.

The sequence in which these strategies is applied is not arbitrary. Managers who are concerned by the level of complexity in their firms sometimes suggest introducing training courses and change programs aimed at increasing collaboration, reducing inter-unit conflicts, and so on. However, such initiatives do not address the root causes of the issue, and one may thus experience that the level of complexity increases further as a result. It seems clear that the ideal sequence is to first establish what the necessary level of complexity is, and then initiate actions to reduce any unnecessary complexity, before strategies to manage the necessary complexity are employed.

Summary and conclusion

A number of studies document that organizational complexity may negatively affect the productivity of individual employees, the performance of projects and processes, and overall financial performance of a firm. Rising levels of internal complexity in large organizations is partly a result of rising environmental complexity, but it also reflects managerial choices, including the implementation of inappropriate organizational designs. Research confirms that firms of similar size and in the same industry differ with regard to the level of internal complexity.

Until recently, there has been a lack of systematic methods for managing or reducing complexity. This situation is changing with the introduction of more precise definitions and of tools that can be used to map and re-structure interdependencies between functions and design parameters. In this chapter, we reviewed two different conceptualizations of complexity. One defines complexity as coupling (i.e., conflict) between functional requirements, positing increased uncertainty as the key implication. The second defines complexity as the existence of interdependencies between design parameters, positing increased coordination cost as the key implication. These definitions are complementary, however, and provide the basis for building a systematic approach to assess complexity and to develop organization design interventions that can support leaders in dealing proactively with complexity.

Design propositions

Objective	*Maximize the effectiveness of large organizations by dealing proactively with complexity.*
2.1	Periodically assess the level of, and consequences of, organizational complexity.
2.2	"MANAGE": Implement systems, tools and processes that can help reduce the impact of *necessary* complexity.
2.3	"REDUCE": Re-design organizational structure, processes, and/or individual roles when complexity is deemed unnecessarily high.
2.4	"PREVENT": When selecting new organizational models, processes, and individual roles, other things being equal, select solutions that minimize complexity, that is, solutions which: a) *minimize coupling between functional requirements;* b) *minimize coordination costs;* c) *(among two or more viable options) have the highest probability of being implemented.*

Review questions

1 How does the definition of complexity proposed in this chapter differ from the definition traditionally employed in organization theory?
2 What are the indicators that suggest that internal complexity is increasing in many organizations?
3 How does complexity affect organizational functioning?
4 What is the difference between a design matrix and a design structure matrix (DSM)?
5 What strategies should managers adopt in order to deal proactively with rising complexity?
6 What is the meaning of the term "coupling"?
7 Does the existence of process interdependencies imply that there is coupling between functional requirements?

Research questions

1 How can we more precisely assess the level of "necessary" versus "unnecessary" complexity?
2 What is the relationship between the perceived level of strategic risk among decision makers and the level of internal complexity in an organization?

3 What indicators could be used to more systematically assess how the level of complexity within organizations changes over time?
4 What are the most effective methods for managing and reducing complexity?

References

Abrahamson, Eric. (2002). DisOrganization theory and DisOrganizational behavior: towards an etiology of messes. *Research in Organisational Behavior, 24*, 139–180.

Anderson, P. (1999). Complexity theory and organizational science. *Organization Science, 10*, 3, 216–232.

Andrews, L. B., Stocking, C., Krizck, T., et al. (1997). An alternative strategy for studying adverse events in medical care. *Lancet, 349*, 309–313.

Aral, S., Brynjolfsson, E., & Wu, D. J. (2006). *Which Came First, IT or Productivity? The Virtuous Cycle of Investment and Use in Enterprise Systems.* Cambridge, MA: MIT Center for Digital Business Working Paper.

Ashby, W. R. (1956). *An Introduction to Cybernetics.* London: Chapman & Hall.

Ashmos, D. P., Duchon, D., and McDaniel, R. R. Jr. (2000). Organizational responses to complexity: The effect on organizational performance. *Journal of Organizational Change Management, 13*, 6, 577–594.

Baldwin, C. and Clark, K. (2000). *Design Rules: The Power of Modularity.* Boston: MIT Press.

Barney, J. (1996). *Gaining and Sustaining Competitive Advantage.* Reading, MA: Addison-Wesley.

Benz, M., & Frey, B. S. (2007). Corporate governance: What can we learn from public governance? *Academy of Management Review, 32*, 92–104.

Bernanke, B. S. (2009). Financial innovation and consumer protection. Speech held at the Federal Reserve System's Sixth Biennial Community Affairs Research Conference, Washington, DC, April 17. Available online from: www.federalreserve.gov/newsevents/speech/bernanke20090417a.htm

Blau, J. R., and McKinley, W. (1979). Ideas, complexity, and innovation. *Administrative Science Quarterly, 24*, 200–219.

Blecker, T., & Kersten, W. (2006). *Complexity Management in Supply Chains.* Berlin: Schmidt Verlag.

Britt, T. W. (2003). Black hawk down at work. *Harvard Business Review*, January, 16–17.

Brooks, F. (1975). *The Mythical Man-Month.* Reading, MA: Addison-Wesley

Burton, R. M., & Forsyth, J. D. (1986). Variety and the firm's performance: An empirical investigation. *Technovation, 5*, 9–21.

Canbäck, S., Samouel, P., & Price, D. (2006). Do diseconomies of scale impact firm size and performance? A theoretical and empirical overview. *Journal of Managerial Economics*, 4, 27–70.

Carillo, P. M., & Kopelman, R. E. (1991). Organization structure and productivity: Effects of subunit size, vertical complexity, and administrative intensity on operating efficiency, *Group & Organisation Management*, 16, 44–59.

Child, J. (1972). Organizational structure, environment and performance: The role of strategic choice. *Sociology*, 6, 1–22.

Chui, M., Manyika, J., Bughin, J., Dobbs, R., Roxburgh, C., Sarrazin, H., Sands, G., & Westergren, M. (2012). *The Social Economy: Unlocking Value and Productivity through Social Technologies*. McKinsey Global Institute. Online report available from: www.mckinsey.com/industries/high-tech/our-insights/the-social-economy

Chun, Y. H., & Rainey, H. G. (2005). Goal ambiguity and organizational performance in U.S. federal agencies. *Journal of Public Administration Research and Theory*, 15, 4, 529–557.

Cross, R., & Gray, P. (2013). Where has the time gone? Addressing collaboration overload in a networked economy. *California Management Review*, 56, 1, 50–66.

Dhawan, R. (2001). Firm size and productivity differential: Theory and evidence from a panel of US firms, *Journal of Economic Behavior and Organization*, 44, 269–293.

Economist Intelligence Unit (2011). *The Complexity Challenge*. London: The Economist Intelligence Unit.

Economist Intelligence Unit (2015). *Taming Organisational Complexity — Start At the Top*. London: The Economist Intelligence Unit.

Eppinger, S. (2001). Innovation at the speed of information. *Harvard Business Review*, 79, 1, 149–158.

Eppinger, S., & Browning, T. (2016). *Design Structure Matrix Methods and Applications*. Cambridge, MA: MIT Press.

Ethiraj, S. K., & Levinthal, D. A. (2009). Hoping for A to Z while rewarding only A: Complex organisations and multiple goals. *Organisation Science*, 20, 1, 4–21.

Fleming, P., & Zyglidopoulos, S. C. (2008), The escalation of deception in organizations. *Journal of Business Ethics*, 81, 4, 837–850

Galbraith, J. (2000). *Designing the Global Corporation*. San Francisco: Jossey-Bass

Gresov, C., & Drazin, R. (1997). Equifinality: Functional equivalence in organisational design. *Academy of Management Review*, 22, 403–426.

Haraldsson, H. V., Sverdrup, H. U., Belyazid, S., Holmqvist, J., & Gramstad, R. C. J. (2008). The tyranny of small steps: A reoccurring behaviour in management. *Systems Research and Behavioral Science*, 25, 1, 25–43.

Heath, C., & Staudenmayer, N. (2000), Coordination neglect: How lay theories of organizing complicate coordination in organizations. *Research in Organizational Behavior* 22, 153–191.

Herring, R. J., & Carmassi, J. (2010). The corporate structure of international financial conglomerates – complexity and its implications for safety and soundness. In A. N. Berger, P. Molyneux, & J. Wilson (eds), *Oxford Handbook of Banking*. Oxford: Oxford University Press.

Hihn, J. M., Malhotra, S., & Malhotra, M. (1990). Volatility and organizational structure. *Journal of Parametrics*, September, 65–82.

Hinckley, C. M. (2003). Make no mistake – errors can be controlled. *Quality and Safety Health Care, 12,* 359–365.

Hoole, R. (2006). Drive complexity out of your supply chain. *Supply Chain Strategy* (Newsletter from Harvard Business School Publishing and the MIT Center for Transportation and Logistics), December–January.

Huckman, R. S., & Zinner, D. E. (2008). Does focus improve operational performance? Lessons from the management of clinical trials. *Strategic Management Journal, 29,* 2, 173–193.

IBM (2010). *Capitalizing on Complexity*. Summers, NY: IBM.

Jensen, M. C. (1983). Organization theory and methodology. *Accounting Review, 56,* 319–338.

Landau, J-P. (2009). Complexity and the financial crisis. Introductory remarks at the Conference on "The macroeconomy and financial systems in normal times and in times of stress," jointly organised by the Bank of France and the Deutsche Bundesbank, Gouvieux-Chantilly, 8 June. Available online from: www.bis.org/review/r090806c.pdf

Le Mée, J. (2000). Interactive axiomatic approach to design. *Studies in the Design Process and Design Education*, Series A, Number 7. New York: The Louis and Jeanette Brooks Engineering Design Center, The Cooper Union.

Malone, T. W. (2004). *The Future of Work*. Boston: Harvard Business School Press.

Meyer, M. W. (2002). *Rethinking Performance Measurement: Beyond the Balanced Scorecard*. Cambridge: Cambridge University Press.

Mortensen, M. (2004). Antecedents and consequences of team boundary disagreement. *Academy of Management Best Papers Proceedings*.

Pandey, S. K. and B.E. Wright (2006). Connecting the dots in public management: Political environment, organizational goal ambiguity, and the public manager's role ambiguity. *Journal of Public Administration Research and Theory, 20,* 75–89.

Peck, H. (2005). The drivers of supply chain vulnerability: An integrated framework. *International Journal of Physical Distribution and Logistics Management, 35,* 4, 210–232.

Perrow, C. (1984). *Normal Accidents: Living with High-Risk Technologies.* New York: Basic Books.

Posner, B. Z., & Butterfield, D.A. (1978). Role clarity and organizational level. *Journal of Management, 4,* 2, 81–90.

PricewaterhouseCoopers (2006). *9th Annual Global* CEO *Survey: Globalisation and Complexity; Inevitable Forces in a Changing Economy.* New York: PricewaterhouseCoopers

Pritchard, J. P., & Armistead, C. (1999). Business process management – lessons from European business. *Business Process Management Journal, 5,* 10–32.

The Radicati Group (2016). *Email Statistics Report, 2016–2020.* Available from: www.radicati.com/wp/wp-content/uploads/2015/02/Email-Statistics-Report–2015–2019-Executive-Summary.pdf

Rettig, C. (2007). The trouble with enterprise software. *Sloan Management Review, 49,* 1, 21–27.

Romano, J., & Nunamaker, F. (2001). Meeting analysis: Findings from research and practice. *Proceedings of the Thirty-Fourth Annual Hawai'i International Conference on System Sciences.*

Saunders, C. (2006). Separation of powers and the judicial branch. *Judicial Review, 11,* 337–347.

Schmalensee, R. (1989). Intra-industry profitability differences in US manufacturing: 1953–1983. *Journal of Industrial Economics, 37,* 337–357.

Schwenk, C. R. (1984). Cognitive simplification processes in strategic decision-making. *Strategic Management Journal, 5,* 111–128.

Serdarasan, S. (2013). A review of supply chain complexity drivers. *Computers & Industrial Engineering, 66,* 3, 533–540.

Simon, H. A. (1962). The architecture of complexity. *Proceedings of the American Philosophical Society, 106,* 467–482.

Suh, N. P. (2005). *Complexity: Theory and Applications.* New York: Oxford University Press.

Suh, N. P. (2001). *Axiomatic Design: Advances and Applications.* New York: Oxford University Press.

Suh, N. P. (1990). *The Principles of Design.* New York: Oxford University Press.

Thompson, J. (1967). *Organizations in Action.* New York: McGraw-Hill.

Tushman, M. L., & Nadler, D. A. (1978). Information processing as an integrating concept in organizational design. *The Academy of Management Review, 3,* 3, 613–624.

Wagner, S., & Dittmar, L. (2006). The unexpected benefits of Sarbanes-Oxley. *Harvard Business Review, 84,* 133–140.

Whittington, R., Pettigrew, A., Peck, S., Fenton, E., & Conyon, M. (1999). Change and complementarities in the new competitive landscape: A European panel study, 1992–1996. *Organisation Science, 10,* 5, 583–600.

Williamson, O. E. (1975). *Markets and Hierarchies: Analysis and Antitrust Implications*. New York: Free Press.

Wong, S., DeSanctis, G., & Staudenmayer, N. (2007). The relationship between task interdependency and role stress: A revisit of the job demands-control model. *Journal of Management Studies, 44,* 2, 284–303.

Worren, N. (2018). Operationalizing the concept of functional conflict. *European Management Review*, forthcoming.

3 Traditional organizational forms

Chapter overview

Background	• Historically, the majority of organizations have been structured according to one of three main principles (i.e., a simple, functional, or divisional form).
	• These are *unidimensional* models in that they are based on only one organizing principle.
	• Typically, firms start with a simple structure and progress to a functional and then a divisional structure as they expand (but there are also exceptions to this pattern).
Challenges	• Each organizational model has strengths and limitations.
	• The strengths and limitations are not visible on an organization chart depicting each model.
Key questions	• How can we best conceptualize each of these organizational models?
	• How can we compare and evaluate the models?
Proposed approach	• Describe the simple, functional, and divisional models in terms of their functional requirements and design parameters.
	• Compare the models in terms of how they contribute to fulfilling different design criteria.
	• Identify the circumstances in which each model is the most appropriate.
	• Consider mechanisms that may compensate for some of the weaknesses of each model.

Introduction

Which organizational model should a firm or institution adopt? New organizational models are developed in response to the unique requirements that firms or institutions are facing. No firm or institution will (or at least should not) attempt to implement a pre-made model "off the shelf." Yet historically, it is also true that most of the organizational models that firms have adopted have been derivations of one of four fundamental models:

1   The simple structure
2   The functional structure
3   The divisional structure
4   The multidimensional structure

In this chapter, we consider the first three models. They are *uni-dimensional* structures, meaning that they are based on one main organizing principle. The fourth alternative is a *multidimensional* structure, which combines different organizing principles (at the same hierarchical level). This alternative is discussed in the next chapter.

The main goal of the current chapter is to describe each of the three traditional models and evaluate their strengths and weaknesses using the conceptual frameworks introduced in the preceding two chapters. We will consider in which situations each model is most appropriate and also discuss more recent variations and extensions of the models.

The simple structure

Most firms are small businesses. There is no standard definition of "small," but if we use fewer than 20 employees as a cut-off, they represent 90% of all firms and 20% of all employment (this holds for the US as well as for EU and OECD countries) If we increase the cut-off to 100 employees, they represent 99% of all firms and 60–70% of employment in most countries (Hurst & Pugsley, 2011; OECD, 2000). Typical examples of small businesses include dentists, plumbers, real estate agents, and family-owned shops and restaurants. Most of them are small because their productivity is directly linked to the particular skills of the employees. They don't have much to gain from expansion and usually don't grow over time. However, a tiny subset (about 4%) of small firms are fast growing *entrepreneurial* companies (Hurst & Pugsley, 2011, p. 88). These are quite different from the other small firms in that they seek to innovate: They start out with an idea for a new product or service, try to develop the concept and attract funding, and hope to grow into a larger firm.

However, these two types of small firms are similar in terms of how they are organized. They tend to have a *simple structure*, which we may characterize as the *absence* of structure (Mintzberg, 1983): Informal roles, little hierarchy, no departments or sub-units, and few rules and procedures. Most of the large firms we know today were once small firms. Microsoft, for example, only had 15 employees in 1978. The employees in Microsoft at this time did not have fixed roles and helped out where there was a need. Problems were solved by arranging brain-storming sessions where all of the employees contributed. As head of the company, Bill Gates had the main responsibility for the business strategy. But he still continued to write code as well. In fact, Gates personally reviewed every line of code the company shipped, and often rewrote parts of it as he saw fit (Wallace & Erickson, 1996).

Let us consider a prototypical small firm in some more detail. What are the functional requirements? For the majority of small firms, we may define two main requirements (see Table 3.1): The firm has to be managed, and customers have to be served. This corresponds with the typical formal structure of small firms, which is simply divided into two levels: Manager (or owner), and employees – all employees report directly to the manager/owner (Figure 3.1). Depending on what type of firm we are considering, there may be additional functional requirements. For example, entrepreneurial firms may need to develop a new product or service, and they may also need to secure funding and identify additional resources. But the basic structure remains the same (see Table 3.2).

How do people in such a firm work and collaborate with each other? The lack of formalized roles and departments implies that employees are *generalists*. They may be assigned any kind of task

Table 3.1 Design matrix for simple structure for small business (as intended)

Functions	Design parameters	
	Manager/owner	Employees
Lead the company (e.g., create strategy and supervise staff)	X	
Serve customers		X

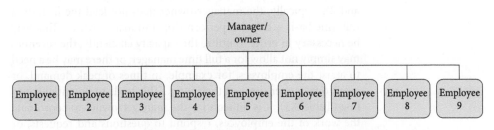

Figure 3.1 Organization chart for firm of 10 people with simple organizational structure.

Table 3.2 Design matrix for simple structure for entrepreneurial firm (as intended)

Functions	Design parameters	
	Manager/owner	*Employees*
Lead the company (e.g., create strategy and supervise staff)	X	
Develop (and produce/deliver) product or service		X

and thus learn about many aspects of the business. There may potentially be dependencies between most or even all employees in the work processes that are performed.

The simple structure has some important advantages compared to more elaborate structures. It requires a minimum of preparation and planning to set up. It can handle unpredictability: There is only one leader, who may be able to make decisions quickly (Mintzberg, 1983). Since there are no middle managers who filter information before it reaches the boss, the leader can stay in touch with every employee and receive information directly from them about the operations. The lack of formalism may be conducive to creating a climate of trust. Instead of following job descriptions or rules, employees make personal commitments toward each other about what they will deliver (Scherr, 1993). The incentives in small firms are what economists have called "high powered" (Zenger & Hesterly, 1997): The incentives depend strongly on factors that each employee has a direct influence on. This may increase the motivation of employees to expend additional effort to succeed (cf. Vroom, 1982). In contrast, in a large firm, the effect of incentives is dulled as the actions of many other people and units may affect the outcome. Finally, for small entrepreneurial and technical firms, the lack of internal differentiation may mean that it is easier to produce an integrated offering, something that is a challenge for larger firms with multiple, specialized departments. It may also facilitate innovation as information flows more freely between people in an informal setting (Murray & Worren, 2003).

Yet there are also a number of tensions inherent in the simple structure. Indeed, the simple structure is actually a complex one, viewed from the perspective of axiomatic design (cf. Chapters 1 and 2). Typically, the manager/owner does not lead the firm on a full time basis – but also performs operational activities. This may be necessary in order to utilize the capacity efficiently; the revenues may simply not allow for a full time manager, or there may be a need to assist the employees, for example, in times of peak demand, or even to take over some of their work. This leads to potential coupling (Table 3.3): It is difficult for the manager/owner to coordinate the work of the employees, respond to questions and requests, or think of new business opportunities, if he/she is himself busy in the

Table 3.3 Design matrix for simple structure for small firm (as typically observed)

Functions	Design parameters	
	Manager/owner	Employees
Lead the company (e.g., create strategy and supervise staff)	X	
Serve customers /deliver services	(x)	X

shop serving customers.[1] Moreover, the employees may also feel that the manager is meddling in their work.

The flat organizational structure (only two levels) has some advantages, but it also has some disadvantages. There is no distinction between junior and senior employees in the simple structure, and consequently no career ladder or promotion opportunities. The simple structure is also quite autocratic. The power over all important decisions tends to be centralized in the hands of the leader, and this may diminish employee motivation over time (Mintzberg, 1979).

The lack of roles and sub-division into departments leads to a very coordination-intensive organization, particularly for entrepreneurial firms that face high uncertainty. As pointed out in Chapters 1 and 2, coordination is not free. Every time that one discovers a need to perform a new task, it will require a discussion about how it should be performed and who the responsible person should be. For a small technical firm, a lot of "cycling back and forth" may occur between people before they can agree on how a task should be solved from a technical point of view. For example, in a small IT firm, the addition of a new module in a software package may affect many of the existing elements of the software and require all of the coders to make adjustments (Clark & Baldwin, 2000).

Leaders of entrepreneurial firms often extol the virtues of informality. The lack of rules and procedures may mean that there is little bureaucracy. But the lack of rules and procedures may also, paradoxically, put a stranglehold on further growth. Every issue requires a new and unique decision, which may not be consistent with earlier decisions. An inconsistent or ad hoc approach to decision making may not be viewed as fair by the employees (bureaucracy is a negatively laden word these days, but it also provides some benefits, including consistency). Moreover, the lack of formalized and specialized roles may lead to uncertainty about what expectations employees have to live up to, and thus they may be unable to focus on a specific task and develop expertise within a given area (Sine, Mitsuhashi, & Kirsch, 2006).

Many small firms continue to operate with a simple structure despite these challenges. Yet there are some that transition to another organization model. When does this happen – what are the

1 In Chapter 6, we discuss the requisite organization perspective developed by Elliot Jaques. From that perspective, the situation described in the text implies that the manager/owner works below the required role level. This is a phenomenon that also occurs in larger organizations.

factors that trigger a shift? There are a number of factors that may render the simple structure unworkable and trigger a search for an alternative organizational model, or alternatively, lead to business failure if the structure is left unchanged. The first, and possibly the most important, is size. A single manager/owner might be able to lead and coordinate a small group of people, but not a larger one. So as the firm grows and more employees are hired, the more acute becomes the need for specialization and sub-division into smaller groups. As one consultant to small businesses remarked:

> We see many companies where all (perhaps 50) staff report directly to a chief executive officer who operates the company rather like a family business (. . .) and is reluctant to define clear roles and responsibilities. In our experience, this is the point at which most companies fail, mostly because they have tried to keep the "warm, friendly, and intimate" feeling from when the company was first established, failing to realize that a shift to professionalism is absolutely essential.
>
> (Föller, 2002, p. 64)

A second factor is related to the nature of the technology. For a young, entrepreneurial firm, considerable effort is usually spent on defining the business model and developing the initial prototype or service concept. But after the development period, when the product or service has reached a certain point of maturity, it is usually possible to codify how it works or how it should be delivered. In this phase, one does not need as much innovation as before – one rather needs the predictability that one gets from documentation and standardization. With experience, one can anticipate and remove many of the interdependencies that lead to a need for close collaboration in initial development phase. One may then be able to create rules and guidelines for how issues are to be resolved, instead of relying on interpersonal coordination and ad hoc problem solving every time a new problem occurs (Clark & Baldwin, 2000). Last but not least, external factors often play a role. The firm may (if it succeeds) take on larger or more discerning customers, or a new investor may join the board of the firm – and may have higher expectations with regards to stability, professionalism, and consistency.

The functional structure[2]

2 The functional structure, which refers to grouping by knowledge or skill, should not be confused with the term *functional requirement*, which refers to an outcome that the organization delivers. Despite the potential for confusion, the term "functional structure" is retained in this book because it is commonly used elsewhere.

Unlike the simple structure, the functional structure is *differentiated*. Employees are specialists who are organized into different departments or other types of sub-units (e.g., teams). Usually, the grouping criterion is professional knowledge or skill: The scientists are placed in *Research and Development (R&D)*. The manufacturing engineers are grouped in *Manufacturing*. The commercial people are placed in *Sales & Marketing.* In a traditional manufacturing firm with a functional structure, there are typically sequential interdependencies. The (unfinished) product moves from one department to the next, each one adding something to it before it is delivered to the customer (Figure 3.2).

Above, we saw that the simple structure is primarily designed to deliver only two main outcomes (related to operations and management of the firm). In the functional structure, these have been decomposed into more detailed functional requirements (Table 3.4). In addition, it performs an additional function – that of establishing common policies and procedures. Overall leadership of the firm is still the responsibility of a general manager or CEO (Chief Executive Officer). But daily supervision of employees is delegated to middle managers (sometimes called functional managers), hence an additional hierarchical layer is introduced (Figure 3.3).

The main advantage of the functional structure is that it encourages development of specialized skills within each of the departments. Employees are supervised by one of their own, rather than by a generalist manager. In a larger firm, there may be career paths within the department (i.e., junior employees have the opportunity to advance to more senior technical or managerial positions). People of similar backgrounds and with similar interests and values are organized together. This may facilitate social interaction and forge a strong identity in each unit.

The prototypical example of a functional unit is the university department: Its mission is to create deep functional expertise (Sosa & Mihm, 2008). But functional structures are used in many other sectors. Pharmaceutical firms, high tech companies, manufacturing firms, as well as hospitals and public sector organizations may be

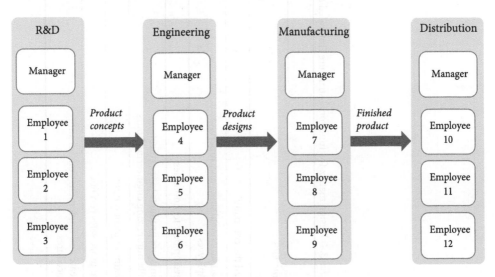

Figure 3.2 Typical workflow in a firm with a functional structure.

Table 3.4 Design matrix for functional structure (intended design)

Functions	Design parameters						
	CEO	Middle managers	Research & Development	Engineering	Manufacturing	Sales and Marketing	Staff
Lead the company	X						
Lead functional units and supervise employees		X					
Develop new technologies			X				
Configure products to specifications while minimizing engineering hours				X			
Maximize plant output					X		
Maximize sales revenue						X	
Create and implement policies and procedures							X

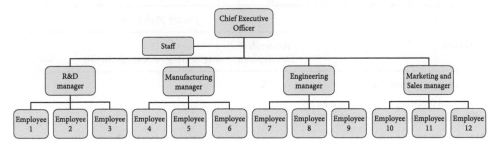

Figure 3.3 Organization chart for firm of 18 employees with a functional structure.

functionally organized. Another advantage is observed in firms with multiple products that are based on the same technology platform. In a firm with a functional structure, the responsibility for different products is allocated to the same unit instead of being split between different units.[3] This means that, say, an engineering department can ensure that all products adhere to the same standards, that they are compatible with each other, and that components are transferred and re-used across products in order to save development time and cost (ibid.).

Unfortunately, the functional structure also has some important limitations. The departments are either cost or revenue centers and are not measured on overall firm profitability. Thus there is a potential contradiction between striving for excellence within one's own discipline and supporting other units or satisfying broader organizational goals. As the size of units increases and more units contribute to producing the finished product or service, it also becomes more difficult to observe individual performance and closely link pay and performance. Hence, the effect of incentives is diminished compared to a small firm with the simple structure (Zenger & Hesterly, 1997). As mentioned above, by grouping specialists in sub-units, one facilitates integration within the departments (e.g., across different products, as just mentioned) but complicates integration across the departments. The members of each department may not communicate very frequently, and when they do, they may even have great difficulty appreciating each other's perspective. Functional departments tend to create separate "thought worlds" (Dougherty, 1992). The employees in the Research & Development (R&D) department in a manufacturing firm may not necessarily focus their efforts on the requirements that people in the marketing & sales department believe are the most important to customers. Those who belong to the engineering department may do their best to introduce new product features, but may ignore requirements regarding manufacturability, and thus cause an increase in manufacturing time and cost (or conversely, manufacturing managers may fail to provide information about plant capacity or constraints to the engineers

3 The text refers to a pure functional structure. Many large organizations have a hybrid model where responsibility for different products has been allocated to different teams *within* a department in the functional structure.

Table 3.5 Examples of goal conflicts (coupling) in functional organizations (see explanation in text)

	Design parameters			
Functions	*Research & Development*	*Engineering*	*Manufacturing*	*Sales*
Develop new technologies	**X**			x
Configure products to specifications while minimizing engineering hours		**X**	x	
Maximize plant output		x	**X**	
Maximize sales revenue	x			**X**

designing the product). Similarly, a lack of customer and market information from the Sales unit may constrain the ability of the R&D unit to develop commercially viable products (Table 3.5).

As mentioned above, new positions are created for middle managers in the functional structure (cf. Figure 3.3). Hence the managerial capacity is strengthened compared to the simple structure. In principle, this should allow the general manager (or CEO) to focus less on operational issues and dedicate more time to long-term planning and strategic leadership, as well as to external relationships such as partnerships with suppliers and alliances with other firms. But in practice, because of the coordination problems we discussed, the general manager is often overburdened with operational issues that are escalated to him/her for resolution. As stated by Hax & Majluf (1981, p. 426): "The general manager must act as the final decision maker and arbitrate disputes among specialties, because he is the only one who is fully accountable for the performance of the organization."

There are, however, various coordinating mechanisms that may be put in place to (at least partly) compensate for these limitations of the functional structure. One may encourage more collaboration across the departments and perhaps reward managers who succeed in coordinating across units and in identifying and implementing business opportunities together with others. Another option is to create a dedicated "integrator role" that is made responsible for coordinating between two or more departments (Galbraith, 1973). A third possibility is to set up cross-functional project teams (i.e., teams with representatives from the different departments). The team leader of the project will be responsible for meeting customer needs (as well as for the economic results of the project) and will seek to integrate contributions from the different specialists. Many knowledge intensive service providers, such as engineering, consulting, and IT firms, organize their specialists in functional departments (sometimes called "groups" or "practices"), but set up cross-functional project teams to deliver client projects.

Yet these coordination mechanisms may not always be sufficient to compensate for the limitations of the functional structure. The functional organization is not designed to accommodate diversity (other than the diversity among the specialties represented by the functional departments themselves). Many firms that move from the simple structure to a functional structure serve *one* customer group and have *one* product, *one* manufacturing site, and *one* distribution system. If the firm decides to develop a wide range of products, target several market segments, or expand internationally, it is not clear who should be accountable for these initiatives. With limited time or resources, it may also be difficult for employees in the functional departments to know which of several product or market segments to prioritize, and to handle all the information necessary to deliver multiple products or services at the same time (Duncan, 1979). The functional structure is also inflexible. A re-orientation of the strategy may necessitate a complete reorganization; all the departments are interdependent (and thus affected by a change) and there is no simple way to add new units (at least not without breaking the basic organizing principle of the functional structure).

The divisional structure

The functional structure was the most common organizational form until the 1950s. But during the 30 years that followed, the majority of firms abandoned this form. In the US, a study showed that the percentage of firms with a functional structure decreased from about 60% in 1949 to 10% in 1970 (Rumelt, 1974). Instead, they adopted a new form: The divisional structure (it also called the multidivisional form or "M-form").[4]

Whereas a functional organization is structured according to inputs (the specialties represented by the departments), a divisional organization is structured according to either the outputs produced (i.e., products) or the markets served (i.e., customer segments or geographical areas). As the name suggests, it consists of units that were traditionally called "divisions," although today it is more common to call the units *business units*. (In large firms, there may be a second layer, so that business units are in turned grouped into different *business areas*.) The divisions are semi-independent units, and usually have their own functional departments (see Figure 3.4).

4 The same pattern has been observed in other countries but the trend started later. In Spain, for example, the move toward divisionalization did not start before the 1990s (the percentage of functionally oriented firms declined from 43% in 1993 to 22% in 2003) (Sanchez & Suarez, 2010)

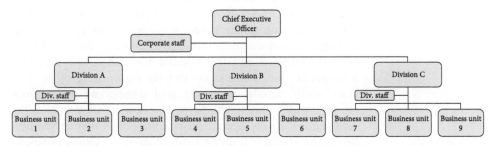

Figure 3.4 Organization chart for multidivisional firm with three divisions and nine business units.

In addition, there is a central administration, called the headquarters (HQ), with the top management as well as some centralized staff functions (e.g., HR, Finance, and IT). (In this respect, it is actually a hybrid model in the sense that it combines two different grouping criteria.) Unlike a department in the functional structure, a division is a profit center and the divisional manager is thus accountable for the overall profitability of the division. Whereas top managers focus on maximizing shareholder value, divisional managers focus on maximizing divisional level profitability. The core idea is that each unit is self-contained, at least in principle. In a manufacturing firm, for example, each division will typically develop, manufacture, and sell its own products (Table 3.6). In addition, each division will usually have its own staff and support teams (although these are also replicated at the headquarters). Considerable decision-making authority is delegated to the manager so that the unit can respond to the specific requirements that it faces (Mintzberg, 1983). All activities related to a particular product, market segment, or geography are grouped in the same unit (i.e., division). The result is a reduction in coordination costs, compared to the functional structure. As stated by Sanchez & Mahoney (1996, p. 64): "The tasks within a multidivisional firm are intentionally designed to require low levels of coordination so that they can be carried out by an organizational structure of quasi-independent divisions functioning as loosely coupled sub-systems."

The creation of semi-independent divisions that are profit centers should reduce goal conflicts (or *coupling*). One implication is that the divisional heads are more likely to pursue goals that are consistent with the goals of the company as a whole, compared to managers in the functional structure (Grant, 2016) (although there are exceptions, which we will discuss below).

Even though divisional managers are in charge of only one segment of the business, they are exposed to the full range of managerial issues (Hax & Majluf, 1981). Hence the career paths in the divisional structures create a pool of general managers that may be capable of leading a new initiative or managing a new unit.

The decentralization of both resources and decision-making authority to the divisional level (with regards to operational decisions) means that the CEO and the executive team (normally located at the headquarters) can take on a more strategic role. One key function of the headquarters is to develop the overall strategy for the firm, which includes determining the overall portfolio of businesses and the mandate for each of the divisions. A second key function is to monitor the performance of the divisions, which includes budgeting, goal setting, and performance measurement. A third function is to allocate financial resources. The headquarters usually operate an internal capital market (Barney, 2010). The executive team approves requests for capital expenditures from the divisional managers and may also seek external

Table 3.6 Design matrix for divisionalized firm (intended design)

Functions		CEO & Executive team	HQ Corporate staff	Division 1	Division 2	Division 3
			Design parameters			
Maximize shareholder value	Develop corporate level strategy, monitor divisional performance, and allocate capital	X				
	Develop and implement policy and procedures		X			
Maximize divisional profitability	Maximize profitability of product A			X		
	Maximize profitability of product B				X	
	Maximize profitability of product C					X

funding to support new business initiatives or to support a struggling division.

The divisional structure was first introduced by the US chemical firm DuPont in 1921. But it gained popularity after the Second World War, when firms grew rapidly and introduced additional product lines. The divisional structure made this expansion possible. But Mintzberg (1983) argued that divisionalization is a structure that not only *supports* diversification; it also encourages further diversification. Divisions can be added (or removed) without having to re-structure the entire firm. Financial resources can be allocated to the initiatives with the greatest growth potential.[5] It is also a robust structure: Since units are in self-contained, the risk is lower that economic problems in one division will reverberate to the rest of the system.[6]

Oliver Williamson hailed the divisional structure as a major organizational innovation (Williamson, 1983). He predicted that firms that adopted the divisional structure should outperform firms that maintain a functional structure. Research has largely confirmed this prediction. For example, Armour and Teece (1978) analyzed a sample of petroleum firms during the period 1955–1973, and found a positive relationship between the adoption of the divisional structure and profitability during the period in which this structure was being diffused among firms in this industry.[7]

Nonetheless, there may also be situations when the divisionalized structure is problematical. With relatively independent divisions, there is always a risk of suboptimization, i.e., that divisions make choices that improve their performance at the expense of the organization as a whole (Miles & Sn ow, 1992). Let us consider three scenarios that have been extensively discussed in the academic literature. The first is related to goal conflicts between divisional leaders and corporate management (Table 3.7a). One example is when corporate management intends to reduce overall purchasing costs, for example, by creating firm-wide agreements with a limited number of external suppliers. Yet for an individual division, switching to a new supplier (perhaps with an inferior offering) may actually increase costs (Argyres, 1995).

A second (and related) issue is goal conflicts across the divisions themselves. As we have seen, an important assumption behind the divisional structure is that tasks can be decomposed in order for the divisions to operate relatively independently. Yet in many firms, the divisions share resources, technologies, and customers. At the very least, this means that decisions and actions by one division will affect other divisions and require compensating actions and decisions in those divisions. Such interdependencies may directly affect the financial performance of the divisions. This is the case, for example, where divisions buy or sell raw materials or components from each other. A division which raises the transfer price of a component will increase its profits, but reduce the profits

5 Yet, the claim that divisionalization leads to further diversification did not receive support in Donaldson's (1982) study.

6 Yet, this is not only dependent on the organizational structure of the firm, as we discuss here, but also on the legal structure. Many firms create separate legal entities for divisions (or business units) in order to reduce risk.

7 They also found that the increased performance did not persist after most of the firms in the industry had adopted the structure. The most likely explanation is that it no longer provided any competitive *advantage*, but at the same, that it conferred *competitive parity* in that continuing with the structure also prevented firms from incurring a competitive *disadvantage* (cf. Barney, 2010).

Table 3.7a Potential conflicts between divisional goals (functions) and those of corporate management

Functions	Design parameters			
	HQ	Division 1	Division 2	Division 3
Maximize shareholder value	**X**	x	x	x
Maximize profitability of product A	x	**X**		
Maximize profitability of product B	x		**X**	
Maximize profitability of product C	x			**X**

Table 3.7b Potential conflict between goals (functions) of different divisions

Functions	Design parameters			
	HQ	Division 1	Division 2	Division 3
Maximize shareholder value	**X**			
Maximize profitability of product A		**X**	x	x
Maximize profitability of product B		x	**X**	x
Maximize profitability of product C		x	x	**X**

of the division buying the component (Zimmerman, 1997) (Table 3.7b).

A third challenge is related to integration. During the last couple of decades, many companies have concluded that margins are higher for *integrated solutions* that address broader customer needs, compared to stand-alone products (Day, 2006; Galbraith, 2002). Consequently, they aim to offer a "bundle" of products or services by configuring a set of products or components from different internal units into a complete solution. The introduction of such a "solutions strategy" implies that one starts orienting oneself toward a different market segment (i.e., customers who prefer buying a complete solution rather than stand-alone components). The different divisions must coordinate in order to sell solutions and configure the different products or components into an attractive and well-functioning system. This is likely to prove difficult in a product-based, divisionalized firm: There is nobody who is accountable for the customer dimension[8] across the various products and who can coordinate across the divisions. Moreover, the leaders of the divisions are measured and rewarded on profitability related to their particular product, and not on the value of the solutions that the firm may be able to configure for a customer (Table 3.7c).

8 However, one may add such a coordinating unit. A first step may be the introduction of a key account manager role or team, which interacts with clients and represents all of the firm's products or services (see Day (2006) and Galbraith (2002)).

Table 3.7c Introduction of new functional requirement related to integration

Functions	Design parameters			
	HQ	Division 1	Division 2	Division 3
Maximize shareholder value	X			
Maximize profitability of product A		X		
Maximize profitability of product B			X	
Maximize profitability of product C				X
Maximize market share in segment A		x	x	x
Maximize market share in segment B		x	x	x
Maximize market share in segment C		x	x	x

How do corporate management react when they are faced with these kinds of challenges? As pointed out by Zhou (2013), many top executives will want to centralize decision making in order to prevent division managers from taking actions that are contrary to the goals of other divisions or that are contrary to those of the entire company. Corporate managers will try to intervene, for example, to make sure that two divisions reach agreement regarding the sharing of a common resource such as manufacturing capacity, or regarding the segmentation of the market between the two divisions with overlapping customer bases. They may also try to alter the reward system by introducing goals related to collaboration or cross-selling across the product categories.

Yet the divisional structure is premised on the idea of decentralization of operating decisions. Too much intervention by corporate managers will deprive division managers of the independence that they need to manage their specific businesses (Miles & Snow, 1992). As pointed out by Argyres (1995, p. 347), intervention by corporate managers may result in the removal of crucial decisions from the division managers' hands. It reduces their decision-making authority, while maintaining similar degrees of responsibility.[9]

This leads us to a paradox with the divisional structure. The divisions are supposed to be semi-independent. Ignoring this principle is problematical, as we have just seen. On the other hand, there must also be a reason for why the divisions belong to the same firm. There must be some synergies between the divisions in order for the whole to be worth more than the parts. If there are no synergies, then top managers should considering selling or spinning off the divisions (Zimmerman, 1997).

Alternative grouping principles

As mentioned, the majority of large firms are already divisionalized. Selecting this structure is just the first step, however. The more

9 The French engineer and management theorist Henri Fayol (1911, cited in Pryor & Taneja, 2010) introduced the principle that there should always be parity between responsibility and authority. If a person is given responsibility without the commensurate authority, it means that he or she must use informal means (e.g., persuasion of colleagues) to acquire resources and escalate decisions (i.e., refer them to a higher level manager) to seek approval. These issues are discussed in more depth in Chapter 6.

difficult task may be to select the *grouping principle*. As mentioned, there are three main alternatives: Divisions may be defined according to products, market segments, or geographical markets.

In a *product-based* structure, the divisions are responsible for a specific type of product or service, or alternatively, a product line or brand. A consumer goods company may have three product divisions: Skin care (e.g., lotions), Home care (e.g., detergents), and Oral care (e.g., toothpaste). An electronics firm may have product divisions responsible for printers, servers, and personal computers. A more recent approach is to structure the organization based on *markets*. Units in such an organization can either be defined by the *market segments* that customers are categorized in or by the *geographical regions* that customers are located in. A bank may be decomposed into three main units: One for individual customers, one for small businesses, and one for large businesses. A multinational company may comprise a number of national subsidiaries; governmental institutions such as the police or the tax authorities may be divided into regions and districts.[10]

When the divisional structure was introduced, most firms adopted a product-based grouping. This variant is appropriate for firms with several distinct products that have few interrelationships. However, with the increasing importance of solutions (combinations of products or services), firms are increasingly adopting a customer- or market-based structure. The appropriate choice thus depends on the nature of the offering and the strategy of the firm. If the main goal is to improve product functionality or cost, a firm should select a product-based model. If the main goal is to become more customer oriented or provide solutions, it should adopt the market-based structure. This is the essence of the contingency-based approach briefly described in Chapter 1: Structure follows strategy (Chandler, 2013; Donaldson, 2001).

We should note that when organizations introduce a new grouping principle, it does not imply that all levels of the organization undergo change and now conform to the new criterion, but that there is a change in the *priority* of several criteria (Thompson, 1967). For example, a large divisional firm may organize its main units according to geography (North America, Europe, Asia). But at the next level, it may be structured by product (Hardware, Software) within each of the geographical units. At the third level, it may be organized by function (Research & Development (R&D), Engineering, Marketing, Sales) (see Figure 3.5).

More recent developments of the divisional structure

From duplication to consolidation of support activities

As we have discussed, divisional autonomy was a key principle in the original version of the divisional structure. Divisions were

10 There are also some additional grouping criteria that we may add to this list, but which are less common. It is possible to structure organization according to its *projects*. An engineering firm may be subdivided into a few large projects, each focused on delivering a specific solution to a client. A hospital may choose to structure its organization based on the *degree of urgency* (e.g., one division for emergencies, one for day surgery, and one for elective care). Many governmental departments are organized according to the *sector* that they oversee (e.g., the department of education may have one unit for primary education, one for secondary education, and one for higher education).

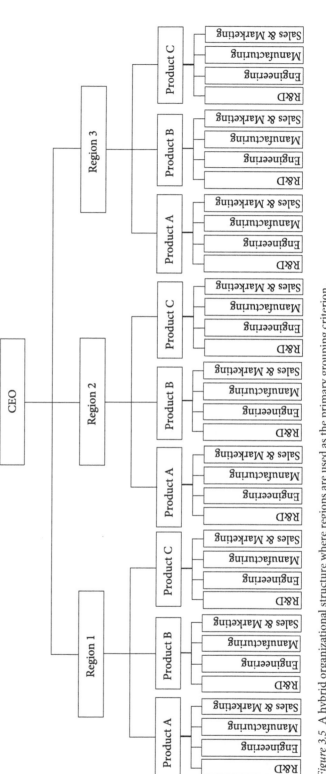

Figure 3.5 A hybrid organizational structure where regions are used as the primary grouping criterion.

supposed to be semi-independent and self-contained. This implied that the manager of a division would have hierarchical control not only over the main functional departments (e.g., R&D, engineering, manufacturing, and sales) but also over support functions. Every division would thus contain departments for finance & accounting, HR, and IT (see Figure 3.6a). Over time, one realized that this led to inefficient duplication, as the support units in many cases carried out similar tasks, such as the processing the payroll and travel expenses. It was concluded that there was little need to customize such support services to each division. The work processes could be standardized, and efficiency could be increased by processing a greater volume of cases (often in the same location). This started a trend in the 1990s where companies would consolidate these administrative tasks into separate Shared Services centers (Figure 3.6b).

Today, practically all large organizations (including many governmental agencies and institutions) operate one or more Shared Services centers. These centers typically provide services related to IT, accounting, HR, and facility management. In some ways, this trend resembled earlier attempts in some firms to centralize administrative tasks. Even before the 1990s, some hotel and retail chains, for example, had centralized support units rather than decentralized support units within each regional division (Mintzberg, 1979). Yet the Shared Services concept differs from traditional centralization in several ways. Units that were centralized in the traditional divisionalized firm were usually placed at the headquarters and managed by a manager belonging to the corporate staff function. In contrast, Shared Services units are supposed to play an *internal supplier* role, and the internal clients (divisions or business units) decide which services they need and pay according to the volume of service that is consumed. The interface is regulated by means of a service level agreement that stipulates the quality level (e.g., availability, response time, etc.) as well as the prices (usually per transaction or unit of service). An important difference is thus that the centralized functional departments used to be funded from the central, corporate budget, whereas the Shared Services function is funded by from the budgets of the divisions or business units. What is common to both centralization and Shared Services centers is that they consolidate activities and resources. But a Shared Services center decentralizes decision making for resource allocation, at least in principle (Strikwerda, 2014).

From competitive to cooperative divisional structures

Similarly, although many firms still have a divisional structure, today there is generally far more emphasis on collaboration between sub-units and between divisions than when the divisional structure was introduced. People may collaborate in many different ways.

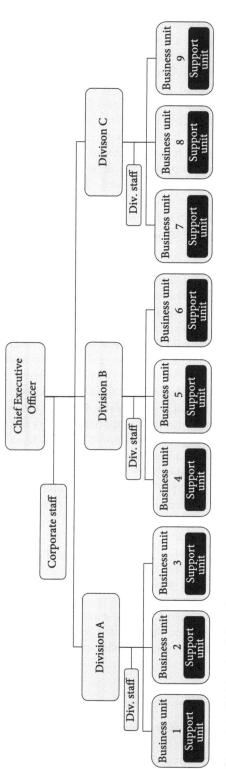

Figure 3.6a Divisionalized firm where each division has a dedicated support unit.

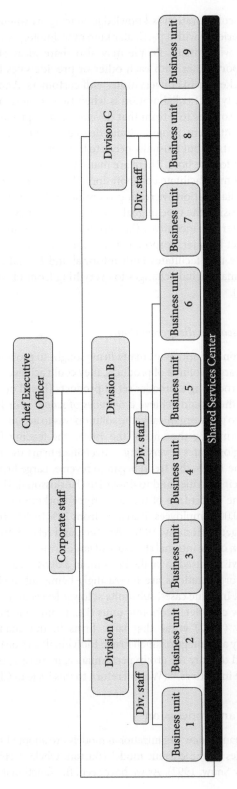

Figure 3.6b Divisionalized firm with Shared Services function.

One type of collaboration is knowledge sharing, as when a person who has experience with a particular kind of technology shares technical advice with others. People may also share ideas about new business opportunities with each other or provide sales leads that they have picked up in conversations with customers. Another, and more formal type of collaboration is when two or more units both contribute resources to a team that develops a new product or that delivers a joint client project. Some degree of collaboration may happen all by itself, but it usually needs to be reinforced by corporate management to take hold. There are many ways in which corporate management may facilitate collaboration. They may promote integration and collaboration by creating a common mission and strategy, and by addressing the type of goal conflicts that we have discussed. They may alter the incentives (i.e., criteria for bonus and promotion) to reflect broader, corporate goals. They may also establish an infrastructure that facilitates both informal and formal collaboration (which may include changes to everything from IT systems to office design).

From rising scale to disaggregation.

11 Economies of scale for a firm implies reductions in the average cost (cost per unit) arising from increasing the scale of production for a single product type. Economies of scope implies lowering average cost by producing more types of products based on the same know-how or assets.

After the Second World War, many firms sought to grow in size. By producing a larger volume of products, they could achieve *economies of scale*. By producing a broader set of products (based on the same know-how), they could achieve *economies of scope*.[11] For firms that were unable to grow organically, the solution was to acquire or merge with other firms. By the end of the 1960s, the leading firms had become conglomerates – very large, diversified firms (Sobel, 1999). Yet during the 1970s, this trend began to reverse. Large firms started to refocus their activities and to downsize (Hoskisson & Hitt, 1995). In the US, the percentage of the labor force working in firms with more than 10,000 employees decreased from 29% to 20% from 1977 to 1987 (Zenger & Hesterly, 1997). Another, and related, trend was a *disaggregation* of the internal structure of large firms. As we discussed above, the division used to be the key unit in a divisionalized organization. But organizations are increasingly being sub-divided into smaller parts. In some cases, sub-units at lower levels of the organization are now complete economic units (i.e., profit centers). Zenger and Hesterly (1997) argue that large firms in this manner may replicate a key advantage of small firms: Individuals can be measured and rewarded directly for group performance, increasing the effectiveness of the incentives.[12] (We will return to this issue in Chapter 5.)

12 Developments with regard to IT (e.g., introduction of ERP systems), cost accounting and benchmarking methods have made it possible to provide accurate and low cost measures of sub-unit performance on many different dimensions (e.g., volume, quality, customer satisfaction, etc.) (Zenger & Hesterly, 1997).

Discussion and conclusion

As a firm expands, new organizational models are adopted to correct for deficiencies in the current model (Burton, Obel, & Håkonsson, 2015; Miles & Snow, 1992). As we have seen, the functional structure emerged as a way of correcting for the lack of formalization and specialization of the simple structure. Increasing size is usually the trigger that leads to the realization that the simple structure is hindering the achievement of strategic goals (typically growth objectives). The divisional structure was in turn introduced to compensate for the inflexibility of the functional structure. Typically, difficulties in handling diversity (i.e., an increasing number of products, geographies, or customer segments) triggers the adoption of a divisional model.[13] This leads to the stages of development depicted in Figure 3.7. We should note that the figure is highly simplified and only shows the most typical progression of a firm. For example, many small firms do not grow and keep the simple structure. There are also examples of large firms (see case example) that have not transitioned to the divisional structure. A more detailed comparison of the three organizational forms with regards to 12 different design criteria are shown in Table 3.8.

The simple, functional and divisional structure are *generic* organizational models. The descriptions in this chapter are obviously simplifications of actual organizational structures that one will encounter in practice. There are several variants and hybrids of these models.

One hybrid is a divisional organization organized as a value chain, which may be seen as a combination of the functional and divisional structure. Such firms have separate divisions, but they are arranged in a value chain so that output from one division is the input for the next division. In other words, there are sequential interdependencies between the units, just as there are between the departments in a functional structure. Firms that are structured in this manner include oil firms[14] (which typically have divisions for exploration and drilling, refinery, and distribution) and aluminum producers (who may have divisions for mining, refining (alumina production), and aluminum metal production).[15]

There are also important variations among small firms. Some of them transcend the simple structure and introduce more formalized and specialized roles, making them resemble the other structures we have discussed. One study assessed the level of role formalization and functional specialization (on a scale from low to high) among 450 small internet firms (with a median size of six employees) and correlated this with later revenues. It found that an increase of one standard deviation in role formalization and functional specialization increased

13 On the other hand, introducing a multidivisional structure when there is only one product will reduce operational synergies: "Use of the multidivisional form in an undiversified corporation would destroy economies of scale in production, purchasing and marketing" (Donaldson, 1986, p. 175).

14 During the last decade, however, the general trend among oil firms has been toward disaggregation (i.e., many oil firms have concentrated on the core activity of exploration and drilling, and sold off other assets).

15 The divisions in aluminum firms also sell by-products directly to the external customers (e.g., bauxite), in addition to providing outputs to the next division in the chain.

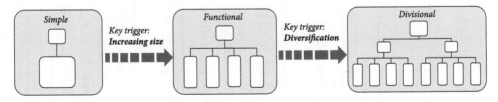

Figure 3.7 Typical evolution of organizational structures over time.

Table 3.8 Comparison between the three organizational forms discussed in the chapter with regards to twelve generic design criteria

V The structure strongly facilitates . . .
+/– The structure may or may not facilitate . . .
– The structure is an obstacle to . . .

Criteria	Organizational structure			Rationale
	Simple	Functional	Divisional	
1. Innovation	V	+/–	+/–	Simple structures allow for informal information sharing
2. Intensity of incentives	V	+/–	+/–	Simple structures have "high powered" incentives
3. Time and capacity for strategic management of the business	–	+/–	V	Divisional structure frees up capacity for strategic thinking
4. Integration among different functional domains	V	+/–	+/–	In a simple structure, all functions are in the same unit
5. Integration among products (in multi-product firms)	+/–	V	+/–	In a functional organization, the same department handles more than one product (but also see criterion 12 below)
6. Consistency in terms of policies and procedures	–	V	V	Functional and divisional structures have dedicated staff units
7. Development of technical excellence	–	V	+/–	Each department in the functional structure houses people with specialized skills (they are not split among divisions)
8. Career paths for specialists	–	V	+/–	In the functional structure, the main career paths are within the departments, which are larger than in a same sized divisional firm
9. Career paths for generalists	–	+/–	V	Divisionalized structures facilitate development of generalist management skills as divisions are self-contained
10. Scalability	–	+/–	V	In a divisionalized structure, the size of the divisions can be increased or new divisions may be added
11. Robustness	–	+/–	V	In a divisionalized structure, business problems may be isolated to one division without affecting the others
12. Accommodation of product or customer diversity	–	+/–	V	New divisions can be established to handle new product categories, customer segments, or geographies

future revenues by more than 50% (Sine et al., 2006). Hence it seems like leaders of small firms can compensate for the weaknesses of the simple structure that are listed in Table 3.8.

The examples in this chapter were based on two simplifying assumptions: The first is that the activities of the firm are performed internally rather than externally. However, one of the most important trends during the last three decades has been the outsourcing of work that previously was done internally to outside partners. Initially, companies outsourced production to lower cost locations, such as China, India, and Mexico. It then became common to outsource some or all of the work previously performed by Shared Services centers (particularly IT) to an outside partner. More recently, there are examples of companies that have outsourced distribution, sales and marketing, and even core functions like engineering, and research & development (Gottfredson, 2005). Anand and Daft (2007) coined the term "hollow organization" to describe a new form of organization that perform only core business processes in-house and outsource all non-core processes (i.e., processes that are not deemed to be critical for competitive advantage). One important change is that a company with only a handful of people may now potentially deliver a large and complex product to a global market. Yet it does not fundamentally change the logic of the approach that we utilize in this book: The company is still responsible for making sure that the same functional requirements are fulfilled as before, but activities are performed by external partners rather than by resources owned by the firm.

Secondly, it was assumed that the sub-units within the firm are permanent (or semi-permanent) rather than temporary. Yet today, many firms rely on projects that are established to deliver a specific product or service customized to the requirements of a particular client. Project-based firms are common within industries such as IT, engineering, consulting, and advertising, as well as in the legal profession. Nonetheless, most project-based firms do not consist solely of projects, but have a traditionally structured line organization that houses the resources and contains staff and support units[16] (see Figure 6.5 in Chapter 6 for a specific example). The line organization may either be a functional or a divisional structure. Establishing projects implies that a second organizing dimension is introduced (with project managers in addition to line managers). Hence, this structure may be analyzed using the principles for multidimensional models described in Chapter 4.

16 There are exceptions, such as film production, were the firm that organizes the project is only a legal vehicle and has no permanent staff (Whitley, 2006).

Case Example: Apple versus Sony and the development of the first iPod

The majority of large firms have adopted the divisional structure, as explained above. Yet there are some exceptions, the

most famous one being Apple, which has a functional structure, even though it has 116,000 employees. However, it has,
considering its size, a relatively limited number of products,
making the functional structure feasible. As explained by
Matthey Yglesias, a journalist for the Vox online newspaper:

> If you look at their executive team you'll find that there's
> no senior vice president for iPhone who works alongside
> a senior vice president for Mac. Nobody is in charge of
> Macs or iPhones or iPads or really anything else, because
> Apple is almost entirely functional. There's a chief design
> officer and a senior vice president of software engineering
> and a senior vice president of hardware technologies (. . .)
> Of course there are also more traditional senior func-
> tional executives like a general counsel and a chief finan-
> cial officer. But the closest thing Apple has to a divisional
> chief with responsibility for a specific line of business is
> (. . .) the senior vice president for retail.
>
> (Yglesias, 2017)

Apple's choice of organizational model may have been a
factor that facilitated its re-emergence as a leading consumer
electronics firm in 2001 – when it succeeded in launching the
iPod, the MP3 player that was the precursor for the iPad and
iPhone.

At the time, it was Sony, and not Apply, that was considered
the leading consumer electronics company. Sony was nomin-
ated as "one of the world's most admired companies" in
Fortune magazine in 1997. Its main hit in the preceding years
had been PlayStation, but it also had large market shares in the
TV monitor, digital cameras and camcorder markets. In addition, it had acquired CBS records in 1988 and Columbia
Pictures in 1989 in order to get access to music and film
content.

Sea-Jin Chang, a business professor at the National
University of Singapore, conducted an in-depth study of Sony
(Chang, 2008). He concluded that Sony was ideally positioned
to develop an iPod device: It had repeatedly developed port-
able music and film players, beginning with the Walkman in
the 1980s. It also owned a vast amount of music and had been
planning a new digital music player long before Apple introduced the iPod; in fact, Sony presented two digital music
players at an industry conference in 1999. However, Sony was
a divisionalized company and two divisions (the VAIO
company and Personal Audio Company) had developed these
devices separately, without any cooperation. Both of the two
devices received negative reviews.

Only in 2004 did Sony succeed in developing a product (called Networkman) comparable to the iPod, but by then, the iPod was already a mainstream product. Because Sony owned a music business, it was more sensitive to illegal copying and sharing of digital than Apple. For this reason, Sony used a proprietary format for the Networkman and made it incompatible with the MP3 standard, which was used in the iPod. As Chang (2008) explains, Sony's in-house music business created negative synergies (i.e., coupling) instead of positive ones.

Sony's organizational structure had been developed during the analog era, when TVs, audio, and computers were independent. But a key element in the digital revolution was convergence: Products that used to be distinct began to overlap and compete. Sony's divisions were organized as separate divisions, and when Sony bought CBS and Columbia Pictures, they continued as independent corporations, led by US executives, and with little supervision by the Sony headquarters in Japan. Apple, in contrast, had a much more integrated organizational structure, combined with a history of effective internal collaboration between specialists from different technical disciplines (Hansen, 2009).

Design propositions

Objective	*Identify the appropriate organizational form that maximizes the effectiveness of small firms (less than 20 employees) without significant growth prospects.*
2.1	Adopt a simple organizational structure.
2.2	Compensate for the weaknesses of this structure by clarifying goals and expectations, create agreements about roles, and by formalizing certain aspects of the business (e.g., HR policies).
2.3	Be heedful of the challenges that arise when the manager/owner steps in and performs operational tasks (see text).
Objective	*Identify the appropriate organizational form that maximizes the effectiveness of small firms (less than 20 employees) with significant growth prospects.*
2.4	Work with only a minimum of formality in the initial phase, when the new product/technology is being developed.
2.5	Start formalizing roles, processes, and procedures when the initial version of the product/technology has been developed.

2.6	As the firm grows to more than 15–20 people, change the structure into a functional form.
Objective	*Identify the appropriate organizational form for medium sized and large firms.*
2.7	Select a functional structure if:
	• There is one main product or a range of product variations based on the same technology platform. • The nature of the product or service (or stage of development) suggests a need for strong functional expertise. • There are multiple products, but they benefit from integration or platform sharing (and multidimensional models are not feasible).
2.8	Select a product-based divisional structure if:
	• There are multiple products. • The different products are based on different technologies or business models. • The firm has a strategy focused on technology leadership. • The firm seeks standardization of products and services across sites/geographies. • [For industrial products] The purchasing process in the client organization is centralized (e.g., performed by a HQ procurement unit).
2.9	Select a customer-based divisional structure if:
	• There are multiple products. • The firm has a solutions strategy (i.e., the firm seeks to sell combinations of products, customized to individual clients (or to market segments), with a significant service element.
3.0	Select a geographically-based divisional structure if:
	• There are multiple products. • Customer needs vary between districts/countries, necessitating regional/local adaptation of products and services. • [For industrial products] The purchasing process in the client organization is decentralized (e.g., performed by local subsidiaries).
3.1	Select a *multidimensional structure* if the importance of the product, customer and/or geographical dimension is equally important (see Chapter 4).

Review questions

1 What are the main differences between the simple, functional, and divisional structure?
2 Who has the Profit and Loss (P/L) responsibility in a firm with a functional structure?
3 Who has the Profit and Loss (P/L) responsibility in a divisionalized firm?
4 In which circumstances is each organizational form most appropriate?
5 What are typical goal conflicts (i.e., coupling) that may emerge in a firm with a simple structure?
6 What are typical goal conflicts (i.e., coupling) that may emerge in a firm with a functional structure?
7 What are typical goal conflicts (i.e., coupling) that may emerge in a firm with a divisionalized structure?
8 What are some recent developments or extensions of the divisionalized form?
9 To what extent can one compensate for the weaknesses of each form?
10 What are alternative grouping principles for divisionalized firms?
11 According to Table 3.8 there the career paths for specialists in divisionalized firms are worse in divisionalized firms than in functionally organized firms. Why may this be so?
12 Why hasn't Apple adopted the divisional structure, despite being a large firm?

Research questions

1 Existing theorizing and research has provided some general guidelines for when a firm should choose a product-based versus a customer-based structure. How can we develop more specific decision criteria?
2 May axiomatic design principles help explain why some variants and hybrids of the traditional organizational forms are viable, whereas others are dysfunctional (Argyres, 1995; Mintzberg, 1983)?
3 In firms with a functional structure, to what extent can the assignment of goals related to integration and collaboration compensate for the tendency to focus narrowly on one's own unit?
4 In firms with a divisional structure, can we preserve clear divisional level accountability, even when there is extensive collaboration across divisions?

References

Anand, N., & Daft, R. (2007). What is the right organization design? *Organizational Dynamics Organizational Dynamics*, 36(4), 329–344.

Argyres, N. S. (1995). Technology strategy, governance structure and interdivisional coordination. *Journal of Economic Behavior and Organization, 28*, 337–258.

Argyris, C. (2005). Actionable knowledge. In C. Knudsen & H. Tsoukas (Eds.), *The Oxford Handbook of Organization Theory*. Oxford, UK: Oxford University Press.

Armour, H. O., & Teece, D. J. (1978). Organizational structure and economic performance: A test of the multidivisional hypothesis. *The Bell Journal of Economics, 9*(1), 106–122. doi:10.2307/3003615

Barney, J. B. (2010). *Gaining and Sustaining Competitive Advantage*. Upper Saddle River, NJ: Financial Times/Prentice Hall.

Burton, R. M., Obel, B., & Håkonsson, D. D. (2015). *Organizational Design: A Step-by-Step Approach*. Cambridge, UK: Cambridge University Press.

Chandler, A. D. (2013). *Strategy and Structure: Chapters in the History of the Industrial Enterprise*. Mansfield Centre, CO: Martino Publ.

Chang, S.-J. (2008). *Sony vs. Samsung: The Inside Story of the Electronics Giants' Battle for Global Supremacy*. Singapore: Wiley.

Clark, K. B., & Baldwin, C. Y. (2000). *Design Rules: The Power of Modularity*. Cambridge, MA: The MIT Press.

Day, G. S. (2006). Aligning the organization with the market. *MIT Sloan Management Review, 48*(1), 41.

Donaldson, L. (2001). *The Contingency Theory of Organizations*. Thousand Oaks, CA: Sage Publications.

Donaldson, L. (1986). Divisionalisation and size: A reply to Grinyer. *Australian Journal of Management, 11*, 2, 173–189.

Donaldson, L. (1982). Divisionalization and diversification: A longitudinal study. The *Academy of Management Journal, 25*, 4, 909–914.

Dougherty, D. (1992). Interpretive barriers to successful product innovation in large firms. *Organization Science, 3*, 2, 179–202.

Duncan, R. (1979). What is the right organization structure? Decision tree analysis provides the answer. *Organizational Dynamics, 7*, 3, 59–80.

Föller, A. (2002). Leadership management needs in evolving biotech companies. *Nature Biotechnology, 20* (July), 64–66.

Galbraith, J. R. (1973). *Designing Complex Organizations*. Reading, MA: Addison-Wesley.

Galbraith, J. R. (2002). Organizing to deliver solutions. *Organizational Dynamics, 31*(2), 194–207. doi:10.1016/S0090–2616(02)00101–8

Gottfredson, M. (2005). Strategic sourcing from periphery to the core. *Harvard Business Review, 83*(2), 132–139.

Grant, R. M. (2016). *Contemporary Strategy Analysis*. Chichester, West Sussex, UK: Wiley.

Hansen, M. T. (2009). *Collaboration: How Leaders Avoid the Traps, Create Unity, and Reap Big Results*. Boston, MA: Harvard Business Press.

Hax, A. C., & Majluf, N. S. (1981). Organization design: A survey and an approach. *Operations Research, 29*(3), 417–447.

Hoskisson, R. E., & Hitt, M. A. (1995). *Downscoping: How to Tame the Diversified Firm.* New York: Oxford University Press.

Hurst, E. G., & Pugsley, B. J. (2011). What do small businesses do? *Brookings Papers on Economic Activity* (Fall), 73–142.

Miles, R. E., & Snow, C. C. (1992). Causes of failure in network organizations. *California Management Review, 34*(4), 53–72.

Mintzberg, H. (1979). *The Structuring of Organizations.* Englewood Cliffs, NJ: Prentice-Hall.

Mintzberg, H. (1983). *Structure in Fives: Designing Effective Organizations.* Englewood Cliffs, NJ: Prentice-Hall.

Murray, F., & Worren, N. (2003). Why less knowledge can lead to more learning: Innovation processes in small vs. large firms. In R. Sanchez (Ed.), *Knowledge Management and Organizational Competence.* Oxford, UK: Oxford University Press.

OECD. (2000). *Small and Medium-sized Enterprises: Local Strength, Global Reach.* Retrieved from www.oecd.org/cfe/leed/1918307.pdf

Pryor, M. G., & Taneja, S. (2010). Henri Fayol, practitioner and theoretician – revered and reviled. *Journal of Management History, 16*, 4, 489–503.

Rumelt, R. P. (1974). *Strategy, Structure, and Economic Performance.* Boston: Harvard University. Graduate School of Business Administration. Divison of Research.

Sanchez, M. J., & Suarez, I. (2010). Towards new organizational forms: Evidence from Spain. *International Journal of Organizational Analysis, 18*(3), 340–357.

Sanchez, R., & Mahoney, J. T. (1996). Modularity, Flexibility, and knowledge management in product and organization design. *Strategic Management Journal, 17*, 63–76.

Scherr, A. L. (1993). A new approach to business processes. *IBM Systems Journal, 32*(1), 80.

Sine, W. D., Mitsuhashi, H., & Kirsch, D. A. (2006). Revisiting Burns and Stalker: Formal structure and new venture performance in emerging economic sectors. *Academy of Management Journal, 49*(1), 121–132.

Sobel, R. (1999). *The Rise and Fall of the Conglomerate Kings.* Washington, DC: Beard Books.

Sosa, M. E., & Mihm, J. (2008). Organization design for new product development *Handbook of New Product Development Management* (pp. 165–197). Oxford: Butterworth-Heinemann.

Strikwerda, J. (2014). Shared service centers: From cost savings to new ways of value creation and business administration. In T. Bondarouk (Ed.), *Shared Services as a New Organizational Form* (pp. 1–15). Bingley, UK: Emerald.

Thompson, J. D. (1967). *Organizations in Action: Social Science Bases of Administrative Theory.* New York: McGraw-Hill.

Vroom, V. H. (1982). *Work and Motivation*. Malabar, FL: Robert E. Krieger Publishing Company.

Wallace, J., & Erickson, J. (1996). *Hard Drive: Bill Gates and the Making of the Microsoft empire*. Chichester: John Wiley.

Whitley, R. (2006). Project-based firms: New organizational form or variations on a theme? *Industrial and Corporate Change, 15*, 1, 77–99.

Williamson, O. E. (1983). *Markets and Hierarchies: Analysis and Antitrust Implications: A Study in the Economics of Internal Organization*. New York; London: Free Press; Collier Macmillan.

Yglesias, M. (2017, Apr 4,). Apple may have finally gotten too big for its unusual corporate structure. Vox.com. Retrieved from: www.vox.com/new-money/2016/11/27/13706776/apple-functional-divisional

Zenger, T. R., & Hesterly, W. S. (1997). The disaggregation of corporations: Selective intervention, high-powered incentives, and molecular units. *Organization Science, 8*(3), 209–222.

Zhou, Y. M. (2013). Designing for complexity: Using divisions and hierarchy, to manage complex tasks. *Organization Science, 24*(2), 339–355.

Zimmerman, J. (1997). EVA and divisional performance measurement: Capturing synergies and other issues. *Journal of Applied Corporate Finance, 10*(2), 98–109.

4   Designing multidimensional organizations

Chapter overview

Background	• Many large organizations today are structured along multiple dimensions, representing markets, products, and internal services.
	• Compared to a unidimensional structure, a multidimensional structure allows greater decentralization, eliminates duplication or multiplication of similar sub-units, better reflects the organization's work processes, and creates a more balanced leadership team.
Challenges	• The organization design literature has over-looked the differences between alternative ways in which to combine different dimensions of large organizations.
	• Managers and consultants also tend refer to any multidimensional structure as a "matrix."
	• There are several ways in which to design multi-dimensional organizations, which differ in terms of their complexity and flexibility.
	• A particular challenge is designing the horizontal linkages between the units representing the different dimensions.
Key questions	• How can the multidimensional organization best be conceptualized?
	• How can we analyze and evaluate the complexity and flexibility of alternative multidimensional designs?
Proposed approach	• Employ axiomatic design principles to distinguish between three multidimensional organizational models: the traditional matrix structure, the front-back model, and the modular organization.

- Distinguish between two types of linkages: reporting relationships and internal customer-supplier relationships.

- Examine the internal and external contingencies that would favor one multidimensional model over another.

Introduction

Identifying the right criterion by which to structure organizations has always been a core issue in organization design. As we saw in Chapter 3, traditionally there have been two main alternatives for medium sized and large organizations: The functional structure and the divisional structure. (There are also three variations of the divisional structure, which can be organized based on products, geographies, or market segments.) Until recently, a fairly common assumption was that it was necessary to select one main criterion, in other words, that organizational structure needed to be *unidimensional*. Strategy experts (e.g., Porter, 1996) have maintained that developing a successful strategy requires the ability to focus, by prioritizing the activities that contribute most strongly to competitive advantage. From this perspective, it seems natural that the relative importance attributed to each criterion (functional excellence, product/service, geography, or market) should be reflected in the organization design. Contingency models (e.g., Donaldson, 2001; Treacy & Wiersema, 1995) prescribed how one should align the organization with the chosen strategy. If functional excellence was the key concern, one should choose a functional organization. If the firm had a high diversity of products, one should choose a product-based, divisional organization. If the firm had a high diversity of geographical units, it should choose a geographical structure. If customer orientation was deemed paramount, it should adopt a market-based structure (Day, 2006).

However, over time, as organizations grew in size and complexity, it gradually became clear that selecting one criterion for structuring an entire organization might lead to compromises that result in suboptimal performance. There were also indications that companies with a unidimensional structure were rarely able to maintain the structure over time; some even oscillated between different (unidimensional) structural configurations. The IT technology firm Cisco is a case in point. From 1997 to 2001, it was organized as three semi-autonomous business lines, one for each main customer type: Large companies, small/medium companies, and Internet Service Providers. Each business line developed and marketed its own product, and had its own sales staff. In 2001, the company chose to introduce a product-based structure, and the three business lines were divided into 11 technology groups. The rationale was to consolidate engineering resources to ensure that technological solutions would be reused across customer segments. Gulati & Puranam (2009) examined the implementation of the new organization more closely. Whereas the new formal structure would suggest that the company operated as a "product centric" company, they instead found that informal networks from the previous customer-oriented organization prevailed. For example, marketing people would continue to approach their old colleagues from engineering to solve problems or to seek advice on how to respond to customer enquiries. It is likely that the informal networks were used to compensate for the fact that new formal structure had placed engineers farther away from the customers. Cisco later seemed to acknowledge that the new structure was inadequate in terms of customer responsiveness, and introduced cross-unit processes in 2004, aimed at achieving integration across the technology groups, and also introduced a set of "business councils" that essentially replicated the older grouping by customer type (albeit at a higher level in the organization).

In conclusion, it is difficult to find one criterion that is appropriate across units that hold different roles and carry out fundamentally different kinds of activities. Of course, as in the Cisco case, people may informally compensate for this weakness, but it is arguably better to find a formal structure that reflects the actual functions that an organization seeks to fulfill. Consequently, many large organizations today are *multidimensional*. Units within the organization that are responsible for the development and manufacturing of products are typically organized by brand or technology platform. Units responsible for sales and customer support are organized by geography (e.g., country) or market segment (e.g., large, medium sized, and small customers). Finally, staff units such as HR, IT, Finance, and Accounting are typically organized functionally (i.e., by knowledge and skills).[1] Initially, organizations simply combined such units by utilizing different grouping criteria at different levels of the hierarchy, creating a hybrid organizational model (as described in Chapter 3). For example, at the lowest level of the organization, units would be grouped by knowledge and skills, then at the next level they would be combined into larger units grouped by product, which in turned would be grouped by geography. With a multidimensional structure, however, it is not necessary to select one dominant criterion at the expense of another, as it is possible to create a design where units representing different dimensions are represented *at the same hierarchical level*. This development is illustrated in Figure 4.1.

It is natural to compare multidimensional organizations to the *divisional* (or *multidivisional*) organization described in Chapter 1. In a pure version of the divisional model, divisions are supposed to be largely independent economic units, with managers that directly

1 We define a multi-dimensional organisation as one consisting of a formal reporting structure where two or more dimensions are represented at the same hierarchical level (see Figure 4.1c). A "dimension" here refers to a set of organisational sub-units having been decomposed based on a certain criterion (e.g., products, customers, segments, functions, etc.). A functional organisation with *informal* coordinating mechanisms such as lateral networks does not constitute a multidimensional organisation as described here.

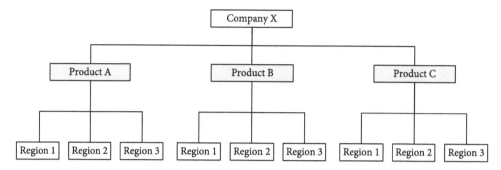

Figure 4.1a Hybrid organization with multiple levels of grouping, with products as the main grouping criterion.

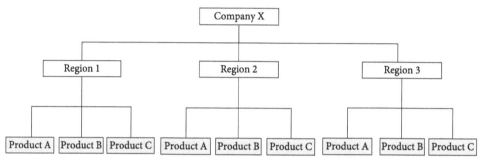

Figure 4.1b Hybrid organization with multiple levels of grouping, with regions as the main grouping criterion.

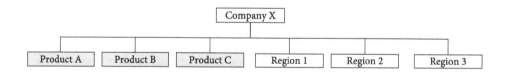

Figure 4.1c Multidimensional organization.

control the resources required to perform their processes. Few firms are organized in this manner today. The majority of large firms have increased resource sharing and coordination between divisions (Hoskisson et al., 1993; Whittington et al., 1999). For example, firms have consolidated administrative functions into Shared Services units and introduced account management processes in order to coordinate sales and marketing. However, the multidimensional models as defined here go a step further by formally decoupling two or more core dimensions (such as products and regions) that are usually organized within the same division or business unit in a multidivisional company.

A multidimensional structure should confer a number of advantages:

- It should make it possible to combine the main advantages of three different organizational models: The customer orientation of a market-based structure, the technology focus of a product-based structure, as well as the economies of scale and competence building derived from a functional structure (if internal units such as IT, HR, and Finance & Accounting are grouped by skills and knowledge).
- It also tends to be flatter: As Figure 4.1a–c shows, two management levels may be collapsed to one in a multidimensional organization.[2] Indeed, large firms have often introduced this design as part of an effort to "disaggregate" their organization by removing management layers, dividing up large units into smaller units, and decentralizing decision-making authority.
- A multidimensional organization avoids the duplication or multiplication of similar sub-units that is required to create a coherent unidimensional structure when sub-units have been defined according to different grouping criteria at different levels (Note that in the hybrid model shown in Figure 4.1a, for example, there are three sub-units responsible for Region 1, whereas only one is required in the multidimensional structure shown in Figure 4.1c.)
- A multidimensional structure will often reflect the main business processes of the organization to a greater extent than a unidimensional organization, which in turn will contribute to a more balanced composition of the leadership team: As indicated in Figure 4.1c, the leadership team may consist of the heads of each of the main units, representing internal service providers, products units, and market units. In a hybrid structure (such as that shown in Figure 4.1a or 4.1b), the composition of the leadership team is always skewed toward one dimension.

2 Managers in a multidimensional organisation often have a larger span of control than managers in a traditional, functional structure. On the other hand, it is possible, where there is large number of sub-units within a dimension, to introduce an additional layer of managers coordinating a set of sub-units. This does not in change the logic of the model described here.

Despite these advantages, one important challenge related to this model is *how to link* the different dimensions – representing internal functions, products, and markets. Most experts would agree that the success of the model is largely dependent upon how well one is able to coordinate across the units responsible for customers, products, and internal functions. However, there has been a tendency to overlook fundamental differences between alternative linking mechanisms. A leading organization design expert, Jay Galbraith, explained that "some form of matrix is usually employed to tie the front and the back together" (2000; p. 243). It has been common in the organization design literature to present the matrix (i.e., a dual authority structure) as the mid point on a continuum from product to functionally-based structures (or alternatively, as the mid point between functional and geographical structures)

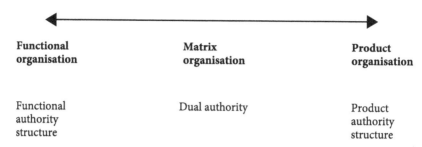

Figure 4.2 Traditional view of the range of organization design options (Galbraith, 1971; 2000).

(see Figure 4.2). Managers and consultants also tend refer to any multidimensional structure as a "matrix."

However, a closer examination reveals that the matrix structure is only one of several alternative ways in which to create a multi-dimensional structure. In the remainder of this chapter we review three different approaches. In addition to the matrix structure we examine the *front-back model* and the *modular organization*. Utilizing design matrices we show how functions are allocated across internal units and discuss the resulting flexibility and complexity of each model.

Scandinavian Telecom

To illustrate alternative ways of designing a multidimensional structure we use an example case from a company that we refer to as ScanTel. The example case is the result of interviews and surveys conducted in a large Scandinavian telecommunications firm in 2007 and was later revised and updated with representatives from the firm. ScanTel's mission is to offer a broad set of services (related to both fixed and mobile telephony, content and infra-structure, etc.) and serve multiple stakeholders (customers, share-holders, employees, etc.) in two main market segments: Consumer (individual/residential) and business. Having evolved from a state-owned monopoly, the firm manages considerable assets (telecom network infrastructure and IT systems).

At the highest level, the functional requirement for this firm can thus be stated as follows:

FR_1 = Create value for stakeholders by offering telecommunica-tion services

This functional requirement can be decomposed into a set of more specific, lower-level functional requirements, as follows:

FR_{11} = Provide cost-effective IT systems and applications that meet the needs of internal clients

FR_{12} = Develop and manage an efficient network infrastructure
FR_{13} = Maximize profits for fixed telephony services
FR_{14} = Maximize profits for mobile telephony services
FR_{15} = Maximize revenue in the business segment
FR_{16} = Maximize revenue in the consumer segment
FR_{17} = Perform enabling and control processes

In the following, we will review slightly different variations of this decomposition. There are often multiple lower level functional requirements that can be chosen that all satisfy the highest level FR. It may be necessary to adjust both the decomposition of functions and design parameters (i.e., unit grouping and/or allocation of responsibilities across units) in order to improve a design. However, an important premise is that the top level function (FR_1) remains constant. This is the case in the following discussion; the three multi-dimensional designs that we describe are alternative ways of realizing this firm's main mission (expressed as FR_1).

The key design parameters for delivering the above functions are as follows (also see Figure 4.3):

DP_{11} = Information Systems (IS) Unit
DP_{12} = Operations Unit
DP_{13} = Fixed Business Unit
DP_{14} = Mobile Business Unit
DP_{15} = Business Market Unit
DP_{16} = Consumer Market Unit
DP_{17} = Corporate Staff Unit

This design is multidimensional according to our definition above as it places units that have been decomposed based on three different grouping criteria at the same hierarchical level (cf. Figure 4.3). There are two products units, defined based on the network infrastructure being utilized to deliver services, either Fixed or Mobile. There are also two market units, defined by the main customer segment that they target: Business and Consumer (i.e., individual/ residential) customers. In addition, there are two important internal units responsible for IT systems and the network infrastructure as well as a central staff unit responsible for HR, Finance, and Procurement.

The key prerequisite for a multi-dimensional model is that one is able to decompose the organization into a set of relatively inde-

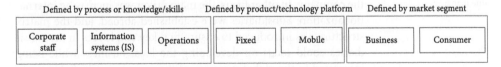

Figure 4.3 Grouping criteria used to define the key units in ScanTel.

pendent sub-units. This in turn requires that some key assumptions, regarding market segments and product interdependencies, actually hold true. As an example, there are five key assumptions behind the model adopted by ScanTel:

1   Business and residential customers have distinct needs and therefore require different product and service packages, pricing plans, etc.
2   Customers in both segments may buy either Fixed or Mobile telecommunication products (or a combination).
3   There are limited interdependencies between Fixed and Mobile technologies, making it feasible to separate these in two units.
4   There are scale effects and other advantages from consolidating product-related processes in the back end units, as opposed to spreading them in the front units.
5   Similarly, IT and operations processes may be consolidated into internal service provider units that serve all product or market units.

Current market trends may challenge these assumptions and make it necessary to revisit the chosen structure. For example, telecom services are increasingly "bundled" (e.g., so-called triple play offerings with a package of fixed telephone services, broadband, and a mobile subscription), which may create a need for tighter integration between different product units. Moreover, the separation between Consumer and Business is not always relevant, as many firms buy telephone services on behalf of their employees, and essentially offer telephone or broadband subscription as an employment benefit. However, even if these trends continue they do not necessarily imply that telecom accompanies should revert to a unidimensional structure, but they will likely lead to a different decomposition of ScanTel's activities compared to the one shown here.

The matrix

The matrix structure emerged during the 1960s and had become quite commonplace in large organizations by the early 1970s.[3] During this period, leaders of many divisionalized firms had become concerned about the duplication of functions (e.g., engineering, production, and marketing) and the lack of coordination across divisions. The matrix structure was implemented to open up the lateral communication channels and better integrate the different parts of the company. In other firms, the main driver was increasing internationalization: Subsidiaries were established abroad, and the matrix structure was introduced to ensure that key employees in the subsidiaries could focus on developing the local business while being integrated in the global structure of the company (Chi & Nystrom, 1998). Managers in the subsidiary would thus report both to a

3 The term "matrix" will here be used in its original meaning, to refer to an organisation where employees have a permanent reporting relationship to more than one manager.

country manager and to a manager in one of the company's product divisions. The classic example is ABB (prior to changes introduced in 1998). A manager in, say, Spain, would report to the country manager in Spain, responsible for sales and customer support. On the second axis the manager would report to a manager in a global business area, which would be organized based on product group or technology (e.g. power transmission, industrial and building systems, financial services, etc.). However, the matrix structure fell out of favor and was abandoned by ABB as well as by other well-known proponents such as Shell and BP several years ago. But it is not yet extinct; some companies have recently starting to adopt matrix structures again, at least in parts of their organization. For example, companies with plants in different countries increasingly see the plants as part of a global supply chain, rather than as country-specific resources. In such companies, a plant manager responsible for e.g., production planning may report both to a local site director and to a supply chain manager in a global supply chain organization. The purpose is to synchronize the global operations and to ensure that common standards apply across different sites. Another variant is the project matrix. Instead of a permanent reporting relationship to two bosses, one here refers to organizations where the "stable" part (e.g., the functional departments) are combined with a "changeable" part (e.g., projects) by means of matrix reporting lines. Employees report to project managers on a day-to-day basis but also belong to functional departments (representing different technical discipline).

There are many ways in which to implement a matrix. To illuminate some of the options that may exist, let us consider how a matrix could be implemented in a company like ScanTel. In reality, ScanTel has several thousand employees, but for the sake of simplicity, we consider the effect of changing the formal structure for 21 people (Figure 4.4). As Figure 4.4 shows, the 21 people include the EVP (Executive Vice President) for each main unit, two managers working in sales and marketing who are already attached to one of the market units, as well as 12 employees that have yet to be allocated to a unit.

How can we use a matrix model to organize this group of 21 people? The first question is at what level a matrix reporting struc-ture should be implemented. The most straightforward solution is to establish dual reporting lines where the 12 employees report both to a manager in a market unit and to one of the product unit directors. Assuming that the volume of work is more or less equal across the product categories, the group of 12 can be subdivided into four groups (see Figure 4.5). The main advantage of this solution is that it avoids the introduction of any additional managerial posi-tions, it simply sub-divides the employees into groups and links them up with the units on both dimensions by adding reporting relationships. In practice, it would mean that both the heads of the product units and the heads of the market units would influence the goals that are set, support and provide resources to the activities

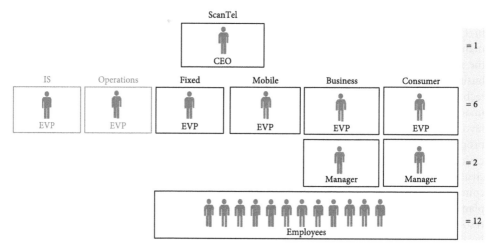

Figure 4.4 People in ScanTel that will be organized by means of a matrix in the subsequent examples (Figures 4.5–4.7).

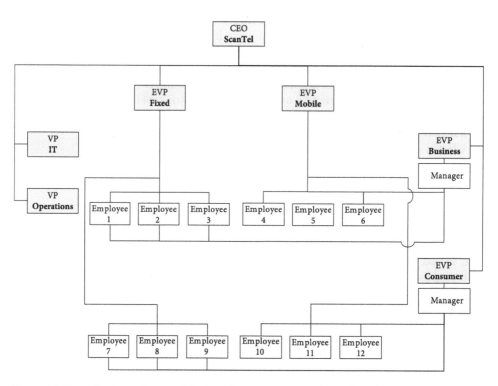

Figure 4.5 Example of matrix created by introducing reporting relationships for employees toward a manager with a market unit manager and the head of a product unit.

performed by employees, and evaluate the performance of the employees.

When two organizational dimensions that are linked in such a manner have an unequal number of hierarchical layers (in this example, the product units have two layers, while the market units have three), it leads to an *unbalanced* matrix: The employees will on the product dimension report to an executive that is one level above the manager in the market unit (see Figure 4.5). Such asymmetrical power relationships present employees and managers with considerable challenges: Not only are employees supposed to handle the different and potentially conflicting expectations from the two axes of the organization, they must do this while keeping in mind the unequal hierarchical status of their managers. The manager in the market unit may experience that he/she is being "overruled" by the EVP in the product unit, or that he/she has no real managerial authority and will need to involve the EVP in the market unit in order to make a decision. Despite these problems, asymmetrical power relationships are relatively common in large and complex organizations (Edmondson et al., 2003).

A balanced matrix can be created in two ways. It is possible to install the matrix one level up, by creating additional managerial positions, and establish dual reporting lines for these positions (Figure 4.6). The managers will then report to bosses that are at the

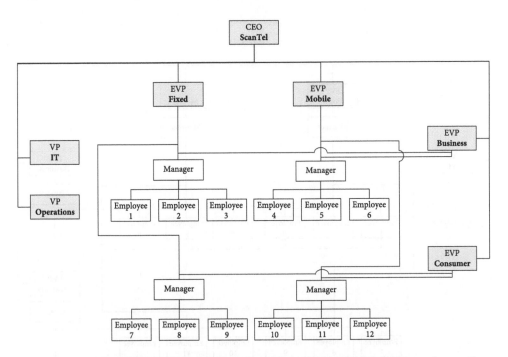

Figure 4.6 Example of matrix where additional manager positions are added. Employees have unitary reporting relationships while the managers report both to the head of a market unit the head of a product unit.

same hierarchical level (the managers' superiors will all report to the CEO). In this alternative, the employees now report only to one boss as the matrix does not encompass level 4 in the organization.

However, creating a balanced matrix in this manner comes at a high cost: The total number of managers would need to increase from two to four. Other things being equal, Mintzberg (1979) estimated that a matrix structure (implemented across an entire company) would require twice as many managers as a purely functional structure. Although Mintzberg's estimate seems to be correct with regard to our example here, it may in fact be too conservative. He mainly cited the increasing cost caused by the added time used for supervision, as bosses in a matrix are supposed to jointly hire, agree on goals for the employee, and evaluate performance. He did not include the need to create additional positions to ensure that the structure obtains a reasonable degree of coherence and consistency: In ScanTel there are only two units along each dimension; the cost of creating a balanced matrix will increase with the number of units.

A third option is to first create an equal hierarchical structure on both dimensions of the organization before introducing the matrix. We started from the assumption that there was one manager attached to each market unit. But new middle management positions could be created, reporting to the EVPs of the product units (Figure 4.7). If the employees instead would report to these middle

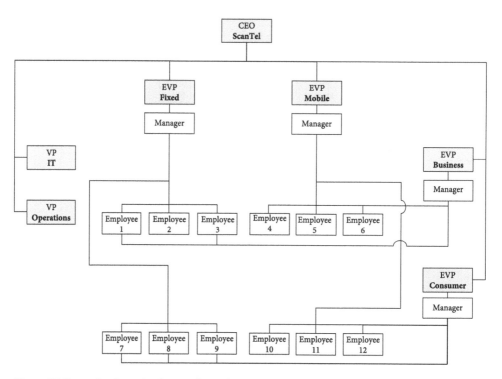

Figure 4.7 Example of matrix where each employee report to a middle manager on each dimension.

managers, we would avoid the asymmetrical relationships described above. However, the assumption would obviously be that the work-load of the organization actually justifies building up a more equal structure on both dimensions of the matrix (or alternatively, that it is possible to transfer resources from one dimension to another to balance out the matrix).

Regardless of which option is selected, a matrix will by its very nature create significant interdependencies between the units that are connected by means of the reporting structure. In a matrix, the ability of a manager or employee to attain his or her goals will to a great extent be dependent upon decisions taken in units repres-enting two organizational dimensions (e.g., market and product units). In some cases the goals pursued by these units may be posit-ively related, but they may also be negatively related, in which case a decision to optimize performance in one unit will undermine the ability of another unit to optimize its performance (Ethiraj & Levinthal, 2009). For example, an employee may report to a superior in a market unit who focuses primarily on product revenue, whereas his superior in the product unit may be measured on profit. The employee is then likely to receive conflicting directions from the two superiors. In a firm like ScanTel, the superior representing the product dimension may encourage the employee to focus on selling complex IT or telephony solutions with high margins. The superior in the market unit may prefer that the employee sell simpler, but higher volume services that contribute to higher revenues. Similarly, if the product unit is responsible for developing new products, the superior on the product dimension may recognize the sales manager's efforts at promoting new and innovative technologies in the market, whereas the superior in the market unit in some cases may resist the introduction of new technologies (particularly if they only address niches in the market or represent unproved solutions that don't contribute strongly to maintaining or increasing revenues). These goal conflicts are the result of *coupling* between functional requirements; in Table 4.1 they are indicated with "x's" in the shaded area.

We should add that coupling may also be due to operational interdependencies that are unrelated to the choice of reporting structure as such. In telecommunications companies, the units that are responsible for IT and telephone network infrastructure have some influence on the achievement of almost all functional require-ments. For example, the introduction of a new pricing scheme, developed by a market unit, may necessitate a significant re-coding effort on behalf of IT, as pricing mechanisms are sometimes "hard wired" in the billing system (which is tightly coupled to the basic telephony network systems). Similarly, increased data traffic from mobile handsets may require network capacity increases, which in turn depend on additional infrastructure investments. Such interdependencies are a serious hindrance for achieving speed

Table 4.1 Assumed design matrix if ScanTel adopts a matrix structure. X signifies a strong relationship between a DP and a FR, and an x a moderately strong relationship. The shaded area corresponds to instances of coupling that are due to the matrix reporting structure

Functional requirements	Design parameters						
	IS	Operations	Fixed	Mobile	Business	Consumer	Corporate staff
1.1 Provide cost-effective IT systems (. . .)	**X**						x
1.2 Develop and manage an efficient network infrastructure	x	**X**					x
1.3 Maximize profits for Fixed telephony services	x	x	**X**		x	x	x
1.4 Maximize profits for Mobile telephony services	x	x		**X**	x	x	x
1.5 Maximize revenue in the Business segment	x	x	x	x	**X**		x
1.6 Maximize revenue in the Consumer segment	x	x	x	x		**X**	x
1.7 Perform enabling and control processes							**X**

and flexibility in many telecoms companies (In Table 4.1, the "x's" in the first two columns of the matrix indicate that the achievement of all functions is dependent upon actions and decisions in the IT and Operations units.)

As with the other two multidimensional forms that we shall discuss, the matrix was intended to allow the combination of two grouping criteria (e.g., product and market) and, in theory, achieve customer focus and economies of scale at the same time. The main change from a purely functional organization is that it opens up the lateral channels of communication, and therefore leads to an increase in both the amount and frequency of information being exchanged between units. Moreover, the matrix significantly alters governance processes by introducing dual reporting relationships. The two managers that intersect in a matrix structure hold joint responsibility for supervising employees, who are supposed to balance the goals of the different dimensions of the matrix. For the individual employee, the main advantage is perhaps that the matrix introduces more variety and contributes to a broadening of one's informal network as one is exposed to a larger number of individuals belonging to different units.

A key issue with matrix structures has been how employees deal with dual authority relationships. However, the primary challenge may not be having two bosses per se, but the fact that the two bosses share jurisdiction over the same work process (e.g., the sales process in the ScanTel), yet are held accountable for different and potentially conflicting goals. When employees at lower levels are unable to resolve conflicts between different goals, they need to escalate the issue to higher levels of management. One key finding from organizations with matrix structures is indeed that higher level managers become overloaded because lower level managers are unable to resolve conflicts and therefore refer conflicts to the executives. In other words, an unintended consequence of a matrix structure is actually to make the organization more centralized and to remove accountability from lower-level managers (Whitford, 2006). More recent organizational models have been developed to try to address this issue.

The front-back model

The front-back model is similar to a matrix in that it consists of decentralized units structured along different dimensions (i.e., decomposed using different criteria). However, whereas the term "matrix organization" may refer to any combination of dimensions (e.g., geography vs. product, project vs. functional, etc.), the "front end" in the front-back model normally consists of market units, whereas the "back end" comprises the product units, responsible for developing or manufacturing products. Another important difference from the matrix is that the front-back model may be implemented without dual reporting relationships. In some cases, the front and back are linked together by an internal customer-supplier interface: The market units identify customer needs, receive orders, and request products and services from the units in the "back end." The internal customer-supplier relations may be largely informal, but the roles may also be formalized in the form of an internal market where units literally buy and sell from each other.

The market units of the front end are usually structured around customer segments at the top level, and then around customers (e.g., by having key account teams for the most important customers) (Galbraith, 2000). The key rationale is to be able to sell all the organization's products or services (cross-selling), to provide a common interface toward the client, or to assemble solutions consisting of products and services from several back end units. Conversely, the back end units should be able to interface with any front end unit to deliver a product. The front-back model is an attempt to derive the advantages of economies of scope and specialization, or what Nadler and Tushman (1997) call leverage and focus. Leverage is gained because resources related to product development and production are consolidated in a product unit, and thus one can more easily derive advantages from scale. For example, a product unit in a home appliances company responsible for refrigerators may be able to re-use engineering designs and share production resources, even though the product is sold in many variants, or even as separate brands, by different market units. Simultaneously, focus is gained as market units are able to concentrate on a set of customers or market segments. Market units, and the various teams within them, should be able to stay in close touch with customers and have the authority to take decisions related to sales and marketing in their respective segments.

A front-back structure is sometimes implemented at lower levels of the organization, even if the overall structure of the company is organized based on geography or product. An example is a large bank that is geographically organized, with subsidiaries in many European countries. However, several of the subsidiaries have organized their corporate banking activities with a front-back structure as shown in Figure 4.8. As is common in this business, a "relationship banker" holds the responsibility for continuous communication with customers, while product specialists develop and deliver the services that the customers require. There is also a Banking Operations unit, which performs "back office" processing, and a staff unit responsible for risk management.

A notable aspect of the front-back organization is that it makes it possible to define roles and responsibilities in a manner that reduces overlaps across units. Or, in axiomatic design terms, it makes it possible – in principle, at least – to create an uncoupled design (Suh, 2001) where each organizational unit performs one main function. The separation of functions is essential because it allows the definition of independent goals and KPIs. Unlike in the matrix organization, sales and revenue related goals may be assigned only to front end units, as product units can be measured on other goals such as productivity, cost, quality, or project execution. The result is a lower degree of coupling, i.e., actions initiated by one unit to fulfill its particular goals (i.e., satisfy the functional requirements) will to a lesser extent hamper the ability of other

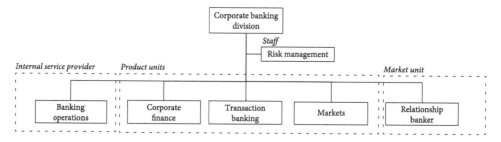

Figure 4.8 Corporate banking division of the national subsidiary of a European bank.

units to reach their goals (i.e., other functional requirements).[4] In the case of ScanTel, we may formalize the functional requirements as follows.[5]

FR_{11} = Provide cost-effective IT systems and applications that meet the needs of internal clients

FR_{12} = Develop and manage an efficient network infrastructure

FR_{13} = Develop and launch new Fixed telephony services

FR_{14} = Develop and launch new Mobile telephony services

FR_{15} = Maximize revenue in the Business segment

FR_{16} = Maximize revenue in the Consumer segment

FR_{17} = Perform enabling and control processes

Figure 4.9 shows the formal reporting lines for employees and Table 4.2 shows the allocation of functions in ScanTel if it were to be organized according to the front-back model.

Even though the front-back model does not require the dual authority structure of the matrix, this does not imply that companies automatically avoid overlapping responsibilities or conflicting goals by implementing the model – the design intent is not always realized. For example, when we conducted our interviews in ScanTel we noted that both front end and back end units had some responsibility for product development, something which managers cited as a source

4 However, as described in Chapter 2, the removal of coupling in terms of functional requirements does not imply that one simultaneously remove *process interdependencies* between the units: In this example, the Market units are clearly dependent upon the Product units to deliver products to customers that the Market unit has secured a sale to.

5 To achieve an uncoupled design, it is necessary to adjust the lower-level functional requirements somewhat (compare the above list of the functional requirements with those for the matrix organisation shown in Table 4.1). The design parameters (organizational units) are the same.

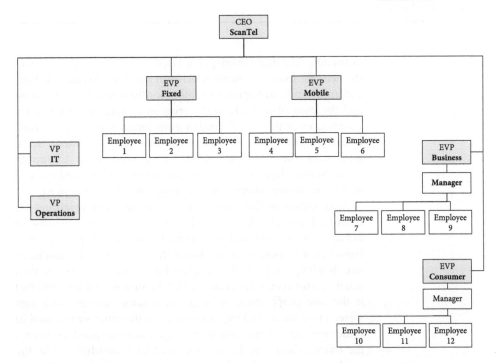

Figure 4.9 Reporting lines for the 21 people shown in Figure 4.4 if a front-back model is implemented in ScanTel.

Table 4.2 Assumed design matrix if ScanTel adopts a front-back organization. X signifies a strong relationship between a DP and a FR, and an x a moderately strong relationship. Compare with Table 4.1

Functional requirements	Design parameters						
	IS	Operations	Fixed	Mobile	Business	Consumer	Corporate staff
1.1 Provide cost-effective IT systems (…)	X						x
1.2 Develop and manage an efficient network infrastructure	x	X					x
1.3 Develop and launch new Fixed telephony services	x	x	X				x
1.4 Develop and launch new Mobile telephony services	x	x		X			x
1.5 Maximize revenue in the Business segment	x	x			X		x
1.6 Maximize revenue in the Consumer segment	x	x				X	x
1.7 Perform enabling and control processes							X

of friction. The more overlapping responsibilities are, the stronger the need for joint coordination between the front end and the back end units. And a strong need for joint coordination between the front and the back often leads to the creation of some mechanism for coordination, either an informal meeting forum or project, or a more formal integrator role. Some organizations that have attempted to implement the front-back model have created an additional, "coordinating" layer between the front end and the back end units. In such cases the organization is gravitating toward a matrix form.

As discussed in Galbraith (2000), a key question regarding the front-back model relates to the balance of power. It is possible to define both the front-end and the back end units as profit centers. However, it is more common to see that one axis is the dominant one, holding the profit/loss responsibility. The other axis is then usually a cost centre. Galbraith (2000) mentioned that the front end is the sole profit centre in some auto manufacturers. Although systematic data are lacking, it seems to be the other way around in some companies. For example, in a large consumer goods company, the official chart was drawn as a front-back structure, while the products units in reality dominated decision making, and directed the activities of the market units. The impression is thus that the front-back structure in many cases represents a "push" model. This means that in the product development process, for example, the market units may provide suggestions based on customer feedback regarding possible new products, but the product units usually have the final say in deciding which technologies to employ or which products to develop.

The modular organization

A third alternative to structuring multidimensional organizations was first articulated by Goggin (1974) and later modified and extended by Russell Ackoff (1994; 1999).[6] The starting point is the distinction between three key functional requirements (Table 4.3). Ackoff reasoned that all organizations require certain inputs, such as people, supplies, and capital. Consequently, there is a need for "input units" that source these inputs and provide them as services to other internal units. Secondly, all organizations produce some outputs, whether they are products or services. "Output units" are defined that perform this function, and will typically be grouped by product category or technology platform. Third, "market units" sell the outputs that are produced to external customers. Markets units may be grouped geographically or by customer segment. In addition, there will usually be an executive office (the corporate centre, or headquarters) comprising the top executives and employees belonging to staff and support units. Key functions for the executives are to develop strategy and set the guidelines for the operations of the subordinate units, invest in the development of units, and monitor performance and conduct audit of units.

Ackoff concluded that there is no need for a matrix to link the different dimensions in a modular organization. Instead, he proposed that there should be supplier-customer relations between

6 Ackoff (1994; 1999) called this model "the multidimensional organisation". To avoid confusion with the two other models described in this chapter, we have chosen the term "modular organisation" instead as it appears to conform with the criteria for defining modular systems (see Sanchez, 1995). It is also sometimes called a "business stream organisation", where *business stream* refers to the output or product units described here.

Table 4.3 Generic functional requirements and design parameters proposed by Russell Ackoff (1994; 1999)

	Design parameters			
Generic functional requirements	*Input units*	*Output units*	*Market units*	*Executive office*
Provide products or services that are principally consumed or used internally	X			x
Provide products or services that are principally consumed or used externally		X		x
Market and sell the products or services provided by the output units			X	x
Perform executive functions				x

people belonging to different units. In other words, if an output unit relies on an input unit for certain services, the head of the output unit becomes the client, rather than the boss, of the employees of the input unit. Similarly, output units are the suppliers to the market units, which are supposed to represent the "voice of the customer" within the company, both by evaluating products and services from the customer's point of view, and by articulating customer needs that may be met by developing new offerings.

The modular structure is similar in some respects to the front-back model described by Galbraith (2000). Like the front-back model, it confers both focus and leverage. Units can be highly specialized (in terms of function, product, or market) yet obtain economies of scale and scope from sharing resources. Input and market units should be able to serve any output (product) unit (although they may not necessarily serve all at any time). Market units should sell all the company's products or services and thus provide a common interface for clients toward the organization.

However, there are also a number of differences. In describing the front-back organization above, we noted that the balance of power may differ from company to company: In some, the front end has the most authority, whereas in others, it is the back end (the product units) that essentially directs the activities of the sales and marketing people in the front end units. In the modular organization, however, the market units always hold the internal client role, and the product units the supplier role, and not vice versa. This is a key element in creating a "pull" system (as in the Lean philosophy) where work processes in upstream (product) units are only initiated based on specific requests from downstream (market) units.

Unlike units in a front-back model, the output (product) units within a modular organization have no fixed assets, and only consist of a few managers (and potentially a small supporting staff). Units not only share production and market resources; they also share *human resources*. Employees are formally organized in a resource pool in one of the input units and hired out on request to output or market units (see Figure 4.10). The model implies the introduction of a dual hierarchy (Malone, 2004), which, despite the name, does not imply a matrix structure. *People managers* lead skills groups within the resource pool. However, once allocated to a project in a business unit, employees work for a *project manager*. The project manager is essentially the *internal client* of the people manager in the resource pool; there is no formal reporting relationship between them. Unlike traditional HR functions, the resource pool in a modular organization becomes a strategic business unit: It is accountable for providing resources that business units require and for developing the skills that the company will need in the future (Worren, 2008).

Units in a modular organization have even greater autonomy than units in the typical implementation of the front-back model.

Although the executive office retains the right to override decisions of individual units, there should in practice be little need for intervention, provided that clear "rules of engagement" have been established with regard to such issues as profit accumulation, capital investment, and protection of intellectual property (see Ackoff, 1999 for further discussion). Apart from resolving issues that are escalated, the role of the executive office (or HQ) is primarily to design and adjust the overall organization, that is, define the units that are necessary and how they should interact. If there is stable, high demand for a service or product delivered by an external supplier, the executive office may ~~decided~~ decide to "insource" this activity and add an internal unit to produce the product or service. Conversely, it may decide to discontinue a unit that produces products or services with little demand. It may also convert an input unit to a product unit, if it turns out that there is a considerable external market for the services that it delivers.

The main difference between the modular and the matrix model is the elimination of dual functions and reporting relationships. Like the front-back model, it allows specialized units with independent performance measures. It shares with the front-back model the concept of standard interface between units, allowing any output (product) unit to transact with any market unit. A modular organization may consist of a great number of individual units, with a great number of possible constellations with regard to collaboration (e.g., product unit A transacting with market unit 1 and 2, product unit B transacting with market unit 1 and 3, and so on).

The modular organization thus confers true *reconfigurability*. Because output (product) units and market units are small and have no fixed assets, such units can easily be added, merged, or disbanded quickly and at a low cost. A firm may choose to disband a unit because there is no longer any demand for the services or products that they produce, or because they are not competitive with external suppliers. Units may be created to serve new markets or because the company believes that it should "insource" a service that has previously been purchased from an external provider.

As pointed out by Ackoff (1994; 1999), combining the modular organization with an internal market economy leads to even greater flexibility. All units will then be profit centers and receive income from the sale of their products and services, and pay for services rendered to them. Ackoff also proposed that units should be free both the purchase whatever they need or sell whatever they produce or provide, either internally or externally.[7] As a consequence, each unit becomes more independent (i.e., it removes *coupling* as defined in axiomatic design theory).

Even if units are not allowed to trade externally, it is possible to use market-based principles to allocate capacity internally. Malone (2004) described how internal markets may be used to allocate manufacturing capacity in a large firm with several plants. The tradi-

7 The main exception is the case where the sale to a competitor of, say, a particular technology, would negatively affect the company's competitive position.

tional approach is based on a centralized process where a person or team at the headquarters allocates capacity based on sales forecasts from market units. In a modular organization, the process could instead be completely decentralized: Market units would be allowed to buy futures contracts for products available at specific times in the future. If the demand turns out be less than anticipated, a market unit may sell future contracts to another market unit. In this manner capacity allocation becomes a self-regulating process that does not require management intervention (although higher level managers obviously need to set up and monitor the process). Interestingly, internal markets should also contribute to greatly decreased complexity, in that the resource allocation process becomes much more transparent: Instead of tracking multiple forecasts and production schedules for a large number of sub-units, an electronic market system would provide information, accessible for all employees, about prices for all products in all future time periods.

If we assume that we may combine the modular organization with an internal market, the functional requirements for ScanTel may be stated as

Generic function	Specific functional requirements for ScanTel
Provide products or services that are principally consumed or used externally	FR_{13} = Maximize profits for Fixed telephony services
	FR_{14} = Maximize profits for Mobile telephony services
Market and sell the products or services provided by the Output units	FR_{15} = Maximize profits in the Business segment
	FR_{16} = Maximize profits in the Consumer segment
Provide products or services that are principally consumed or used internally	FR_{11} = Maximize profits for IT services
	FR_{12} = Maximize profits for network services
	FR_{17} = Perform enabling and control processes
	FR_{18} = Maximize competence utilization

Figure 4.10 shows the formal reporting lines of employees in ScanTel and Table 4.4 the mapping between functional requirements and design parameters (organizational units). Note that we have added a functional requirement related to the maximization of competence (FR_{18}), which has been allocated to a new organization unit (the People Unit, i.e., a resource pool).

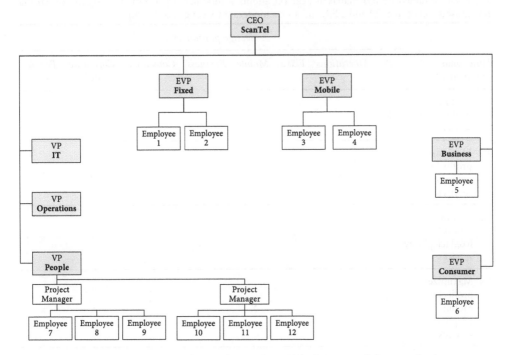

Figure 4.10 Possible reporting lines for employees if ScanTel adopts a modular organization.

Discussion

When the modular organization first was conceptualized, it represented a theoretical possibility. Yet it anticipated fundamental changes that have been taking place during the last couple of decades.

The organization of many project-based firms, such as engineering, IT, and consulting firms, often resembles the modular form. One example is PwC, the professional services firm for accounting, tax, and management consulting. Its organization comprises three dimensions: Industry teams, Professional services, and Support services. The managers responsible for PwCs industry teams (e.g., Government and public services; Telecommunications, Insurance, etc.) are measured on revenues, market position, and customer retention. But they have virtually no resources under their control, and must request resources from the professional services units when they are awarded client projects (Strikwerda & Stoelhorst, 2009).

In some organizations, the internal value chain is becoming virtualized in that units are free to source their input from any source, internal or external. An extreme example would be companies in commodity-based industries, such as electrical energy. The sales department of an energy company is not dependent on the capacity of the company's own power stations in order to serve a customer: Once a contract is established with a customer, the energy is simply sourced from the energy commodity market. There are similar

Table 4.4 Assumed design matrix if ScanTel adopts a modular organization. X signifies a strong relationship between a DP and a FR, and an x a moderately strong relationship

Functional requirements	IS	Operations	Fixed	Mobile	Business	Consumer	Corporate staff	People unit
				Design parameters				
1.1 Maximize profits for IT services	X						x	x
1.2 Maximize profits for network services		X					x	x
1.3 Maximize profits for fixed telephony services			X				x	x
1.4 Maximize profits for Mobile telephony services				X			x	x
1.5 Maximize profits in the Business segment					X		x	x
1.6 Maximize profits in the Consumer segment						X	x	x
1.7 Perform enabling and control processes							X	x
1.8 Maximize competence utilization							x	X

examples in other sectors. Smaller telecom companies are often "virtual" companies that lease network capacity from larger telecom companies. Engineering companies similarly make use of external contractors in times of high demand for their services. Reducing dependencies toward internal suppliers in this manner decreases the probability that a unit's performance will be affected by, for example, a lack of capacity in another internal unit.

Despite the advantages reviewed so far, there are a number of issues related to the modular organization that should be examined more carefully. Perhaps the most important issue is clarifying to what extent the different functions of the respective dimensions (input, output, and market) really are separable. If market units are separated from output (product) units, is it enough that market units identify customer needs and market trends, and transfer this information to output (product) units in the form of product specifications? Or is it necessary for members of output (product) units to interact directly with customers to understand their preferences, or customize solutions to their particular needs? This is the situation in corporate banking: Although the relationship manager (representing the market unit) may sell and initiate the sale of a financial service, the actual service is often performed by specialists from one of the product units, who interact directly with client personnel (although they may primarily interact with client personnel at a lower level than the relationship manager). Vice versa, when sales people estimate the costs for a complicated engineering project when responding to a customer request, is it enough for them to rely on information supplied by an output (product) unit, or do they need a deep understanding of the technology to be able to estimate the costs correctly? Or put differently, is it really possible to design a "standard interface" in modular terms between an output (product) unit and a market unit, or does the interface have to be more permeable (Kogut & Bowman, 1995)?

Several options exist when it is not possible to fully separate output (product) units and market units (or the "front end" and the "back end" in the terminology of the front-back model). A company may simply integrate market units within output (product) units, essentially reducing a three-dimensional organization to two dimensions. Sales and marketing resources will then be organized in the same unit as those responsible for developing and delivering products and services, but the company will find it more difficult to maintain a common interface toward clients across products and to sell solutions that include combinations of products or services from different output (product) units. Another option is to maintain three dimensions but place more responsibility in the market units. Homburg et al. (2000) observed that key account managers are increasingly responsible for costs in serving accounts as well as the revenues generated (on the other hand, this responsibility is not always accompanied by real authority over internal resources that influence the costs).

However, before altering – some would say diluting – the logic of the model in this manner, one may consider whether there are mechanisms that could compensate for the separation of functions that the model entails. Continuing the example of a sales process in an engineering firm, at least three possible options exist. The first is to document and standardize processes. Many engineering firms have developed standard execution methodologies consisting of repeatable processes, procedures, and tools (often called work packages).

These may not only specify how to execute a project, but also contain estimates of time and cost associated with different activities. Over time, these estimates can be updated to reflect actual time and cost of implementing projects. In this manner, there may be less of a need for sales people to be deeply involved in the technical process, as long as they can access and correctly interpret the historical data. Another approach is to establish a cross-functional sales team that involves employees in both a market unit and an output (product) unit. This is a natural approach, particularly in the absence of reliable, historical cost data, for example, when the project involves new technologies or other uncertainties. Finally, it is possible to rotate personnel between output (product) and market units. This approach secures that those selling products have sufficient technical insight as well as informal networks to draw on when there is a need for closer collaboration with engineers during a sales process.

A second issue concerns the concept of an internal market. As described above, combining the modular structure with an internal market should contribute to greatly increased flexibility. However, the main challenge is determining the boundaries of the market. Critics of the internal market model have been concerned that it may lead to internal fragmentation. As Peter Senge has noted, "free markets don't always promote a common good, especially when the common good goes beyond the simple transactions on which the market's actors are focused" (1993, p. 91). Fostering collective action among a group of semi-autonomous units is often a challenge. It seems clear that a clear definition – and acceptance – of the executive office's role and authority is required in order to avoid fragmentation in a modular organization. An important consideration is whether a decision, policy, or process is "modular" (i.e., aimed at enhancing unit performance) or "architectural" (aimed at enhancing the performance of the overall system). As an example, in implementing a common IT system across different business units, costs may be reduced for the organization overall because of pooling of resources (i.e., use of the same software, procedures, training courses, etc.), even though costs may increase for some individual units that previously used simpler, local IT systems. But more importantly, a common IT system may also contribute to increased internal information sharing or allow more efficient transactions across interfaces – and thus influence the ability to forge collaboration across functions, units, and geographies. If so, we are clearly talking about *architectural level* processes – which the corporate centre of a modular organization needs to have the authority to select and implement.

Summary and conclusion

Many large organizations today are structured along multiple dimensions, representing markets, products, and internal functions. Until now, one has overlooked the differences between alternative ways in which to link units representing the different dimensions of such organizations. In this chapter we have seen that there are in fact three alternative ways in which to create multidimensional designs: The traditional *matrix* structure, the *front-back* model, and the *modular* organization. Although these models may look superficially similar, they represent significantly different principles with regard to reporting relationships, coordinating processes, and allocation of resources (Table 4.5). By acknowledging the differences between these models, we provide new design options for managers seeking to reduce complexity and improve the flexibility of large organizations.

Table 4.5 Comparison between matrix, front-back, and modular organizational structures

	Matrix	*Front-back*	*Modular*
Number of dimensions	• Two or more	• Two or more	• Two or more
Reporting structure	• Dual (or in some cases triple) reporting structure	• Is sometimes a matrix, but the structure allows unitary reporting combined the creating of customer-supplier relations between roles	• Unitary reporting combined with customer-supplier relations units
Key Performance Indicators	• Profit and loss may be on both dimensions, and may overlap	• Profit and loss may be on both dimensions • The structure allows independent KPIs	• Profit and loss may be on both dimensions • The structure allows independent KPIs
Organization of resources (i.e., where people belong)	• Within each unit	• Within each unit	• In separate resource pool (neither in product nor market unit)
Organization of "front end"	• No particular requirement	• Always defined according to market segments	• Always defined according to market segments
Key advantage	• Increases lateral coordination	• Clarifies sub-unit roles • Reduces complexity	• Maximizes flexibility
Key limitation	• High complexity due to overlapping functions and goals • Creating a balanced matrix results in higher cost (more management resources) • Easily leads to asymmetries in the composition of leadership teams	• Low degree of resource flexibility • One dimension (product or market) will usually dominate • Intent of model often undermined during implementation	• Requires a high degree of process maturity • Requires minimum size in each location, or high geographical mobility among staff • May increase risk of fragmentation

The matrix organization is the oldest model and appears to be the most costly, complex, and inflexible of the three alternatives. Its complexity stems both from the dual authority relationships and from the existence of overlapping goals. The front-back and modular organization provide viable alternatives for leaders that consider different options for structuring large organizations. There may be a few exceptions, where it is hard to avoid a matrix structure. In most organizations there is a need to align corporate functions at different levels, and one common method to achieve this is establish a dual reporting structure for managers of staff functions (i.e., those responsible accounting and finance, HR, etc.) where they simultaneously report to both the line manager of the business unit in which they work, as well as to the head of the respective corporate function. However, unlike the traditional matrix, there exists in such cases only a "dotted line" relationship on the second dimension; the primary reporting relationship is toward the line manager of the business unit.

The highest level of flexibility will be attained by adopting the modular organization design. The modular organization is explicitly based on a "pull" philosophy, similar to the Lean philosophy (Womack & Jones, 1996). "Pull" essentially means that no upstream unit should produce a good or service until the (internal) customer downstream requests it. In the modular organization, this principle is extended even to human resources. Instead of having an "inventory" of human capital in each department, waiting to be utilized, the modular organization organizes resources in a common pool and provide these resources "on demand" to product and market units.

However, it is also clear that the modular organization may not be the appropriate choice for all firms. Exploiting the potential flexibility of a modular organization requires a relatively high degree of process maturity, with well defined interfaces. It also requires clear internal transfer pricing principles, an IT infrastructure that supports efficient transactions between sub-units, as well as accounting processes that allow individual sub-units to monitor their economic performance. Another element of the modular organization is to organize people in a common resource pool. This concept is chiefly relevant for project-based firms of a certain size, or with workers who are geographically mobile. (A large project-based firm may establish one resource pool per location; a smaller project-based firm with several offices may require employees to travel between projects for various internal clients.) For firms that carry out more stable or continuous processes, the front-back model should be the preferred choice. The front-back model relies on the well-established line organization where people are organized within one specific unit. It is possible that these two models represent different evolutionary stages in the development of large firms: Firms seeking to combine a product and a market focus may start by adopting the front-back model and later evolve to a modular design as the organization attains a higher level of process maturity.

Design propositions

Objective	*Design an organizational model that maximizes the effectiveness of multibusiness organizations (organizations delivering multiple products or services, or addressing multiple markets).*
4.1	Create a multidimensional model that: • Is built up of a set of relatively independent sub-units, each performing one distinct function; • Contains units representing the different dimensions/grouping criteria (e.g., internal services, products, and markets) at the same hierarchical level; • Principally use customer-supplier relations to link units (as opposed to dual reporting lines).
Objective	*Identify the appropriate multidimensional model to fit internal and external contingencies.*
4.2	Design the organization according to the front-back model if: a) The business environment is relatively stable and the firm relies on continuous processes to produce standard product; b) The level of process maturity is low to moderate; c) There is a limited need for internal mobility of resources.
4.3	Design the organization according to modular principles if: a) The business environment is highly dynamic and/ or the firm is project based; b) The firm would benefit from high internal resource flexibility and mobility; c) It is possible to establish the appropriate internal interfaces, systems and processes to support effective sub-unit transactions.
Objective	*Reduce implementation barriers and fully exploit the value of a multidimensional model.*
4.6	Ensure that the design intent is realized during implementation by avoiding overlapping or conflicting functions

4.7	Ensure that there is an enabling infrastructure to support effective sub-unit interaction and transactions (if the model includes an internal market).
4.8	Avoid fragmentation by clearly establishing the authority of the executive office to take decisions related to the architecture of the system.

Review questions

1 What are the main advantages of a multidimensional structure compared to a unidimensional structure?
2 How does a multidimensional structure allow a firm to realize economies of scope?
3 What are the key differences between the matrix, front-back, and modular organization?
4 Why do matrix reporting relationships create coupling between functional requirements?
5 What are the main preconditions that must be in place in order to implement the modular organization as defined by Russell Ackoff?
6 Can a multidimensional structure be implemented even in a small organization?
7 Compared to a traditional organization, do you think the modular organization will lead to more internal competition between managers, or to more cooperative behavior?
8 What do you think are the advantages and disadvantages for employees of being organized within a resource pool?

Research questions

1 To what extent is it possible to design a "standard interface" in modular terms between output (product) units and market units?
2 How can modular organizations be designed to exploit the advantages of flexibility while at the same time foster the "collective action" required to maintain coherence?
3 How can market-based resource allocation processes best be implemented in large organizations?
4 What is the evidence with regard to the effects of resource pooling?
5 How can we operationalize the concept of the modular organization and track the degree of adoption of this model?
6 What are the performance effects of adopting multidimensional models?
7 Is the need to reorganize reduced in multidimensional organization (i.e., do such organizations maintain their structure over a longer period of time compare to unidimensional organizations)?

References

Ackoff, R. (1999). *Re-Creating the Corporation: A Design of Organizations for the 21st Century.* New York: Oxford University Press.

Ackoff, R. (1994). *The Democratic Corporation.* New York: Oxford University Press.

Baldwin, C. Y., & Clark, K. B. (2000). *Design Rules – Vol. 1: The Power of Modularity.* Cambridge, MA: MIT Press.

Barney, J. (1996). *Gaining and Sustaining Competitive Advantage.* Reading, MA: Addison-Wesley.

Chi, T., & Nystrom, P. C. (1998). An economic analysis of matrix structure, using multinational corporations as an illustration. *Managerial and Decision Economics*, 19, 141–156.

Day, G. S. (2006). Aligning the organization with the market. *MIT Sloan Management Review*, 48, 1, 41.

Donaldson, L. (2001). *The Contingency Theory of Organizations.* Thousand Oaks, CA: Sage Publications.

Edmondson, A. C., Roberto, M. A., and Watkins, M. D. (2003). A dynamic model of top management team effectiveness: Managing unstructured task streams. *The Leadership Quarterly*, 14, 3, 297–325.

Ethiraj, S. K., & Levinthal, D. A. (2009). Hoping for A to Z while rewarding only A: Complex organizations and multiple goals. *Organization Science*, 20, 1, 4–21.

Galbraith, J. (1971). Matrix Organization Designs: How to combine functional and project forms. *Business Horizons*, February, 29–40.

Galbraith, J. (2000). *Designing the Global Corporation.* San Francisco: Jossey-Bass.

Gulati, R., & Puranam, P. (2009). Renewal through reorganization: The value of inconsistencies between formal and informal organization. *Organization Science*, 20, 2, 422–440.

Goggin, W. C. (1974). How the multidimensional structure works at Dow Corning. *Harvard Business* Review, 55, 1, 54–65.

Homburg, C., Workman, J. P., & Jensen, O. (2000). Fundamental changes in marketing organization: The movement toward a customer-focused organizational structure. *Journal of the Academy of Marketing Science*, 28, 4, 459–478.

Hoskisson, R.E., Hill, C.W.L., & Kim, H. (1993). The multidivisional structure: Organizational fossil or source of value? *Journal of Management*, 19, 269–298.

Kogut, B., & Bowman, E. H. (1995). Modularity and permeability as principles of design. In B. Kogut & E. H. Bowman, *Redesigning the Firm.* New York: Oxford University Press.

Malone, T. W. (2004). *The Future of Work.* Boston: Harvard Business School Press.

Mintzberg, H. (1979). *The Structuring of Organizations: A Synthesis of the Research.* New York: Prentice-Hall.

Nadler, D., & Tushman, M. (1997). *Competing by Design: The Power of Organizational Architecture.* New York: Oxford University Press.

Porter, M. E. (1996). What is strategy? *Harvard Business Review,* November–December, 61–78.

Sanchez, R., & Heene, A. (2004). *The New Strategic Management: Organization, Competition and Competence.* New York: John Wiley & Sons.

Sanchez, R. (1995). Strategic flexibility in product competition. *Strategic Management Journal,* 16, 135–159.

Senge, P. M. (1993). Internal markets and learning organizations: Some thoughts on uniting the two perspectives. In W. E. Halal et al., *Internal Markets: Bringing the Power of Free Enterprise Inside Your Organization.* New York: John Wiley & Sons.

Strikwerda, J., & Stoelhorst, J. W. (2009). The emergence and evolution of the multidimensional organization. *California Management Review,* 51, 4, 11–31.

Suh, N. P. (2001). *Axiomatic Design: Advances and Applications.* Oxford: Oxford University Press.

Treacy, M., & Wiersema, F. D. (1995). *The Discipline of Market Leaders.* Reading, MA: Addison-Wesley.

Whitford, A. B. (2006). Unitary, divisional, and matrix forms as political governance systems. *Journal of Management Governance,* 10, 435–454.

Whittington, R., Pettigrew, A., Peck, S., Fenton, E., & Conyon M. (1999). Change and complementarities in the new competitive landscape: A European panel study, 1992–1996. *Organization Science,* 10, 5, 583–600.

Womack, J. P., & Jones, D. T. (1996). *Lean Thinking: Banish Waste and Create Wealth in Your Corporation.* New York: Simon & Schuster.

Worren, N. (2008). Managing the company's resource pool. *People & Strategy,* 31, 1, 42–49.

5   Designing sub-units

Chapter overview

Background	• Before a high level architecture can be implemented, it needs to be operationalized by (re-) designing the lower level units that comprise the organization (e.g., business units, departments, and teams).
Challenges	• Leaders often proceed directly to a discussion about the organizational structure of sub-units, without first agreeing on the goals (i.e., functional requirements) of the sub-units.
	• Decisions about sub-unit structure are sometimes made without taking into account work process interdependencies, leading to unnecessary coordination costs.
	• At the same time, there may be several, competing design criteria that make it difficult to select the optimal grouping of roles or activities.
Key questions	• How can a sub-unit be designed in a manner that maximizes the chance that its particular functional requirements will be realized, while at the same time ensuring alignment with the purpose of the overall organization?
	• How can a sub-unit (and the teams and roles within them) be designed in order to minimize coordination costs?
Proposed approach	• Develop a clear mission or mandate for the sub-unit that can be the basis for identifying lower-level functional requirements.
	• Involve stakeholders representing higher level units and other units at the same level in establishing the mission or mandate.

- Employ an analytical, "bottom up" approach in analyzing actual work flow interdependencies to identify optimal grouping of activities.

- Consider the relationship between work processes and formal structure in order to select between partitioning (dividing a unit into smaller sub-units) and integration (increasing the level of interaction between, or formally merging, two or more units).

Introduction

In the previous chapter, we considered the design of the overall *architecture* of the organization. The overall architecture usually contains a specification of the main business areas, business units, or functions (depending on the size of the organization). In this chapter, we examine how the overall architecture is operationalized by designing (or re-designing) the sub-units comprising the organization. If we use the multidimensional models discussed in Chapter 4 as the starting point, there will essentially be four types of sub-units that will need to be defined:

- Sales (or market) units – responsible for marketing and selling products or services
- Product (or output) units – responsible for development and manufacturing/delivery of products or services
- Internal service providers (or input units) – responsible for providing support, operating the infrastructure, or performing administrative services for product and market units
- Executive office and staff units – responsible for strategy development, policy formulation, and compliance.

Each of these units may in turn be divided into smaller sub-units (departments, teams, etc.) and finally into individual jobs. In other words, the design process can be viewed as a successively more detailed specification of the sub-systems of the organization.

This chapter will address the twin aspects of the design methodology introduced in Chapter 1: The definition of functional requirements, derived from the sub-unit's *mission or mandate*, and the specification of design parameters that will ensure that the functional requirements can be achieved. Although we mentioned five types of design parameters in Chapter 1, we here focus on the sub-unit's *operating model*, that is, the main processes and work groups/teams. (In chapter 7, the focus will be broadened to include other design parameters.)

Defining the sub-unit mission and functional requirements

In designing sub-units, a key challenge is to ensure that the sub-unit's purpose contributes to the achievement of the organization's purpose *and* that the organization enables the sub-unit to achieve things that it would otherwise not be able to achieve. (If that is not the case, the sub-unit in question will perform better and be more valuable outside than inside the organization.) As stated in Ackoff (1994): "'An enterprise conceptualized as a social system should serve the purposes of both its parts and the system of which it is a part" (p. 31).

However, as we have discussed in the previous chapters, the organization's purpose may not always be clear. The strategies and missions developed by higher level managers are sometimes incomplete and may contain considerable ambiguity. Sub-unit managers who participate in the design of their unit will often need to develop and test alternative interpretations of missions or mandates, and interact with multiple constituents that must agree and accept the mission or mandate before it can be implemented.

In the following, we will consider the design of Subsea Tech, a business unit within a large engineering group that delivers oil platforms and subsea installations to the offshore oil industry. Subsea Tech is one of several business units within a *business area* (division) in this firm. The business units are legally independent companies, but the business area owns a majority stake in each unit. Subsea Tech designs and manufactures three mechanical devices: Hydraulic pumps, compressors, and actuators. The pumps are used to inject water into an oil well to increase pressure and to increase the flow rate out of the reservoir. Compressors are devices that increase the pressure of a gas by reducing its volume. Actuators are devices for moving or controlling a mechanism such as a valve. (These devices are placed on the seabed and connected to other modules and to the pipe through which the oil is transmitted.) The main clients are other business units in the same firm, which integrate these components into larger subsea solutions (Subsea Tech is thus currently defined as an *input unit*). The formal structure of Subsea Tech is shown in Figure 5.1. Fabrication is by far the largest sub-unit within Subsea Tech, and the one we will focus primarily on in this chapter.

In the terminology introduced in previous chapters, a *mission* (or *mandate*) expresses the top level functional requirement of the sub-unit. Once one has agreed on the mission/top level functional requirement, one can decompose it into more detailed functional requirements. How can we formulate an effective mission for Subsea Tech? Mission statements are sometimes criticized for being public relations attempts at improving the corporate image that bear little relation to how the organization actually works. (There

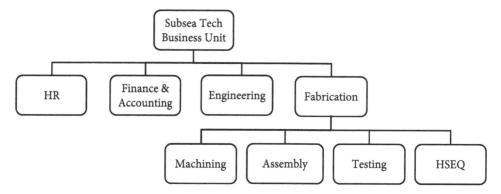

Figure 5.1 Organizational structure of the Subsea Tech business unit described in the text.

is some empirical support for this view, see Wright, 2002.) How can we formulate a mission that actually creates clarity about Subsea Tech's purpose, and that provides guidance in the subsequent phase when roles, processes, and formal structures are to be carved out? According to Haeckel (1999), an effective mission should express the organization's *Reason for Being* (why it exists), be unambiguous with regards to the *primary constituency,* and specify *the outcomes* that the unit must provide that constituency. Let us consider some alternative ways of formulating Subsea Tech's mission statement:

1 Subsea Tech exists to earn profits by delivering high quality subsea system components.
2 Subsea Tech exists to design and manufacture high quality subsea system components to internal customers while earning profits for our owners.
3 Subsea Tech exists to maximize subsea system performance for the group's end customers by delivering cost effective and highly reliable subsea system components.
4 Subsea Techs exists to provide employees with an attractive work environment and career opportunities by developing advanced components profitably for the oil industry.

What we see is that relatively minor differences in wording imply a rather different organizational purpose. In Table 5.1 each statement has been analysed by means of the framework proposed by Haeckel (1999). The primary constituent is the owner (the business area) in the first statement, the internal customers in the second statement, the end client in the third statement, and the employees in the fourth. The first three statements mention "subsea system components," while the last statement includes the term "advanced components." In other words, the last statement would suggest that

Table 5.1 Example of an analysis of alternative mission statements for Subsea Tech (based on framework proposed in Haeckel, 1999)

Action	Primary constituency	Qualifiers	Outcome
1. EARN profits	Owner	Deliver high quality system components	Profits
2. DESIGN and MANUFACTURE high quality subsea components	Internal customers	Profits	Quality components
3. MAXIMIZE subsea system performance	End customers	Cost effective and reliable components	High performing subsea systems
4. PROVIDE attractive work environment and career opportunities	Employees	Advanced components for the oil industry Profitability	Work environment and career opportunities

the business unit has a more general purpose (developing *components*), while the first three statements suggest that the business unit should specialise in delivering components for *subsea system installations* (which it may consider the most promising market, and one that demands the specialised expertise that Subsea Tech possesses). Also note that only the second statement specifies that the purpose of the business unit is to "design and manufacture." The other statements suggest that the overall purpose is to "deliver" or "develop" rather than design and manufacture. The second statement may thus be preferred if one would want to open up the possibility of outsourcing the fabrication process at some point in the future. Last but not least, only the second statement indicates that Subsea Tech should limit itself to internal customers; the other three statements mention end (external) customers. In other words, a fundamental question that would need to be clarified is whether Subsea Tech should remain an input unit, or be allowed to market and sell its products directly to external customers.

Which of these alternative interpretations is the most appropriate one? The owner (the business area), the external customers, the internal customers (other business units in the group), the employees, and the managers of Subsea Tech may each have different interests and preferences. It will be difficult to minimize complexity, and identify an effective design, unless one can get the stakeholders to agree on the fundamental purpose of the unit. The business unit leader may proactively engage the relevant constituents in interpreting and clarifying the mission. Participation by managers within the business unit should help the leader identify what Subsea Tech's unique contribution to the organization may be. A dialogue with executives at business area and group level is required in order to ensure that the mission that is adopted is aligned with higher level missions and strategies. Communication with other business units (including the current internal customers) will ensure that the unit selects a mission that is consistent and complementary to those of other sub-units within the group.[1]

In this particular case, let us assume that it is the second statement that is accepted and adopted. In other words, the top level functional requirement becomes:

FR$_1$ To design and manufacture high quality subsea system components for internal customers

This functional requirement can be further broken down into two more detailed functional requirements corresponding to the core work processes performed in Subsea Tech:

FR$_{11}$ Design components and sub-systems
FR$_{12}$ Manufacture components and sub-systems

There are also some functional requirements related to support processes:

FR$_{13}$ Recruit, develop and retain people
FR$_{14}$ Perform financial planning, reporting and control
FR$_{15}$ Ensure compliance with Health, Safety, Environment & Quality (HSEQ) policy

Defining the sub-unit operating model (design parameters)

The next question is how *design parameters* should be defined to ensure that these functional requirements can be realized. If the mission statement is clear in terms of the constituents served and the desired outcomes, it should simplify the process of designing the required operating model. In this case, it is clear that there is a need for design parameters (i.e., organizational units) that can be accountable for achieving the core FRs listed above. The mission statement may also be interpreted as excluding some design options. It establishes that Subsea Tech will both design and manufacture components (outsourcing is thus not an option). It also specifies that it serves internal customers; if this were not the case, a business development or sales unit would probably be needed to market and sell the products externally. Despite these constraints, there is still more than one operating model that may enable Subsea Tech to realize its mission as stated here. In particular, there are several alternatives for organizing the teams within the fabrication units (currently defined as machining, assembly, and testing). Below, we shall consider

1 Of course, if fundamental disagreements are encountered during this process, it may in be necessary to escalate the decision about the selection of the mission statement to the key stakeholder (e.g., higher level executives, sponsors, or board members).

Table 5.2 Design matrix representing Subsea Tech's initial organization

Functional requirements	Design parameters			
	Engineering	*Fabrication*	*HR*	*Finance*
1.1 Design components and sub-systems	X			
1.2 Manufacture components and sub-systems		X		
1.3 Recruit, develop and retain people			X	
1.4 Perform financial planning, reporting and control				X
1.5 Ensure compliance with Health, Safety, Environment & Quality (HSEQ) policy		X		

different options in some detail, and discuss how one may select the most optimal one. But if we start with the current organization depicted in Figure 5.1, Subsea Tech has four main units:

DP$_{11}$ Engineering
DP$_{12}$ Fabrication
DP$_{13}$ Finance
DP$_{14}$ HR

The resulting design matrix for the current organization is shown in Table 5.2.

Identifying potential conflicts (coupling) between functional requirements

In the preceding chapters, we have discussed Suh's (1990; 2001) axiom of minimizing complexity by reducing conflicts (or *coupling*) between the functional requirements. This implies that each sub-unit or team has its own functional requirements (or missions or mandates) and can pursue its objectives without interfering with those of other sub-units or teams. In order to identify potential conflicts between functional requirements, one needs to consider each functional requirement in turn, and ask whether the accountable unit (the corresponding DP) can work to achieve the functional requirement independently, without a negative impact on other functional requirements.

In this case, there will inevitably be coupling, as there are more functional requirements than design parameters: The fabrication sub-unit is not only responsible for manufacturing the product, but also carries out the activities related to HSEQ compliance (Health, Safety, Environment & Quality). We know from the mission statement above that quality is an important criterion and thus specific processes or roles may be required for this purpose. Currently, these

2 The example in the text describes a rather obvious conflict of interest. However, there are several other sources of coupling that are more subtle. See chapter 2 (Example 2.1) and chapter 8.

processes and roles are placed within the fabrication unit (cf. Figure 5.1 above). In other words, the fabrication sub-unit itself creates guidelines related to HSEQ, provides safety training to workers, and perform worksite audits to ensure that the guidelines are followed. Such a model leads to a potential conflict of interest. The main goal of fabrication is to produce components and sub-systems and earn a profit. HSEQ procedures and HSEQ staff are costs that the head of fabrication may be tempted to minimize. Even more seriously, if HSEQ staff report to the head of fabrication, they may be reluctant to raise potential safety or quality issues that may result in a cost increase or a production delay. The solution is to allocate FR_5 to a dedicated HSEQ team. This implies that the HSEQ staff will form a separate department and report directly to the head of the business unit (Figure 5.2)[2] and that we get a design matrix with entries along the diagonal only (Table 5.3).

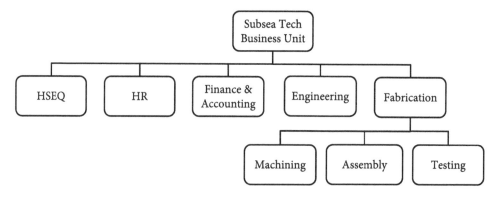

Figure 5.2 Revised organizational structure for Subsea Tech.

Table 5.3 Design matrix for Subsea Tech after the establishment of a separate HSEQ department

	Design parameters				
Functional requirements	*Engineering*	*Fabrication*	*HR*	*Finance*	*HSEQ team*
1.1 Design components and sub-systems	X				
1.2 Manufacture components and sub-systems		X			
1.3 Recruit, develop and retain people			X		
1.4 Perform financial planning, reporting and control				X	
1.5 Ensure compliance with Health, Safety, Environment & Quality (HSEQ) policy					X

Identifying and analysing interdependencies

The core design principle of grouping roles and sub-units to minimize interdependencies across units (Thompson, 1967) was described in Chapter 1. By grouping related tasks or roles together, one facilitates coordination within the unit. Application of this principle will also lead to the establishment of sub-units that are accountable for the performance of a "whole" task (e.g., the development of a finished module or component). Such units may to a great extent operate purposefully and autonomously, that is, be capable of setting goals, managing their own resources, and solving problems that arise in the course of the work, without the need for escalation to higher levels of management. In some cases, sub-units are even "complete economic entities" that are measured on their financial performance (Zenger & Hesterly, 1997).

We may consider the opposite case, where related tasks and roles are *not* grouped together, leading to significant interdependencies across sub-units. In this situation, coordination will be more costly, as one will need to communicate and reach agreement with people outside one's own unit in order to finalize a task. It will be more difficult to define accountability, as decisions made in one sub-unit will have ramifications for some or all of the other sub-units. It will also lead to a more complicated role for managers, as they will no longer control the resources or have authority over all of the employees who perform tasks related to the sub-unit's mission or mandate, as the employees (some or all of them) are now located in other sub-units (Kilman, 1983).

The principle of grouping related roles together is probably not far from the lay theories that many managers hold, even if they have never been exposed to organizational theory. Nevertheless, when one examines the relationship between work processes and the formal structure in organizations carefully, one often finds examples of ineffective grouping (for an empirical study, see Sherman & Keller, 2011). Managers may agree, in principle, that the minimization of coordination cost should be a priority, but in practice, many grouping decisions are made on the basis of largely intuitive reasoning or custom. Von Hippel (1990) interviewed managers in aircraft manufacturers and engineering firms, and found that managers rarely analyzed the work tasks and how they related to each other before making decomposition and grouping decisions:

> We have always designed aircraft bodies by dividing them into a series of cylindrical sections and assigning each section to a different task group. No one now at the company has thought about why we do this or whether it currently makes sense from any point of view. It is just the way we do it.
>
> (von Hippel, p. 410)

Von Hippel (1990) concluded that in some firms, certain ways of organizing are so traditional as to appear fixed, even though decomposition and grouping clearly represent variables that can be affected by management decisions. At the same time, it is important to acknowledge that it may be difficult to find an optimal grouping even if managers are determined to apply systematic methods in finding the best organizational design for a unit. It is not always obvious what the key interdependencies are which should form the basis for the grouping. And there may also exist conflicting demands, which means that one is forced to prioritise among alternative grouping criteria.

Unlike the formal reporting relationships depicted on organization charts, work process interdependencies often remain implicit. Yet it is hard to improve something that is not described or documented. To ensure that work process interdependencies become a part of the decision process regarding the formal structure, they need to be identified and analysed.

There is little disagreement with regard to the definitional framework. As proposed by Thompson (1967), we can distinguish between three types (and levels) of interdependency (Figure 5.3).[3] *Pooled interdependency* refers to a low level and indirect form of interdependency, such as when two units rely on the same pool of resources. For example, business units seeking investments may both rely on the same corporate funds; the work processes within several sub-units may depend on the same IT system. *Sequential interdependency* is a medium level of interdependency and means that two processes or units have a direct connection, so that the output of one process or unit is the input to the other (strictly, speaking, in this relationship one unit is *dependent* on the other). The typical example is the relationship between different units along the value chain in a manufacturing firm. Finally, *reciprocal interdependency* means that there is a two-way, iterative relationship, in that the output of one process or unit is the input to the other process or unit, and vice versa. Examples include the relationship between a project manager and a project member working on a consulting assignment or

3 Donaldson's (2001) concluded that the three interdependencies identified by Thompson correspond to a scale of increasing task uncertainty. Hence one can see view them as "levels of interdependency".

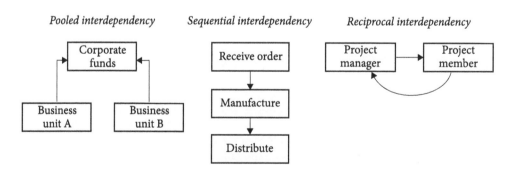

Figure 5.3 Examples illustrating Thompson's (1967) framework for levels of interdependency.

between a surgeon and a nurse during an operation. Reciprocal interdependency may sometimes involve ambiguous or uncertain information, making it difficult to use procedures and plans to coordinate the interaction (Donaldson, 2001). Reciprocal interdependency requires what Thompson (1967) termed *mutual adjustment* or what some later theorists have described as ad hoc coordination or interactive problem solving (von Hippel, 1990). Mutual adjustment is the most costly form of coordination because it means that more time needs to be spent on coordination with others, leaving less time to do perform the actual tasks. Mutual adjustment usually requires that one is engaged in a direct and continuous dialogue with each other and each party must be prepared to change its plans and priorities based on the feedback from the other. In an experimental study, it was found that participants that collaborated on solving tasks with reciprocal interdependencies required twice as much time to coordinate their efforts, compared with participants who were collaborating on tasks with pooled or sequential interdependencies (Nuñez, Giachetti & Boria, 2009).

For this reason it will usually be the first priority to contain reciprocal interdependencies within the same formal unit. Remaining sequential and pooled interdependencies between the units that are formed can then be handled by other means, such as by joint planning, rules, and procedures. In other words, we can restate Thompson's (1967) design principle as that of forming sub-unit boundaries around roles or processes with reciprocal interdependencies.

Until recently, there was a lack of tools and methods that could help operationalize these concepts. It is one thing is to agree on a design principle in theory, but another to ensure that it can be implemented in actual design processes. An important advance in this regard is the introduction of the design structure matrix (DSM) (Steward, 1981; Eppinger, 2001), sometimes also called task structure matrix (Baldwin & Clark, 2000). The DSM is a square matrix with one row and column per activity. The DSM allows a compact representation of elements and relationships in a system and is a useful tool for representing and analysing work flow interdependencies (Browning, 2009).

To construct a DSM, one first identifies the key tasks or process steps. One then identifies interdependencies between the tasks by asking participants who they interact with: "Who do you need input from (e.g., physical components, information, approval, etc.) in order to complete your tasks?" And conversely "To whom do you provide outputs?" In a small organization (such as a single department or team) one can gather this information by conducting interviews with each of the participants in the process. In a larger organization one can use an electronic survey questionnaire (Worren, Soldal, & Christiansen, 2017). The information that is gathered is then mapped using the DSM. There are four possible

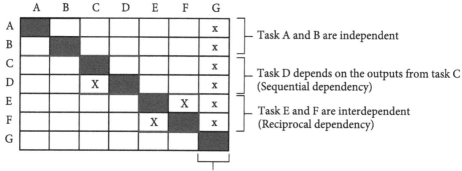

Task A and B are independent

Task D depends on the outputs from task C
(Sequential dependency)

Task E and F are interdependent
(Reciprocal dependency)

Task A–F are all (weakly) dependent upon G
(Pooled dependency)

Figure 5.4 Different bilateral relationships expressed in a DSM.

ways to characterize the relationship between tasks by using the DSM (Oosterman, 2001) (Figure 5.4):

- Neither task A nor task B may be involved in an interaction (independence).
- Task A may require the output of task B or vice versa (sequential dependence).
- Task A requires outputs from B, and B requires output from A (comparable to reciprocal interdependency as defined above).
- Task A and B are both dependent upon a shared resource (pooled dependency).

Once the interdependencies have been captured, one can consider different ways of clustering the tasks in order to minimize interdependencies across units. Intuitive methods can be used for systems consisting of a small number of elements. In the example provided in Figure 5.5, six elements have been clustered into two units, with no remaining interdependencies across the two units. For more complex processes, there now exist software packages[4] that can assist in identifying the optimal clustering of elements (and thereby the size and number of groups of elements) based on interdependencies.

There are two main types of DSMs. What we have described so far is a "task-based" DSM where the elements (rows) represent steps in a work process. But the matrix elements may also represent organizational units (this is sometimes called a "team-based" DSM). The same principles apply, except that a team-based DSM does not imply a time sequence (in contrast, in a task-based DSM, the elements are listed in chronological order, with early activities listed in the upper rows (i.e., A precedes B, and B precedes C). A restructuring of a team-based DSM will only indicate an alternative *grouping* (clustering) of roles or sub-units, whereas a restructuring

4 A number of DSM software tools exist that can take such data as input and apply an algorithm to find an optimal configuration of elements. Some of the available tools are listed on this web page: http://www.dsmweb.org These tools are generally intended to support product design rather than organization design. However, the author is involved in an initiative to develop a DSM tool aimed at supporting organization design decision (see Worren, Soldal & Christiansen, 2017).

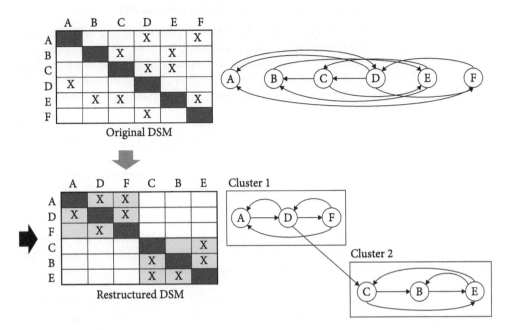

Figure 5.5 Example of clustering of DSM elements. Comparison to a graph representation of the same data.

of a task-based DSM will indicate an alternative *task sequence* as well as an alternative grouping.

In Figures 5.4 and 5.5, an "X" is used in the examples to denote the presence of an interdependency. However, in more sophistic-ated applications, one also distinguishes between interdependencies of different strength or frequency. Members of a work unit may be asked to indicate on a scale from 1 to 3 *how frequently* they need to receive information from other people in order to complete their tasks. Alternatively, they may be asked to indicate *how important* the different interdependencies are for their ability to perform their work tasks or achieve their goals.

It is obviously the case that the interdependencies that are identi-fied need to be valid for the subsequent analysis to produce appro-priate groupings. If one asks people what information they need to complete their tasks, different people may interpret "information" in different ways. Various types of information, such as formal data and friendly communication, may be mixed up (Oosterman, 2001). However, this concern may be at least partly be mitigated by the fact that the DSM collects information about *bilateral* relations. One asks two people about the same interdependency and may validate the information by evaluating whether the required *inputs* that have been identified by some participants match the *outputs* that other participants state that they feel responsible for providing (see Browning, 2009 for an example).

Locating sub-unit boundaries (interfaces)

To consider in more detail how to group roles and define sub-unit boundaries, let us return to the Subsea Tech example. It will be recalled that Subsea Tech designs and manufactures three main products (hydraulical pumps, compressors, and actuators). In order to illustrate the key concepts, some simplifying assumptions will be made:

- We focus on two main sub-units: Engineering and Fabrication (we ignore other units such as HR, HSEQ and Finance & Accounting).
- We assume that there are only three employees in each of the four sub-units/teams (in reality, there are many more).
- We assume initially that the workload is relatively stable over time and similar across the teams.
- We highlight work process interdependencies and leave out interdependencies due to the hierarchical structure (i.e., between employees and their managers).

The two main functional requirements of Subsea Tech are to design and manufacture components. The manufacturing operation was further divided into: Machining (fabrication of metal components), welding and assembly, and testing. In the current organization, each process is carried out by a separate team at the manufacturing plant (see Table 5.4 and Figure 5.1 above).

The work process is by and large sequential, and each worker within the team specializes in a particular procedure. For example, in the Machining team, the first worker receives engineering drawings and raw materials (corrosion-resistant steel), and goes on to set the parameters in computer-assisted machines. The second worker performs the initial turning and milling, and the component is then transferred to another machine where the third worker performs drilling operations. But the three workers also need to coordinate between them as every product is slightly different and may require some adjustment in the procedures used, or even the sequence of different operations.

Table 5.4 Design matrix for engineering and fabrication in Subsea Tech

Functional requirements	Design parameters			
	Engineering department	Machining team	Assembly team	Testing team
Design components	X			
Perform machining process		X		
Perform welding and assembly process			X	
Perform testing process				X

		Engineering			Machining			Assembly			Testing		
		E1	E2	E3	W1	W2	W3	W4	W5	W6	W7	W8	W9
Engineering	E1	■	X	X									
	E2	X	■	X									
	E3	X	X	■									
Machining	W1			X	■	X	X						
	W2				X	■	x						
	W3				X	X	■						
Assembly	W4						X	■	X	X			
	W5							X	■	X			
	W6							X	X	■			
Testing	W7									X	■	X	X
	W8										X	■	X
	W9										X	X	■

Figure 5.6 Interdependencies between employees belonging to four functional (discipline-based) teams (three engineers and nine workers in the manufacturing plant).

Let us examine the boundaries between the units. In the DSM shown in Figure 5.6, the four teams are indicated as bold squares. The blocks of X's in the matrix indicate that the work within each team is interdependent. But we also see three interdependencies outside the blocks, which represent sequential interdependencies between the teams (e.g., the product must be assembled before it can be tested).

Although this structure represents a well-proven, functional (discipline-based) grouping, we may still, as suggested by Baldwin and Clark (2006), ask why the boundaries are located as they are, and the consequences that would follow from altering the boundaries.[5] The first phase of the process is to *design* the products. In this phase, the three engineers (E1, E2, E3) capture the technical specifications, perform calculations, and produce drawings and models using computer assisted design tools. The boundary between Engineering and the next team, Machining, is located at the point at which the physical hand-over of manufacturing specifications occurs (the sequential dependency indicated in Figure 5.6 between Engineer 3 (E3) and Worker 1 (W1)), which provides the information that the Machining team needs to initiate the fabrication of the products. The boundary between the two teams is a natural one, for several reasons. One could imagine, as an alternative, that the boundary was pushed forward and that the Machining team also included Engineer 3 (E3). This would mean that the Machining team would receive unfinished engineering designs as an input, and would have to complete them

5 The example in the text is based on Litterer (1973) and extended based on later work by Baldwin & Clark (2006) and Zenger & Hesterly (1997). Although the example is fictitious it reflects several aspects of real manufacturing firms.

before initiating the manufacturing process. It would probably also imply more diffuse accountabilities, as the output from the Engineering team would to a lesser degree constitute a distinct, measurable deliverable: How would you monitor and evaluate partially completed engineering drawings and manufacturing specifications? On the other hand, moving the boundary downwards, by including Worker 1 (W1) or 2 (W2) in the Engineering team, would mean that the deliverable to be transferred would include completed drawings, plus a partially completed mechanical component. In general, the boundaries between units that are linked together by sequential interdependencies are usually located at the junctures with *a measurable output* (Zenger & Hesterly, 1997). By circumscribing activities with a measurable output, one allows monitoring of output levels and evaluation of efficiency. Monitoring and evaluation allows the introduction of performance-based incentives – members of the unit can be rewarded based on their productivity. Once you can measure the output you also have the opportunity to introduce a (financial) transaction at the transfer point (Baldwin & Clark, 2006): In a large manufacturing firm, the designs could potentially be valued and sold at an internal transfer price to the internal client (the manufacturing plant). In sum, locating the boundaries around activities with a measurable output allows the creation of "complete economic entities," even at lower levels of the organization (Zenger & Hesterly, 1997).

Evaluating alternative grouping criteria

We have confirmed that a functional (discipline-based) grouping may provide logical boundaries between the teams in Subsea Tech's fabrication facility. Yet this is not the only possible grouping under all circumstances. In fact, there exists several possible grouping criteria and the key task for organizational designers is to identify the relative priority of the different criteria.

Let us consider an alternative way in which to group the three manufacturing teams. So far we have assumed that the fabrication process is largely sequential, and that a team effort is required, in that the three workers in each team need to coordinate with each other in the execution of the process that the team is responsible for (however, each worker specializes in a sub-process, such as milling). We have also assumed that each worker is able to perform his/her particular sub-process to manufacture all of the products (pumps, compressors, actuators). However, let us consider the situation that emerges if the firm decides to introduce multi-task machines that can perform several processes (e.g., turning, milling, drilling, etc.), combined with a "job enlargement" scheme where each worker is given additional training in order to operate the machines and perform *all of the tasks* that his/her team was previously responsible for. At the same time, let us assume that the scope of work is limited to one of the products (i.e., each worker must now specialize by focusing on either pumps, compressors, or actuators). The result is a shift in the interdependencies: Each worker is now independent from the other members of the functionally defined (disciplined-based) teams – he or she does no longer provide outputs to, nor receive inputs from, the other two workers that used to be part of his/her team. (On the other hand, new interdependencies will arise toward the other workers working on the same product.) The component can move from one step of the manufacturing process to the next when one worker has completed his or her job. The three products can also be worked upon in parallel. The interdependencies that arise in this situation are depicted in Figure 5.7.

As we see in Figures 5.7 and 5.8, the interdependencies are in this case poorly aligned with a functional (discipline-based) grouping. To rectify this, one may structure the organization by *product*. A product-based structure creates "manufacturing cells" where each cell is made responsible for the fabrication of one product (see Table 5.5 and Figures 5.9 and 5.10). Note that a product-based structure would satisfy the criteria discussed above with regard to boundary definition, to an even greater extent than the functional (discipline-based) organization. It avoids the sequential interdependencies between the teams. Moreover, a finished product – which is the output produced by a team in a product-based structure – is not only measurable internally, but also externally, as it may be valued and priced based on comparison with other offerings in the market.

We thus have two alternative groupings. Is the product-based structure the optimal one? Not necessarily. As noted above, the functional (discipline-based) structure implies significant *sequential* interdependencies across the three departments in terms of the work process: The product must pass through three separate departments in order to be manufactured. A decision in the first team that results in a delay in the machining process will most likely affect the assembly

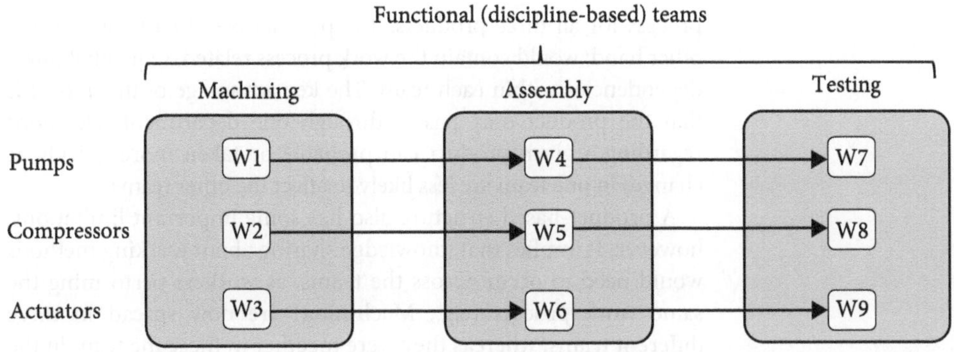

Figure 5.7 Interdependencies created by introducing multi-task machines combined with job enlargement and product focus. Interdependencies within teams disappear, while new ones emerge between the teams.

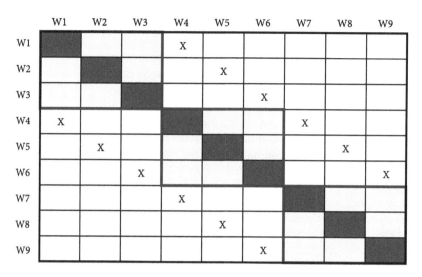

	W1	W2	W3	W4	W5	W6	W7	W8	W9
W1				X					
W2					X				
W3						X			
W4	X						X		
W5		X						X	
W6			X						X
W7				X					
W8					X				
W9						X			

Figure 5.8 DSM depicting the situation after the introduction of multi-task machines combined with job enlargement and product focus (compare to Figure 5.6). The same information is presented in Figure 5.7.

Table 5.5 Design matrix for product-based decomposition (compare with Table 5.4)

	Design parameters		
Functional requirements	*Pump team*	*Compressor team*	*Actuator team*
Manufacture pumps	X		
Manufacture compressors		X	
Manufacture actuators			X

process for all three products. The product-based structure, on the other hand, would contain the work process related, sequential interdependencies within each team. The key advantage of this model is that the product only passes through one department. Decisions regarding a given product can probably be taken more quickly as changes in one team are less likely to affect the other teams.

A product-based structure also has some important limitations, however. It implies that knowledge sharing about working methods would need to occur across the teams, as workers performing the same work process (e.g., Machining) are now spread in three different teams, whereas they were together in the same team in the functional (discipline-based) structure. (Note: such interdependencies due to a need for knowledge sharing or coordination about working methods were omitted from Figure 5.7 and 5.8.) But the

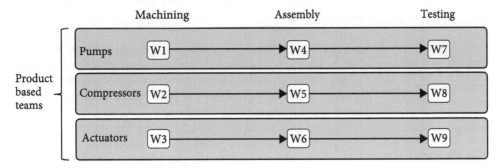

Figure 5.9 Alternative, product-based grouping of manufacturing teams. Compare with Figure 5.7 above.

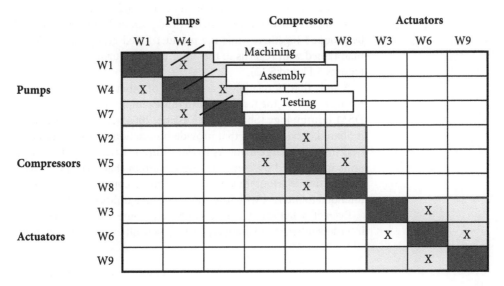

Figure 5.10 DSM for alternative, product-based grouping of manufacturing teams. Compare the grouping of roles (W1, W4, W7 etc.) to that in Figure 5.6. The same information is presented in Figure 5.9.

most important limitation is that the model presupposes that each of the sub-units is able to utilize its capacity effectively over time. Empirical research has shown that one of the key obstacles to implementing cell-based manufacturing is identifying part families with enough demand volume and demand stability over time (Johnson & Wemmerlöv, 2004). In a product-based (cell) structure, capacity imbalances may occur at times, such as when the worker performing testing in the Compressor team is idle due to lower demand for its product, while the worker performing the same process in Pumps team is overworked. If demand for the different products fluctuates over time, it may be more cost effective to "pool" resources; one way

6 One indication of this
neglect is that neither
Litterer (1973) nor
Mintzberg (1979)
mentioned resource
utilisations
considerations when
discussing the same case
as described here.

to do this is to revert to the more traditional functional (discipline-based) structure.

Resource utilization is sometimes considered an "operations management problem" rather than an organization design problem.[6] Yet, as we see in this case, it is possible to imagine that it may be economically infeasible in some cases to group reciprocally interdependent positions together in the same unit, even if that may be optimal from a work process perspective.

To fully understand the impact that a proposed change in the formal structure of an organization will have, one thus needs to evaluate the effect of alternative groupings on both work process interdependencies and resource utilization. A possible outcome of such an evaluation is the introduction of a hybrid model, i.e., a grouping based on a combination of two criteria. Based on such a rationale, the managers at the plant in Subsea Tech might conclude that workers performing one of the processes, such as testing, should be grouped together, while the product-based grouping should be maintained with regards to the other manufacturing processes (see Figures 5.11 and 5.12).

A unit that is related to a number of other units in the same manner, such as the testing unit in this example, is called a "bus" in DSM terminology (Sharman & Yassine, 2004). A familiar example is Shared Services units that provide transactional services to business units in a large firm. As in our example here, Shared Services units are created by consolidating resources that were previously dispersed in various business units into a common unit that is intended to interact with internal clients in a uniform way.

Even if a hybrid structure is chosen, some weaker, "residual" interdependencies (Mintzberg, 1979) will often remain that have

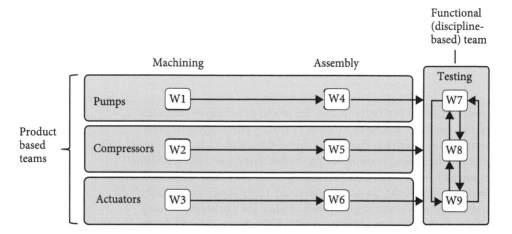

Figure 5.11 Product-based grouping of machining and assembly workers combined with functional (discipline-based) grouping of workers performing testing. Compare to Figure 5.7 and 5.9 above.

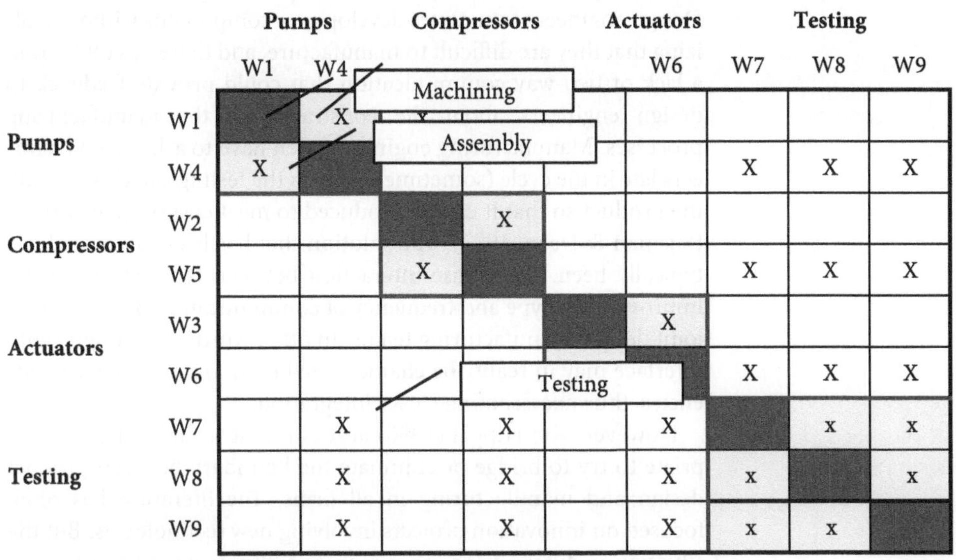

		Pumps		Compressors		Actuators		Testing		
		W1	W4	W2	W5	W3	W6	W7	W8	W9
Pumps	W1	■	X							
	W4	X	■					X	X	X
Compressors	W2			■	X					
	W5			X	■			X	X	X
Actuators	W3					■	X			
	W6						■	X	X	X
Testing	W7		X		X		X	■	x	x
	W8		X		X		X	x	■	x
	W9		X		X		X	x	x	■

(Overlay boxes on the matrix: "Machining", "Assembly", "Testing".)

Figure 5.12 DSM for product-based grouping of machining and assembly workers combined with functional (discipline-based) grouping of workers performing testing.

not been picked up by the grouping criterion chosen as the basis for the formal structure. We already mentioned that there may some interdependencies due to a need for knowledge sharing among workers performing the same process. Such interdependencies will need to be managed by employing different, compensatory means. If a plant selects a product- or "cell"-based grouping, as in the case just described, workers performing the same process may find other, informal means, such as discussion forums, to share experiences and ideas regarding their working methods. Similarly, instead of reverting to a functional (discipline-based) structure, a plant manager may find alternative ways to compensate for uneven resource utilization levels across the product-based teams (manufacturing cells): The plant manager may implement a capacity planning system to predict the required resource levels, or implement procedures that allow foremen to "borrow" resources from each other in order to utilize the total capacity of the plant.

Alternative characterisation of interdependencies

In the example described we assumed that the interdependences between engineering and manufacturing were *sequential*: The engineers complete a product design and hand it over to manufacturing where the fabrication process takes place. However, this characterization of interdependence has been challenged by a number of scholars, and the "design-build" interface has become a classic issue in the technology management literature. The key argument is that this conception of interdependence has led to organizational "silos." Design engineers sometimes develop new components without realizing that they are difficult to manufacture, and there has often been a lack of two-way communication that could provide feedback to design engineers about the constraints of the manufacturing processes. Manufacturing engineers often have to ask design engineers late in the cycle (sometime as late as the testing stage) to modify the product so that it can be produced to meet cost or quality goals (Susman & Dean, 1992). The solution that has been advocated has typically been to increase interaction between the two groups by improving the type and frequency of communication or by creating joint design-manufacturing teams. In other words, the design-build interface may in reality be characterized by *reciprocal* interdependencies, thus necessitating closer integration.

However, von Hippel (1990) argues that it would not be appropriate to try to bridge or eliminate the boundary between product design and manufacturing in all firms. The literature has often focused on innovation projects involving new technologies. But the situation is different for more mature technologies and processes. Many firms employ modern manufacturing technologies that are capable of producing a range of new designs. Von Hippel cites book printing as an example: Book authors do not have to write their books with the needs of the printer in mind. For this reason there will not usually be a need for interactive problem solving or two-way communication between printers and authors. (But he also notes that a graphics designer trying to do something that pushes the limits of existing printing processes may well find close coordination with the printer to be valuable.)

A firm that experiences problems with the design-build interface should not only consider the boundary between design and manufacturing but also how the process itself may be improved. The product engineers and the manufacturing engineers could work together to agree on *standards for manufacturability* that specify some general rules for how new components are to be developed given the existing manufacturing processes. It may thus be possible to reduce the need for coordination by establishing common standards that the engineers can consult when designing new products (Baldwin & Clark, 2000). These standards essentially remove interdependencies and take the place of on-going coordination between individuals belonging to different teams.

The introduction of software systems sometimes has a similar effect. As an example, consider the task of scheduling a meeting among several participants. If one does not know the other participants' availability, one will usually have to contact each of them in order to find a time suitable for all. With software tools (e.g., Microsoft Outlook), this task is greatly simplified in that the software will indicate the times when all the invited participants are available. As long as everybody updates their calendar and has some available time, one does not need to expend much effort to schedule the meeting. Similarly, the need for interaction between designers and manufacturing engineers may be reduced if engineers have access to component databases that list approved components with descriptions of their physical properties, functional characteristics, manufacturing requirements, and so on.

Determining group size

Unit size will, in principle, follow from the decomposition that one arrives at after defining unit boundaries. The basic building blocks of the organization correspond to the grouping of interdependencies that are identified in the DSM; the optimal unit size from this point of view is the size that maximizes intra-unit and minimizes cross-unit interdependence. Nevertheless, one still has the option of combining the different building blocks or adjusting the size of a unit by altering the interdependencies that formed the basis for the grouping. For this reason it can be useful to briefly review the main approaches that have been proposed in the literature with regard to the optimal size of sub-units.

At an operational level, the required sub-unit size will in some cases be derived from estimates of "minimum critical mass." For example, a consulting firm considering geographical expansion may want to know how large new offices must be in other to justify the cost of establishing and running the office. It may calculate the minimum size of an office based on knowledge of the typical utilization rate of its consultants, the cost of renting office space, and the cost of support personnel to run an office. The conclusion may be that an office may have at least 10 or 15 people in order to justify its costs.

A more strategic approach, mainly relevant to the definition of the main business units, is to match the size of internal units with the size of the market segment (e.g., Eisenhardt & Brown, 1999; Christensen, 1997): A small business unit may not possess the technical or financial resources required to compete in a large market. A large business unit, on the other hand, will have difficulty targeting niche opportunities for growth. (Large and integrated firms often have difficulties justifying investments in emerging technologies because they initially represent only a small fraction of the firm's potential revenues.)

A third approach is advocated by some authors who believe that there are psychological and biological laws governing the efficient size of social sub-systems. This approach is usually based on considerations of cognitive or social psychological constraints to working in large and complex systems. Nicholson (1997; 1998) suggested that there are evolutionary reasons for why human beings prefer to be part of "herds" of no more than 15–20 people within larger "clans" of around 150 people. Most studies point to the advantage of small group size on participation and group cohesiveness. Units that reach more than 10 members tend to fraction into cliques (smaller groups). For much of human evolution, individuals lived their lives within a clan system and would rarely if ever encounter a stranger, i.e., someone from outside the kinship network of the clan. Our psychology is as a consequence geared to a known and finite social universe and the social information processing capacity may therefore correspond to what we encounter in a typical clan. The ABB case is frequently cited. In its heyday, ABB was a federation of approximately 1,500 business units, each of which consisted of only 150 people. Eisenhardt and Brown (1999) similarly noted that Microsoft tries to keep its applications businesses at or below 200 people.

On the other hand, some scholars have pointed out that a decrease in the average size of units comes at the price of an increasing number of units overall, leading to a sharp rise in the number of interfaces. The basic trade-off is thus often presented as one of choosing between having a few large sub-systems that are in themselves complex but provide few sub-system interfaces, or dividing the system into the smallest possible units, but at the price of having numerous individual units with many sub-system interfaces (see Figure 5.13) (Chroust, 2004). A sub-unit manager in a complex organization may spend half of his or her time coordinating with other units, and may easily become bogged down as the number of interfaces increases (Rechtin, 1991).

In reality, the trade-off between size and number of units will depend on the particular nature of the interfaces. It is considerably more time-consuming to handle reciprocal interdependencies than sequential or pooled interdependencies. Sub-unit managers may be able to handle a large number of interfaces relatively easily if they involve standard processes; for example, an internal IT department may be perfectly capable of delivering services to a large number of

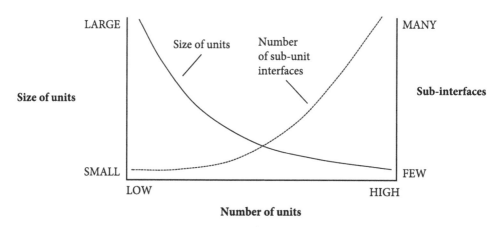

Figure 5.13 Trade-off between size of units and number of units.

internal clients, as long as it delivers a standardized service and transacts with each internal client in more or less the same manner (i.e., there exists a *standard interface* between the unit and its internal clients). The internal structure of the unit also influences its possible size. A work unit with a high degree of reciprocal interdependence among its members will require more intense supervision by the unit manager. Consequently, such units will need to be relatively small for the manager to have adequate capacity for supervision (Mintzberg, 1979). On the other hand, a manager may be able to supervise a large number of people – or oversee a large number of sub-units – if the level of interdependency is low. In some retail banks, for example, there are dozens of branch managers reporting to the same divisional executive. (We return to the issue of span of control in Chapter 6.)

Aligning formal structure with work process interdependencies

Effective grouping involves *partitioning* of processes that are characterised by sequential or pooled interdependency, and *integration of* processes with reciprocal interdependences (Figure 5.14). Partitioning entails the creation of one or more structural boundaries (e.g., by dividing a unit into two sub-units), whereas integration involves the removal of one or more boundaries (e.g., by merging two sub-units). There are potential pitfalls associated with both options. A lack of coordination (often attributed to organizational "silos") is often the result if one partitions a process with reciprocal interdependencies. The appropriate solution would be to increase interaction across the boundary of the units concerned or to eliminate the boundary altogether. On the other hand, one will usually not obtain any benefit from integrating processes that are independent, or that only have sequential or pooled interdependencies, into one unit. In fact, it may produce unwanted costs. Combining two or more different, weakly related units may frustrate efforts at creating a common purpose and a clear group identity. Integration increases the size of units and implies that the manager of the combined unit will be responsible for a potentially large set of weakly related processes. The integrated structure may produce a number of interaction points that result in time being spent on unnecessary and unwanted coordination. Members might be expected to participate in joint meetings and interchange information via e-mail, leading to information overload. Decisions processes may slow down as more stakeholders may have a say in the outcome. Integration may also lead to more diffuse accountability and make it more difficult to assign credit or blame to individuals or teams within the combined unit.

As indicated in Figure 5.14, the organizational designer has two main levers at his or her disposal: To adjust the formal structure to fit the interdependencies, or to manipulate the interdependencies

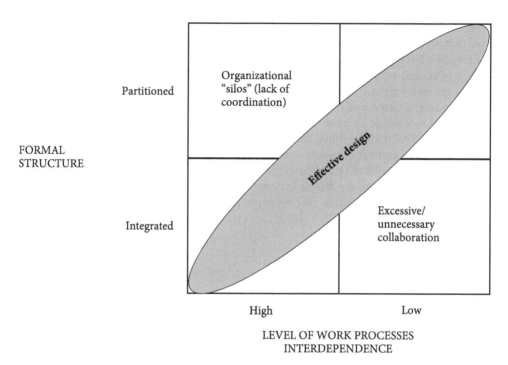

Figure 5.14 The relationship between formal structure (grouping) and work process interdependencies.

to fit the current organizational structure. The latter option is less frequently discussed but is equally important. As we touched on when discussing the design-build interface, common standards and "design rules" can be introduced that help participants in a process anticipate interactions and thereby reduce the level of reciprocal interdependence.

This reasoning also points to why ineffective groupings exist or why a grouping that might be perceived as effective today moves out of "fit" over time. First, the structural design decisions may simply be taken without considering work processes. Decisions about organization design are often made by senior managers, who may not be able (or have the necessary data) to identify the actual interdependencies at lower levels of the organization. But even if data are available, or a more operational level manager takes the grouping decision, it will be difficult to make the correct judgment in those cases where people develop new technologies or perform novel processes with unknown interdependencies. In such cases the appropriate strategy is to have a flexible structure that can be adapted as the project evolves. Even in more stable organizations, however, where it is easier to predict interdependencies, the design can gradually move out of "fit." Over time, people document and standardize the different steps of a process, learn to anticipate interdependencies between activities, and often develop rules and procedures that reduce the need for coordination or remove the interdependence altogether. This is part of what is referred to as "process maturity" (Curtis, Hefley, & Miller, 2002). The formal structure needs to be adapted in step with increasing maturity of the work processes.

In making grouping decisions, one does not need to restrict oneself to the interdependencies that are recognized and well understood today. A strategic approach to grouping should include pragmatic ways of considering *potential* interdependencies, that is, interdependencies that *can or should be developed* (or removed) to achieve some purpose (e.g., improved organizational performance) (Ensign, 1998). An excellent example is described in McKelvey and Kilmann (1975), who used a statistical technique similar to the DSM approach described here. McKelvey and Kilmann participated in the organization design of a business school at a large university. The dean and faculty wanted to change the structure of the school. The key challenge was to identify the right sub-units (which were called study centres, essentially groups of researchers). The goal was to maximize the homogeneity of research interests within the group (in order to encourage mutual support and collaborative research projects) while minimizing task-based interactions across the groups. In accordance with this goal, they developed a questionnaire where the faculty members were asked to indicate who, among the other faculty members, they thought would contribute to their own research activities over the next years, and, consequently, should be part of the same study center (a seven point scale was used, from "not at all," to "none I'd like more"). A statistical technique called factor analysis was then used to identify the optimal groupings.[7] McKelvey and Kilmann also later verified that the actual organization that was implemented was in accordance with the suggested grouping. This example demonstrates how the DSM approach can be used to map potential or ideal interdependencies that are required to support a design objective. Moreover, whereas the DSM may be perceived as a purely analytical tool to be used in "expert driven" processes, this example shows that the DSM can be part of a participatory process that takes into consideration the preferences of individual members of an organization.[8]

Summary and conclusion

The process of forming sub-units can be viewed from two perspectives: Whereas the decomposition of functional requirements focuses on the ends, the definition of the design parameters (including a unit's operating model) specifies the means. In practice, one often needs to iterate between the two modes of design.[9] One may start by using a "top down" approach, by breaking down a high level mission into functional requirements, but combine this with a "bottom up"

7 Today, more sophisticated methods exist that use computer algorithms to cluster DSM data (for an example, see Yu, Goldberg, & Yassine, 2007).

8 One difference from the approach described in Worren et al. (2017) is that McKelvey & Kilman (1975) clustered people, whereas Worren et al. (2017) assumes that one should cluster roles first, before one allocates people to the roles (because people may be allocated to new role as a result of a reorganization). However, this is less relevant in an academic setting, as that described in McKelvey & Kilman (1975), where the professors would maintain their roles after the reorganization.

9 There are several reasons for why designers may iterate between FRs and DPs. As described in chapter 1, in decomposing a system, the design parameters that are chosen at one level often determine the functions that are relevant at the next level of decomposition. There are also instances where the same function can be achieved by several alternative design parameters. Finally, as functions are typically more abstract than design parameters, some managers may prefer to start with the design parameters and define the function second ("we need an accounting department for sure … but what should its mandate be?").

approach later to analyse work processes and group related roles into sub-units (Mintzberg, 1979).

The key choice facing organizational designers is whether to *partition or integrate* a given set of sub-units (or teams or roles, depending on the unit of analysis). When considering the functional requirements (i.e., missions and mandates), the key principle is to partition, or separate, sub-units (or roles, processes) with conflicting requirements (coupling). When considering the design parameters, the general rule is to partition when there is a low level of interdependence and to integrate when there is a high level of interdependency (as long as the functional requirements are independent). The design structure matrix (DSM) is a tool that facilitates the analysis of interdependencies and the identification of correct groupings. Organizational designers may also be able to manipulate the interdependencies themselves by re-designing the process in a manner that reduces the need for coordination.

Competing grouping criteria may sometimes exist. For example, decisions makers may have to choose between a grouping that optimizes work process interdependencies and one that maximizes resource utilization. There is no universal prescription in such cases, but the recommended approach is to explicitly evaluate all the costs and benefits of a proposed design solution. Once a decision has been taken about the primary grouping criterion, compensatory means should be developed to address the remaining, "residual" interdependencies between roles or sub-units.

In our discussion in this chapter, we have focused mainly on the relationship between the work process interdependencies and the formal structure. In Chapter 7 we broaden our focus by considering *different types* of interdependencies that arise as a consequence of sub-unit grouping and how these can be managed on a more continuous basis.

Design propositions

Objective	Create clarity with regards to a sub-unit's functional requirements (FRs)
5.1	Create an overall mission or mandate for the sub-unit that identifies key outcomes, the primary constituent, and constraints.
5.2	Involve key stakeholders in interpreting and clarifying the sub-unit mission.
5.3	Ensure that the mission is aligned with the higher level organizational architecture of the firm and that it is consistent and complementary to the missions of other sub-units at the same level.

5.4	Use the mission as the basis for defining lower-level functional requirements for processes, teams, departments, etc.
Objective	*Minimize coupling between functional requirements [Cf. Design proposition 2.4a]*
5.5	Consider interrelationships between the functions of different sub-units (or between departments, teams, roles, etc.).
5.6	Create a formal structure that separates sub-units (or departments, teams, roles, etc.) with conflicting or incompatible goals.
Objective	*Define an operating model that minimizes coordination costs [Cf. Design proposition 2.4b]*
5.7	Identify work process interdependencies by collecting data "bottom up" (i.e., from employees in the organization who perform the processes).
5.8	Create a formal structure that integrates the elements (sub-units, departments, teams, roles) that are most highly interdependent (provided that their functions are not coupled, cf. proposition 5.6) and separates elements (sub-units, departments, teams, roles) that are independent or weakly interdependent.
5.9	Create a plan (or ensure that plans are created) for managing the interdependencies that remain across units in after the proposed grouping of sub-units, departments, teams, or roles.
5.10	To reduce the need for coordination, consider whether some interdependencies of low to moderate criticality and uncertainty may be removed by introducing plans, procedures, or common standards.
5.11	Adjust the proposed grouping to reach an adequate group size, depending on the level of interdependency within the group and the number of interfaces overall.
5.12	Evaluate the benefit of implementing the proposed grouping against any potential additional costs stemming from e.g., reduced scale or resource utilization.

Review questions

1 Why is it valuable to invest time in clarifying the mission or mandate of a sub-unit as part of a design process?

2   What are the key elements of mission statements according to Haeckel (1999)?

3   How can potential conflicts (coupling) between functional requirements be identified?

4   What different types of interdependencies exist according to Thompson (1967)?

5   How may these interdependencies be represented in a design structure matrix (DSM)?

6   How may interdependencies between different tasks or roles be identified?

7   Why are interdependencies sometimes neglected?

8   How can one ensure that the formal structure of an organization (or a sub-unit) is aligned with the work process interdependencies?

9   A large organization has a rule that every department should consist of at least 15 employees. Two departments, HR and Finance, have only 10 employees each. Consequently, management decides to merge the two departments into one, even though they have little in common and are responsible for different work processes. Where would you place this department in the diagram shown in Figure 5.14?

10 A firm produces only two products that are highly interrelated technically. The firm has been growing steadily and now has several hundred employees. The CEO believes that as a medium sized firm, it should have a divisional structure. Hence the CEO decides to split the units responsible for production, marketing, and sales into two parts. After this reorganization, where would you place the new units (e.g., the two production units, or the two marketing units) in the diagram shown in Figure 5.14?

11 What considerations are important when determining the size of units?

12 Try to obtain an organization chart for a fairly large firm or governmental organization (e.g., by accessing its internet site). What is its main function? What grouping criteria have been used to define the units? Have consistent criteria been used at the same level, and at different levels hierarchically?

Research questions

1   Managers must sometimes choose between a grouping that optimizes work flow and a grouping that optimizes resource utilization or that provides economies of scale. Is it possible to develop a formal, quantitative methodology that could support managers in making such trade-offs?

2   Several metrics have been proposed for assessing the degree of modularity (sub-unit independence) of a system represented in a DSM (see e.g., Höltttä-Otto et al., 2012). However, so far, we lack

a scale-independent metric that can be used to characterize systems of varying sizes and complexity. How can such a metric be developed?

3 Algorithms have been developed to cluster DSM data and reduce coordination costs (e.g., Yu et al., 2007). However, they rely on assumptions and we lack empirical data about the actual coordination costs related to optimal versus sub-optimal grouping. How can we estimate coordination costs? What factors may increase or decrease coordination costs?

4 In his doctoral dissertation, Bas Oosterman (2001, p. 57) voiced some concerns about the DSM. He pointed out that the DSM matrix does not clearly distinguish between what needs to be coordinated from the coordination activity itself (an "X" in a cell may refer to either). How could the conceptual framework underlying the DSM be improved to address this concern?

5 Zenger & Hesterly (1997) described the trend toward disaggregation of large firms. What is the most effective way to proceed when designing "complete economic units" at lower levels of the organization?

References

Ackoff, R. (1994). *The Democratic Corporation.* New York: Oxford University Press.

Baldwin, C., & Clark, K. (2000). *The Power of Modularity.* Boston: MIT Press.

Baldwin, C., & Clark, K. (2006). Where do transactions come from? Unpublished working paper, Harvard Business School.

Browning, T. (2009). Using the Design Structure Matrix to Design Program Organizations. In Sage, Andrew P. and William B. Rouse, Eds., *Handbook of Systems Engineering and Management,* 2nd edn. New York: Wiley.

Christensen, C. M. (1997). *The Innovator's Dilemma: When New Technologies Cause Great Firms to Fail.* Boston: Harvard Business School Press.

Chroust, G. (2004). The empty chair: Uncertain futures and systemic dichotomies. *Systems Research and Behavioral Science, 21,* 227–236.

Curtis, B., Hefley, W. E., & Miller, S. (2002). *People Capability Maturity Model: Guidelines for Improving the Workforce.* Reading, MA: Addison-Wesley.

Donaldson, L. (2001). *The Contingency Theory of Organizations.* Thousand Oaks, CA: Sage Publications.

Eisenhardt, K., & Brown, S. (1999). Patching: Restiching business portfolios. *Harvard Business Review,* May–June, 72–82.

Ensign, C. (1998). Interdependency, coordination, and structure in complex organizations. *The Mid-Atlantic Journal of Business, 34,* 1, 5–22.

Eppinger, S. D. (2001). Innovation at the speed of information. *Harvard Business Review*, January, 149–158.

Haeckel, S. H. (1999). *Adaptive Enterprise: Creating and Leading Sense-and-respond Organizations.* Boston: Harvard Business School Press.

Hölttä-Otto, K., Chiriac, N. A., Lysy, D., & Suk Suh, E. (2012). Comparative analysis of coupling modularity metrics. *Journal of Engineering Design*, 23, 10–11, 790–806.

Johnson, D. J., & Wemmerlöv, U. (2004). Why does cell implementation stop? Factors influencing cell penetration in manufacturing plants. *Production and Operations Management*, 13, 3, 272–289.

Kilmann, R. H. (1983). The costs of organization structure: Dispelling the myths of independent divisions and organization-wide decision making. *Accounting, Organizations and Society*, 8, 4, 341–357.

Litterer, J. A. (1973). *The Analysis of Organizations.* New York: John Wiley & Sons.

McKelvey, B., & Kilmann, R. H. (1975). Organization design: A participative multivariate approach. *Administrative Science Quarterly*, 20, 24–36.

Mintzberg, H. (1979). *The Structuring of Organizations.* Englewood Cliffs: Prentice-Hall.

Nicholson, N. (1997). Evolutionary psychology: Toward a new view of human nature and organizational society. *Human Relations*, 9, 1053–1079.

Nicholson, N. (1998). How hardwired is human behavior? *Harvard Business Review*, 76, 4, 134–147.

Nuñez, A. N., Giachetti, R. E., & Boria, G. (2009). Quantifying coordination work as a function of the task uncertainty and interdependence. *Journal of Enterprise Information Management*, 22, 3, 361–376.

Oosterman, B. J. (2001). Improving product development projects by matching product architecture and organization. Unpublished doctoral dissertation, University of Groningen.

Rechtin, E. (1991). *Systems Architecting: Creating & Building Complex Systems.* Englewood Cliffs, NJ: Prentice-Hall.

Sherman, J. D., & Keller, R. T. (2011). Suboptimal assessment of interunit task interdependence: Modes of integration and information processing for coordination performance. *Organization Science*, 22, 1, 245–261.

Sharman, D. M., & Yassine, A. A. (2004). Characterizing complex product architectures. *Systems Engineering*, 7, 1, 35–60.

Steward, D. (1981). The design structure system: A method for managing the design of complex systems. *IEEE Transactions on Engineering Management*, EM–28, 3, 71–74.

Suh, N. P. (1990). *The Principles of Design.* New York: Oxford University Press.

Suh, N. P. (2001). *Axiomatic Design: Advances and Applications*. New York: Oxford University Press.

Susman, G. I., & Dean, J. W. (1992). Development of a model for predicting design for manufacturability effectiveness. In G. Susman, Ed., *Integrating Design and Manufacturing for Competitive Advantage*. New York: Oxford University Press.

Thompson, J. D. (1967). *Organizations in Action*. New York: McGraw-Hill.

von Hippel, E. (1990). Task partitioning: An innovation process variable. *Research Policy, 19*, 5, 407–418.

Worren, N., Soldal, K., & Christiansen, T. (2017). Organizing from the ground up: Developing a DSM based tool for organization design. Paper presented at the 19th International Dependency and Structure modelling conference, Espoo, Finland, September 11–13.

Wright, N. J. (2002). Mission and reality and what not? *Journal of Change Management, 3*, 1, 30–44.

Yu, T.-L., Yassine, A. A., & Goldberg, D. E. (2007). An information theoretic method for developing modular architectures using genetic algorithms. *Research in Engineering Design, 18*(2), 91–109.

Zenger, T. R. & Hesterly, W. (1997). The disaggregation of corporations: Selective intervention, high-powered incentives, and molecular units. *Organization Science, 8*, 3, 209–222.

6   Defining the vertical structure

Chapter overview

Background	• Defining the accountabilities of key jobs at different organizational levels is a core task in organization design.
	• For this purpose one may use requisite organization (RO), a framework originally developed by Elliot Jaques in the 1970s.
	• RO places the main emphasis on appropriate definition of formal, vertical structures or "accountability hierarchies."
Challenges	• Some of the assumptions behind RO may seem to be at odds with the realities of modern organizations, characterized by:
	– Reliance on teams and horizontal coordination
	– Lack of predictability and subsequently lower emphasis on long term planning
	– Less reliance on predefined positions and greater ability of individual workers to shape their own jobs.
	• Yet even flexible, project-based organizations need a minimum of structure and clarity with regard to accountability.
Key question	• Is it possible to adapt RO to the realities of modern organizations so that it can serve as a framework for defining vertical structures?
Proposed approach	• Clarify RO concepts to avoid common misunderstandings.
	• Increase applicability of RO by describing jobs in terms of outcomes as opposed to activities.

- Combine RO with the concept of the modular organization to create a layered structure in flexible, project-based firms.

Introduction

The preceding chapters have mainly focused on the horizontal dimension of organizations, in considering how to design the overall architecture of firms and the interfaces between organizational sub-units. However, one must obviously attend to both the horizontal and vertical dimension when designing organizations. One does not have an implementable design before one has identified the required number of management layers and defined the responsibilities of key positions at different levels. In this chapter, we will consider how to approach such issues. We will also discuss how an early framework for hierarchical/vertical structuring – originally developed for organizations in relatively stable market environments – can be adapted to the demands of today's flexible, project-based organizations.

The ideal hierarchy

Compared to the situation 30 or 40 years ago, it is clear that organizations today rely less on hierarchical control and more on self-directed teams (Zenger & Hesterly, 1997; Whittington et al., 1999; Devine, 1999). Yet the vast majority of organizations remain hierarchically structured (Leavitt, 2005). The key question is thus how we can design hierarchies to serve the needs of both the organization and its internal and external stakeholders.

Let us first consider the basic logic for structuring hierarchical systems. One can easily define the principles behind an "ideal" hierarchical system (see Table 6.1). But it is also true that the structure of most organizations tends to depart somewhat from this ideal. Over time, roles are added or removed, responsibilities altered, and reporting lines changed to accommodate new business opportunities as well as individual preferences, and such adjustments are not necessarily carried out in a coherent or consistent manner. An initial task in a re-design project could be to identify the main logical inconsistencies in the current formal structure. In the subsequent phases a key priority may be to avoid the introduction of new inconsistencies when developing a new design. A useful list of criteria is Abrahamson's (2002) summary of common deviations from an ideal hierarchical structure (Table 6.2).

However, it is not a deviation from an ideal hierarchical structure per se that is a problem, but the consequences that sometimes result from such a deviation. It may be perfectly acceptable for a subordinate to report to two bosses, if the subordinate experiences that there is relative clarity about goals and priorities in his or her

Table 6.1 "Ideal" hierarchical structure

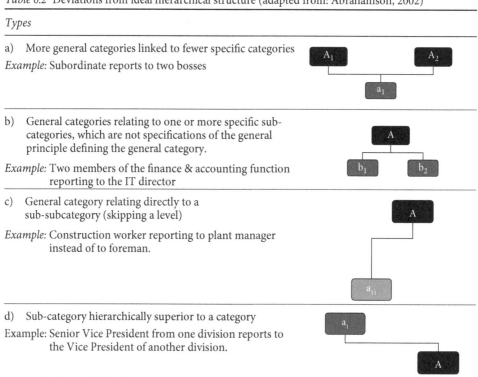

Fewer, more general categories, subdivided into several, specific sub-categories

Table 6.2 Deviations from ideal hierarchical structure (adapted from: Abrahamson, 2002)

Types

a)   More general categories linked to fewer specific categories

Example: Subordinate reports to two bosses

b)   General categories relating to one or more specific sub-categories, which are not specifications of the general principle defining the general category.

Example: Two members of the finance & accounting function reporting to the IT director

c)   General category relating directly to a sub-subcategory (skipping a level)

Example: Construction worker reporting to plant manager instead of to foreman.

d)   Sub-category hierarchically superior to a category

Example: Senior Vice President from one division reports to the Vice President of another division.

job. It may not be acceptable to have two bosses if it results in conflicting priorities and thus negatively impacts the subordinate's ability to perform his or her job. Similarly, it may not be a major problem if a senior vice president reports to a vice president, if this confusion is only due to an idiosyncratic use of titles in different units of the firm. It may be more problematical, however, if the vice president is in fact responsible for more complex tasks than the senior vice president, who may then be unable to provide guidance and support to his direct report (let alone provide the necessary coordination toward other units that interface with the unit managed by the senior vice president). Idiosyncrasies in hierarchical structures also create challenges for large organizations that intend to standardize their operations or introduce common, company-wide processes. A company may be planning a new reward system for all executives at level 1–3 of the company (i.e., the CEO and those at the two levels below) but may find that the official chart does not reflect the actual job functions and level of responsibility of the different executives, and that people at level 4 in some units carry more responsibility than those at level 3 in other units. Similarly, to ensure compliance with external accounting regulations, a company may need to introduce a clear separation of duties in terms of who requests and who approves financial expenditures. But it may find that the currently defined reporting structure is too ambiguous or incomplete to serve as a basis for defining such responsibilities.[1]

The requisite organization approach

Of course, correcting errors in the design of the formal structure is not enough to assure that it actually fulfills its purpose. How do we design hierarchies to maximize motivation, productivity, and performance? This question was addressed in depth by the late management theorist Elliott Jaques, who, between 1950 and his death in 2003, published a number of works aimed at describing the optimal design of hierarchical structures. He referred to organizations as "accountability hierarchies", pointing out that they are essentially systems for getting things done. His key purpose was to create organizational models that enable a large number of people to work together yet preserve unambiguous accountability, place people with the necessary competence at each organizational layer, and ensure that each manager adds value the work of his or her subordinates.

Although he was trained as a psychotherapist, Jaques concluded that problems in working relationships are often caused by dysfunctional systems rather than by dysfunctional people. He was skeptical of interventions aimed at changing the attitudes and behavior of individuals. For example, he believed that confusion and mistrust in working relationships (such as between manager and employee, or between members of different internal units) often develop as a result of inappropriate or missing specification of roles and reporting relationships. The key intervention he advocated was thus to create more clarity with regard to accountability and authority. He also proposed that organizations should carefully match the capability of individuals with the requirements of different roles. Jaques initially referred to this approach as *stratified systems theory (SST)* in that it sought to determine the optimal number of layers (strata) in complex organizations and the key individual capabilities required to perform roles at different strata.[2] (Among practitioners today, the approach is more commonly referred to as requisite organization (RO).)

1 Sherman (2005) describes a company with 17,000 employees that decided to examine its existing reporting relationships in more detail. They found out that they had 400 people who didn't report to anybody, and 35 who reported to each other.

2 Jaques did not limit his analysis to the *manifest* organization (the organization as officially presented on the organization chart) but considered the *extant* organization as well (how the organization actually functions). For example, an organization chart may depict four different hierarchical layers while a closer analysis of the real authority relationships would suggest that there exist only three.

Organizational strata

Organizational layers and managerial hierarchies are traditionally defined based on indicators related to size. For example, an organization may use the number of people reporting to a manager and the magnitude of his or her sales or profits in order to determine at what level of the organization the manager's role should be placed. Jaques argued, however, that a more relevant criterion for structuring organizations would be the *complexity of tasks*. More specifically, RO is built on the following assumptions:

1   Tasks that are performed in an organization vary in terms of their level of complexity.[3]
2   Sharp discontinuities in task complexity exist that separate tasks into a series of steps (or strata).
3   Similarly, the capacity for working at different levels of task complexity differ among individuals, and may also be categorized as a series of steps (or strata).

3 It is important to distinguish this notion of task complexity (related to individual roles and job requirements) from the notion of organizational complexity (a characteristic of an entire organization) used in Chapter 2 of this book.

Solving tasks of low complexity involves the processing of fairly tangible information and only requires the ability to follow an assigned plan or procedure, while tasks of high complexity require the ability to handle ambiguous information, devising alternative routes to a goal, consider multiple, interrelated issues in parallel, and predict the long term consequences of actions. The essence of RO is to consider the requirements of roles at different levels in relation to the capacity people have for handling the task requirements: "As [task complexity] gets greater, the feeling of weight of responsibility increases, and the greater the working-capacity you must have in order to cope" (Jaques, 1989, p. 37). Jaques believed that the most effective employees have a capability that matches the requirements at the level they are at. Common sense would lead us to predict that employees faced with tasks that demand higher capacity than they possess will perform poorly and also may experience stress and anxiety. But RO also leads us to predict the reverse: That it may be dysfunctional if individuals have a working capacity (i.e., competence) that exceeds the requirements of the work tasks at their level. The working capacity required at senior levels may be a liability at lower levels where direct judgment and quick action are needed. A lack of challenge in the job may also lead to frustration for the individual (Popper & Gluskinos, 1993).

4 More specifically, the level of a role can be assessed by considering the time-span of the task assigned to a role with the longest time horizon (Jaques, 1989).

To quickly determine the complexity of a given role, Jaques invented the use of "time span", which is basically the planning horizon required to perform a role successfully.[4] The role of leading a large organization may require a time span of 10 or more years, while the role of production worker may only require a time span of one day. Jaques concluded that there are at most seven different strata, suggesting that even a large organization may need no more than seven hierarchical levels, from the shop floor to the CEO role (the key characteristics of the strata are summarized in Table 6.3). Because task complexity is the key criterion for placing roles at different strata, Jaques proposed that certain roles responsible for complex tasks, such as research & development, should be placed near the top of the hierarchy and report to the COO or CEO, even in the case where the individuals holding the roles have no subordinates.

Assignment of tasks to different levels

The organizational strata proposed by Jaques may serve as a guide when re-designing an organization and determining the number of management layers. But the framework may also serve as a guide when assigning tasks to roles at different levels of the organization, in a manner that matches complexity of the tasks with the capability and accountability of the person at that level. The CEO may develop plans with a 20 year time horizon, but should be able to identify

Table 6.3 Summary of the organizational strata proposed by Elliott Jaques

Domain	Level	Typical title	Time span	Key tasks
Systems/strategic	VII	Chief Executive Officer	20 years or more	Interpret environmental trends, understand impact of alternative scenarios, conceptualize long term mission and strategy, initiate structural changes
	VI	CFO; COO etc.	10–20 years	Set broad direction for entire systems/organizations, build consensus among internal and external constituents for required changes
General management	V	Executive vice president; business unit president	5–10 years	Manage uncertainty, make continual adjustments to changes in the business environment
	IV	General manager; department manager	2–5 years	Handle several interacting projects, manage interdependencies between sub-units
Operations	III	Unit manager	1–2 years	Make trade-offs between short term and long term goals; interpret trends (e.g., quality data)
	II	Supervisor	3–12 months	Exercise diagnostic judgment and initiate actions to deal with identified problems /obstacles
	I	Production worker; operators; clerk	1 day–3 months	Perform well defined tasks

tasks with a shorter time horizon that need to be completed to realize the 20 year plans. The CEO may assign these tasks to business unit executives who operate with a 10 year horizon. They may in turn define a set of projects to be completed within 5 years, which can be delegated to their subordinates.

Definition of "manager"

There are various conceptions of what it entails to be a manager. For example, a manager may be viewed as somebody who coordinates the work of others, as somebody who coaches others and evaluates their work, or as somebody who has formal authority over employees. According to Jaques, these definitions are not necessarily wrong, but they don't capture the essence. He defined a manager as *someone who is held accountable for the outputs of others (the subordinates)*. This in turn means that the manager must be able to put together a team of subordinates who are capable of producing the outputs that are required, and ensure that they collaborate effectively in pursuing the goals that have been set. In other words, unlike the subordinates, the manager is not an individual contributor, but somebody who is judged by the results of his or her team.

A common question in most organizations is who a given employee "reports to." This is a surprisingly difficult question to answer for many employees (particularly in organizations with multiple dimensions): The person that the employee "reports to" may be the manager of the employee's department or group, or it may be the project manager that the employee is working for right now, or the internal client that is funding the project. Given the definition he proposed, Jaques suggested that one should turn the question around, by asking who is accountable for the performance of the employee: One may work *with and for* many managers, but only one should be held accountable for the effectiveness of any given employee – and that person is the employee's manager.

Unlike senior managers, middle managers often have little formal authority. It is not untypical for a middle manager to be appointed as leader of a team, only to discover that a higher level manager has already chosen the team members and decided how they should approach the task. In addition, it may not necessarily be the case that the existing team members are capable of doing the work that they are assigned. In this situation, the manager cannot be held accountable for the results, according to Jaques. To ensure accountability, the managers need a minimum level of authority. This authority includes at least the following four elements:

1 The right to veto any proposed candidate to the team or unit who, in the manager's opinion, does not have the right skills or knowledge for the job

2   The authority to define roles in the team/unit and assign tasks to its members
3   The authority to provide feedback, including performance appraisals, and make decisions about raises and merit rewards
4   The authority to, after fair warning and coaching, initiate removal from the team or unit of anyone who are incapable of doing the work

Hence the goal is not to maximize managerial authority, but to ensure that there is just that amount of authority that is needed to discharge the accountability (Jaques, 1990). We should also note that authority is two-ways in a modern society: A prospective employee decides whether to accept an offer of employment in an organization or not (or an offer to become member of a team within the organization). If he or she accepts, and the manager assigns a task to him or her, the task must lie within the employee's "zone of acceptance" for the employment relationship to continue. A common misunderstanding is to assume that authority is used to issue specific commands. In most cases, a manager will describe the role, assign a task, and/or specify a goal. The employee will usually have discretion in finding the method for reaching the goal, within some constraints (Foss & Foss, 2002).

An absolute condition set by Jaques was that *managers should always be in the next higher stratum* from their subordinates in terms of their working capacity. He predicted that the manager would be unable to provide effective leadership if he/she is at the same level as the subordinates:

> Such a manager cannot set adequate context; gets involved in too much detail; breathes down the subordinate's neck; seems to be comfortable doing work that the subordinate ought to be doing; does not add any value; is inclined to take all the credit for what goes well, and to blame subordinate for everything that goes wrong (...) It is the exact opposite of what managerial leadership ought to be.
>
> (Jaques & Clement, 1991, p. 42)

It is interesting to note that the phenomenon that Jaques describes is essentially an example of *coupling* as defined in the preceding chapters (Table 6.4). The only difference from the cases discussed elsewhere in this book is that we are here talking about vertical as opposed to horizontal relationships. The solution to remove the coupling in this case is to ensure that that roles and responsibilities are properly defined and that individuals with the appropriate competencies are selected for the job.

Jaques claimed that the actual organization often would work according to the strata defined in RO, even if the formal organization chart suggested otherwise. For example, he observed that if the

Table 6.4 Consequence of a lack of separation in strata

Functional requirements	Design parameters	
	Manager	Subordinate
Perform managerial tasks	X	x
Perform subordinate tasks	x	X

manager of a group of employees does not possess a cognitive capacity superior to his or her employees, the employees will frequently consider another manager, at the level (stratum) above their own, to be "the real manager." In contrast, what Jaques termed "requisite" organization is one where the extant (actual) organization is aligned with the formal structure of the firm (Dive, 2004). The number of levels in such an organization reflects the actual differences in task complexity across the different levels. Promotion is a move from one level of accountability to another. And the manager who appears on the organization chart is the person that the direct reports actually turn to for advice and supervision.

Span of control

The number of subordinates per manager is called the "span of control." An organization with broad spans of control (i.e., a higher number of direct reports for each manager) will have few vertical layers. Conversely, an organization with narrow spans of control will have more vertical layers (Figure 6.1) (Littener, 1973). Hence, when determining the shape of the formal structure, one will need to consider the vertical and the horizontal dimension simultaneously.

Jaques and other proponents of RO have often argued that the span of control is generally too narrow in most organizations (i.e., there are too many layers). When the span of control is too narrow, people with seemingly distinct titles in fact perform work at the same level of complexity; which limits the accountability of each individual manager and slows down the speed of decision making. Dive (2004) describes the case of Unilever PLC, a firm with 170,000 employees and 20,000 managers, which, during the 1990s, used the RO concepts[5] to simplify its hierarchical structure. In order to verify the required number of levels, interviews were conducted with a number of managers. The aim of the interviews was to identify the unique accountabilities at each level. This was done by asking the managers what decisions they made, that their subordinates couldn't make, and also what decisions the managers made, that their boss did not need to make. Based on these results, 17 existing job grades were reduced to only five work levels, which became the basis for performance management, compensation, and leadership development (Dive, 2004).

5 More precisely, Dive (2004) used the Levels of Work approach, which is derived from Jaques' RO approach (Kinston & Rowbottom, 1989).

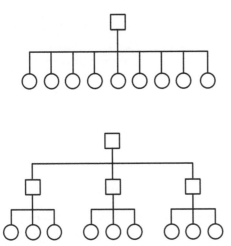

Figure 6.1 Comparison between broad and narrow span of control.

The Unilever case is one example of a broader trend of "delayering" that occurred between 1985 and 2005. In this period, large firms systematically eliminated layers in the hierarchical structure, particularly at the top of the organization. In the US, the average span of control for CEOs almost doubled from 1985 to 2005 (from 4.7 to 9.8 direct reports on average) (Wulf, 2012).

Some empirical research exists that confirms that delayering may produce positive results. As mentioned in Chapter 1, in a study of 663 Swiss firms between 2000 and 2004, Kuhn (2011) found that delayering significantly increased firm performance. Meier (2000) studied the span of control in 678 school districts in Texas. He collected data at two levels: The teacher to administrator ratio and the central office administrator to school-level administrator. He found that larger spans of control were associated with higher performance, measured as the percentage of students in each school district who pass standardized reading and mathematics tests each year.

Yet in some cases, one seems to have gone too far. As a result of budget cuts during the last two decades, public sector organizations have been forced to cut management layers to become more cost-effective. Studies performed in both Canada (Wong et al., 2015) and Sweden (Wallin, Pousette, & Dellve, 2014) have shown that increasing the span of control can lead to some unintended consequences. Higher span of control is associated with "work overload" (i.e., managers reported that they have too many responsibilities given the time available). In the Canadian study, which surveyed managers in 14 hospitals, it was also found that higher span of control was associated with self-reported adverse outcomes (i.e., medical errors, infections, and injuries).

These results are not necessarily contradictory, however. As suggested in Meier (2000), the relationship between span of control

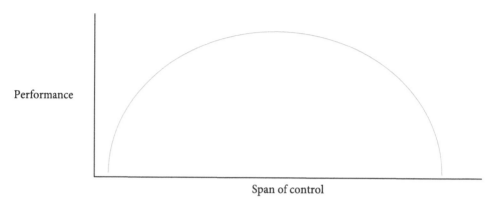

Figure 6.2 The theoretical relationship between span of control and organizational performance. (Adapted from Meier, 2000).

and performance may be quadratic (Figure 6.2). As span of control increases (from zero or one), performance also increases. First of all, costs are reduced because mwanagement positions are removed. In addition, the motivation of employees may increase as a result of higher autonomy (a manager with many subordinates will have less time for close supervision). However, the performance gains are subject to diminishing marginal returns. At even higher spans of control, the addition of new subordinates may reduce performance. It may lead to work overload for the manager, who will have insufficient capacity for supervision of employees or for coordination of the work that is performed. Increasing the span of control also reduces the opportunities for promotion, which in turn may reduce motivation and effort among employees.

The applicability of requisite organization concepts in modern organizations

The requisite organization approach remains popular among some consultants and HR managers. By and large, however, it receives little attention today and is almost completely ignored in the academic literature.[6] This paucity of interest in Jaques' work is perhaps not surprising: With its focus on deliberate planning and hierarchical structure, it does not seem to be a good fit for those seeking methods and frameworks for managing flexible, project-based organizations. Nevertheless, Jaques addressed some fundamental managerial challenges and offered innovative and intriguing solutions to problems faced by many – if not most – organizations. To identify the potential value and the possible imitations of RO it is worthwhile examining some of the core assumptions in more detail and consider to what extent these depart from current assumptions about organizing large firms.

6 For example, RO is not even mentioned in Mintzberg (1979), Pfeffer's (1979/1989), or Morgan (1998), three well known books reviewing organization theory (Morgan (1998) does mention earlier works of Jaques unrelated to RO.)

Requisite organization is essentially a system for defining and structuring jobs. But the concept of a job has changed over time as a result of the introduction of new organizational forms. Jobs used to be fairly stable and well defined entities, which made it possible for managers to carefully design all key aspects of job before hiring a new employee: Identifying the tasks and responsibilities of the job, defining the required skills to perform the tasks, and position the job at the right organizational level depending on the nature and complexity of the tasks. Indeed, there is a whole discipline, with specific tools and techniques, dedicated to the issue of job design (e.g., Parker & Wall, 1998).

In large organizations today, however, there is typically much less specification of jobs than before; more depends on the individual holding the role. The typical output of job design – a job description – may no longer be a meaningful tool. Haeckel (1999) noted that collaboration and communication processes in organizations basically revolve around negotiation and fulfillment of ad hoc commitments (see Chapter 7). To improve clarity in terms of what is expected of the individual job (role) holder, he suggested that each employee maintains an updated list of commitments that he or she has made to other employees, a list of the commitments that others have made to him/her, and the status of both. Compared to the tasks and responsibilities in the typical job description, such commitments will usually be more specific, focused on a concrete deliverable or goal, rather than on a repetitive task or permanent area of responsibility. Moreover, whereas job descriptions represent vertical agreements (between a subordinate and his/her manager) commitments are usually made horizontally, between people accountable for producing specific business outcomes (Haeckel, 1999).

Even in organizations where formal job descriptions still exist, the scope and content of the roles that people perform gradually expand, contract, or change focus. Some authors have proposed that employees are *architects of their own jobs* (Wrzesniewski & Dutton, 2001). Employees influence both the number and nature of tasks that are performed, exercise discretion in terms of selecting who they should interact with, and even alter the very purpose and identity of their own role. An employee with energy and initiative will be able to craft his or her own role.

The changing concept of jobs also affects career structures and employment relationships more generally. RO includes frameworks for creating career trajectories (career paths) and systematic methods for assessing future potential and defining criteria for promotions (i.e., succession planning). Similar frameworks and methods have been popularized by other authors (e.g., Charan, Drotter, & Noel, 2001)[7] and form the basis for the HR and leadership development processes in many large firms. The goal for many of these firms has been to create long term succession plans to ensure that they had the leadership talent ready when they needed it. As an

7 Charan, Drotter, & Noel (2001) do not cite Jaques, but the concepts they present are largely based on General Electric's management structure and leadership competencies, which were defined by a consultant who was influenced by Jaques' work, according to Craddock (2007).

example, Exxon Mobil reportedly hired its CEO for the year 2010 in 1988 already, in order to develop, assess, and prepare the candidate for the top job (McManis & Leibman, 1988). Current authors, however, are skeptical of the ability of firms to create long term career plans for its people or develop specialized skills that fit future strategic needs. It is difficult to predict who will have relevant skills in the future if the business environment is undergoing rapid change. Capelli (2008), for example, noted that the uncertainty faced by many companies necessitate frequent updates and changes to the succession plans, as strategies and jobs change (and as individuals leave the organization). Rather than attempting to align people with a particular strategy, some authors have suggested that one should instead develop a broad skill base that allows the company to create the capability to implement a wide range of strategies (Snow & Snell, 1993).

Discussion

Few would contest that jobs, career paths, and leadership development processes have undergone change as a result of the emergence of new and more flexible ways of working. But do these observations necessarily invalidate the key assumption behind the requisite organization approach?

We should note first that although the concept of jobs has changed, it has not vanished: The reality is that organizations are still structured around jobs (Sparrow & Cooper, 2003). But the general emphasis among practitioners and management thinkers has shifted to a more individualistic and "people oriented" view. Some modern management thinkers even seem to believe that structures may emerge as they may, if one only has the right set of people.[8] Such a view does contradict Jaques, who strongly favored "structure first": Mission followed by structure followed by selection and education. He defined an organization as a set of roles, not as a collection of people, although roles are occupied by people. He argued that unless structure comes first, there would be no consistent way of identifying who should lead whom or ensure that those who do not fulfill role requirements are removed, if necessary (Jaques & Clement, 1991).

Yet it is easy to misunderstand the purpose of systems of vertical structuring such as RO. For example, Jaques in no way assumed that information would only flow along the formal reporting lines of the organization, or that actual working relations would be perfectly aligned with the formal structure of an organization. On the contrary, Jaques acknowledged that many employees would participate in cross-functional projects, work with and for managers at several levels and possibly in several internal units of the organization. In fact, Jaques outlined principles for structuring a range of role arrangements, including those related to advisory relationships

8 For example, Jim Collins (2001), the author of the best-selling management book *Good to Great*, stated that leaders should first "get the right people on the bus," and only then decide where to drive it (i.e., what strategy and structure to pursue).

between colleagues and temporary assignments for managers in other parts of the organization.

On the other hand, it is precisely the complexity of such work processes and working relationships that often lead to a deterioration of accountability and a lack of clarity with regard to goals and priorities (as we discussed in Chapter 2). But Jaques insisted that one should be able to define a clear, coherent and consistent *accountability hierarchy*, even in large and complex organizations. In other words, one could argue that the concepts in RO are all the more relevant, the more complex the overall organizational structure is.

Although the RO concepts may at first sight appear to be an elaborate excuse for a "top down" management philosophy, Jaques actually saw RO as a prerequisite for achieving fair treatment of employees and for implementing systematic people development processes. He recommended that managers should be judged not only on their ability to attain business related outcomes (e.g., sales and profits targets) but also on their effectiveness as leaders, including their ability to create an effective working environment, utilize the existing skills and competencies, and develop their people.

Jaques believed that people's working capacity would mature throughout life, although the rates of progression would be different from person to person. (In general, the higher a person's potential working capacity, the faster the rate of maturation and the later in life it continues to grow.) Thus in addition to placing people in the right strata based on their current working capacity, an important additional task is periodically assessing their future potential. Jaques offered an intriguing and important idea for how this process should be carried out. He suggested that one should follow what is sometimes called the "grandfather principle", namely that the manager's manager, rather than an employee's direct manager, should be responsible for assessing the employee's future potential. The manager's manager works at a higher stratum and thus has a broader overview of the requirements at different levels and the future opportunities that may exist in the organization. Although the practice is widespread, Jaques deemed it illogical asking a line manager to assess the potential of his or her current subordinates. If the potential of a subordinate is deemed high and the employee is promoted, he or she will in many cases become a subordinate of the manager's manager. (The line manager's favorite employee may not be the one that the manager's manager judges to be the most qualified to join his or her team.) According to RO, it is also the manager's manager who should monitor the manager's leadership performance. In sum, a proper implementation of RO would *make leaders accountable for developing their people.*

Extending RO to project-based organizations

We mentioned above that whereas RO presupposes that there are predefined roles in an organization, there is typically no permanent definition of jobs in fast-changing organizations, such as project-based firms. The more dynamic the organization, the greater the need to periodically re-assess the purpose of different roles; in many role relationships it may also be up to the job holders themselves to agree on the boundaries between their roles and their respective responsibilities. But even if we accept that it is harder to design jobs in advance, and that creative employees in any case will (and should) shape their own roles, we may simultaneously acknowledge that there needs to be "minimal critical specifications" of roles and accountabilities in a hierarchical system.[9] It may be possible to bridge these seemingly contradictory concerns.

9 The principle of "minimal critical specifications" states that "While it may be necessary to be quite precise about what has to be done, it is rarely necessary to be precise about how it is done" (Cherns, 1976, p. 786).

One may increase the applicability of RO in dynamic organizations by modifying how individual jobs are designed. It is customary to define individual jobs by listing the *activities* that the individual is supposed to perform. For example, a job description for a Chief Financial Officer (CFO) may contain lists of activities such as "prepare budgets", "oversee accounting practices", and "monitor financial performance." Such job descriptions are often quite detailed and lengthy, which means that they are difficult to maintain. Traditional job descriptions also do surprisingly little to clarify the purpose of the job or even why the role exists at all (Haeckel, 1999). An alternative is instead to define jobs in terms of accountabilities and outcomes. Outcome-oriented job descriptions focus on the desired results, while leaving the job holder to decide which activities are required to attain the outcomes that have been agreed.

Haeckel (1999) maintained that accountabilities only exist in connection with commitments between people: A person must be accountable to someone, which means no one can be generically accountable for sales, manufacturing, or quality. He proposed the following generic format for specifying accountabilities: 'In the role as [role name], [name of person] is accountable to [customer] for [outcome]' (Haeckel, 1999, p. 146).

The desired outcome may be more fully described by adding the customer's conditions of satisfaction, i.e., the criteria for acceptable performance, such as delivery time or quality level. Often it is possible to substitute a long list of activities with one or two sentences that express the purpose of job in this manner (see Table 6.5 for examples). Evaluation of performance will then be based on the ability to deliver the specified outcomes rather than on the ability to carry out tasks skillfully which is the likely focus when jobs are defined in terms of activities. Outcome oriented job descriptions provide management with a tool for the definition of jobs, while at the same providing allowing the individual job holder to shape the content of the job and create new ways to respond to unexpected events.

Table 6.5 The difference between activities and outcomes, exemplified by excerpts from three job descriptions

Role	Activities/tasks	Outcomes
Sales executive	• Develop sales and marketing strategy • Oversee development of sales and marketing materials • Plan customer visits • Develop proposals • Negotiate contracts • …	• Acquire 2 new major accounts • Increase customer retention • Ensure customer satisfaction
Manager responsible for Health, Safety and Environment	• Develop HSE policy • Communicate HSE guidelines to business unit staff • Conduct audits to ensure compliance with HSE policy • Monitor and report HSE incidents • Regularly review HSE performance in leadership team • …	• Create proactive HSE culture, as measured in HSE attitude survey • Minimize frequency and severity of incidents
Payroll clerk	• Compile employee time, production, and payroll data from time sheets and other record • Record employee information, such as exemptions, transfers, and resignations, to maintain and update payroll records • Compute wages and deductions and enter data into computers • ….	• Salary and benefits paid without errors or delays

The relevance of RO is not limited to traditional line organizations. In fact, RO can support the design of highly flexible, project-based organizations. One example is firms where employees are organized in a resource pool (a key feature of the modular organizational form described in Chapter 4.) This is a model that traditionally has been used by many professional services firms, but there are also examples of its use in other industries. Some project-based engineering firms use resources pools to organize its engineers, and some hospitals organize nurses in "float pools" (Worren, 2008).

As an internal service provider, the resource pool assigns people to projects based on requests from internal clients (e.g., projects or business units). Once an employee has been assigned to a project initiated by a business unit, the employee works for a project manager in the business unit on a day-to-day basis. However, the permanent reporting relationship of employees is to a *people manager* belonging to the resource pool. A larger resource pool may be divided into several skill groups, each led by a skill group leader (people manager). A manufacturing company may define skills groups representing different technical and commercial disciplines, such as marketing, engineering, operations. There will usually be slightly different roles and competency requirements within each skill group, leading to a set of alternative career paths.

It is common to define role/career levels in a resource pool, based on competence requirements for the different career paths. The competence requirements that are defined for each level support selection decisions, assessment of performance, and also provide criteria for promotion within the career track (or transfers to other skill groups). For example, in a consulting firm, consultants may enter the firm as junior consultants, and advance to consultant and project manager once they demonstrate that they perform according to the requirements defined for those levels. In an engineering firm, there may be different career levels such as junior and senior engineers, chief engineer, and so on. The role/career levels may have a structure similar to the strata defined in RO. The main difference is that the role structure and the competence requirements in a resource pool will relate to the type of tasks that one will be responsible for in temporary projects, rather than the more permanent tasks of a line management role in the organization. One example would be the requirements for project managers, which are usually defined based on the duration, size, and complexity of projects that one is able to manage (Table 6.6).

Applying RO principles in the design of the resource pool means that it becomes possible to maintain a layered role structure even in a flexible, project-based firm (Figure 6.3). This also means that systematic people development processes can be implemented. The resource pool is the "home base" and a stable core in an otherwise changeable structure. The people managers in the resource pool are responsible for supporting staffing decisions, providing feedback to the individual employee, and creating individual development plans based on the employees' own preferences and development needs. It

Table 6.6 Example of roles and competence requirements used to define levels (strata) of resource pool

Level	Role	Requirements
V	*Project director/ program manager*	• In-depth knowledge and skills of tools and processes used to plan, organize, and control projects. • Able to lead large, complex projects, often involving several technical disciplines, or programs of longer duration consisting of multiple, interrelated projects
IV	*Project manager*	• In-depth knowledge and skills of tools and processes used to plan, organize, and control projects. • Able to lead short projects of low to medium size and complexity
III	*Project team member*	• Familiar with basic project management tools and processes • With increasing experience, able take responsibility for separate deliverables/work streams within a project.

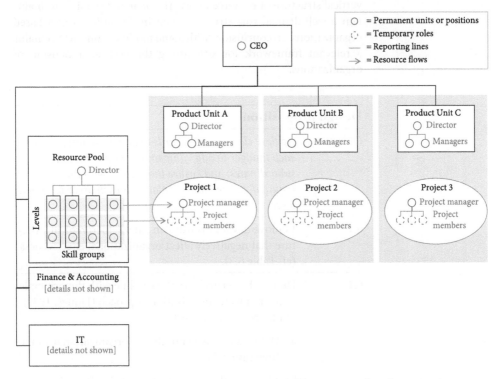

Figure 6.3 Resource pool structured according to RO principles in project-based organization.

may not be possible in such an organization to develop detailed and long-term succession plans, but a resource pool should, at a more aggregate level, be able to forecast the overall demand for different role categories, which can form the basis for longer term recruitment and development plans.

Summary and conclusion

The key concepts of requisite organization provide a useful "lens" by which to view an organization, and a clear set of normative criteria for structuring vertical relations, which complements the other design tools and frameworks described in this book. But RO is largely ignored by academics today and is often associated with the design of traditional, "hierarchical" organizations. Yet we have seen in this chapter that it may be possible to adapt and extend RO to the demands of modern organizations. By specifying jobs in terms of outcomes rather than activities, one creates a structure for accountability while at the same time providing job holders with the autonomy to define the best way to perform their tasks. Another alternative is to combine RO with the concept of the modular organization described in Chapter 4, by applying RO in defining the vertical structure of resource pools. This makes it possible to maintain a well-defined role structure even in dynamic, project-based organizations. In conclusion, with some modifications, RO remains a relevant framework for structuring the vertical dimension of organizations.

Design propositions

Objective	*Achieve clarity with regards to accountability, allow each manger to add value to the work of his or her subordinates, and ensure that people with the required competence are placed at each organizational level.*
6.1	Remove deviations from an "ideal" hierarchical structure that negatively affect organizational effectiveness (cf. Table 6.2).
6.2	Design the vertical structure in line with the principles in the requisite organization approach (Jaques, 1989; Jaques & Clement, 1991), i.e.:

a) Define a requisite number of organizational strata (maximum 7).

b) Place people into each stratum that have the required working capacity to handle the level of task complexity encountered at that level.

c) Ensure that each role reports to a role located in the next higher stratum.

d) Hold managers accountable for the results of their immediate subordinates.

e) Ensure that managers have minimum managerial authority, including the right to veto appointments of new subordinates and the right to initiate removal from the team.

f) Designate the manager's manager as accountable for assessing future potential and evaluating the manager's leadership effectiveness.

6.3	In project-based organizations, apply the same principles as above but with the following modifications:

g) Organize people who perform ad hoc activities or temporary projects in a resource pool.

h) Structure the role /career levels of the resource pool according to the RO principles.

Review questions

1 What is a manager?
2 What is an organization?
3 What is the optimal span of control?
4 One of the basic principles in requisite organization (RO) approach is that managers should be one level above their sub-ordinates in terms of ability to handle task complexity. What is the rationale behind this principle?
5 How can we extend RO to project-based organizations?
6 Draw a diagram of the hierarchical layers of an organization that you know or can obtain information about (e.g., your employer or your university). To what extent does the formal structure correspond to an ideal structure according to RO?
7 What does the word accountability entail? To what extent are managers in the average organization accountable, in the sense of the word used by Jaques?
8 Are large organizations able to place the right people at the right level? What indications do we have to suggest that this may or may not be the case?
9 What concerns would you expect that managers and employees might have with regard to the application of RO concepts in their organization? To what extent are these concerns well founded? To what extent may they be addressed by revising some elements of RO?

Research questions[10]

1 What are the effects, on individuals and organizations, of mismatches between individual working capacity and task requirements?
2 What is the reliability and validity of time-span as a proxy for task complexity?
3 What are the most reliable and most convenient methods for assessing an individual's working capacity?
4 To what extent does the introduction of a structure based on RO improve the perceived fairness of key HR processes related to appraisals, succession plans, reward, and promotions?
5 What are the key prerequisites for institutionalizing the role of the manager's manager as advocated by Jaques?
6 Did Jaques pay sufficient attention to the non-cognitive aspects of leadership, such as emotional intelligence?
7 To what extent is individual working capacity as defined by Jaques correlated with organizational capabilities? To what extent may strong institutional processes and systems compensate for either low individual working capacity, or mismatches between person and role?

10 One should note that these research questions are not entirely new; a number of empirical studies on RO were conducted during the 1960s, as documented in the annotated bibliography of RO research by Craddock (2007). However, the issues mentioned deserve renewed attention as there has been very little systematic research in this area during the last couple of decades.

References

Abrahamson, Eric. (2002). Disorganization Theory and disorganizational behavior: Towards an etiology of messes. *Research in Organizational Behavior*, 24, 139–180.

Capelli, P. (2008). *Talent on Demand: Managing Talent in an Age of Uncertainty*. Boston: Harvard Business School Press.

Charan, R., Drotter, S., & Noel, J. (2001). *The Leadership Pipeline*. San Francisco: Jossey-Bass.

Cherns, A. (1976). The principles of sociotechnical design. *Human Relations, 29*, 8, 783–792.

Collins, J. (2001). *Good to Great*. New York: HarperCollins Publishers.

Craddock, K. (2007). *Requisite Organization – Annotated Bibliography*, Fourth edition. Available on-line: http://globalro.org/pick-up/RO-Intro.pdf

Devine, D. J. (1999). Teams in organizations. *Small Group Research*, 30, 6, 678–711.

Dive, B. (2004). *The Healthy Organization*. London: Kogan Page.

Foss, K., & Foss, N. J. (2002). *Authority and Discretion Tensions, Credible Delegation and Implications for New Organizational Forms. Working Paper*. DRUID, Copenhagen Business School, Department of Industrial Economics and Strategy/Aalborg University, Department of Business Studies.

Haeckel, S.H. (1999). *Adaptive Enterprise: Creating and Leading Sense-and-Respond Organizations*. Boston: Harvard Business School Press.

Jaques, E. (1989). *Requisite Organization: The CEO's Guide to Creative Structure and Leadership*. Arlington: Cason Hall & Co publishers.

Jaques, E. (1990). In praise of hierarchy. *Harvard Business Review*, 68, 1, 127–133.

Jaques, E., & Clement, S. D. (1991). *Executive Leadership: A Practical Guide to Managing Complexity*. Arlington: Cason Hall & Co publishers.

Kinston, W., & Rowbottom, R. (1989). Levels of work: New applications to management in large organizations. *Journal of Applied Systems Analysis, 16*, 19–34.

Kuhn, D. (2011). *Delayering and Firm Performance: Evidence from Swiss firm-level Data*. Working paper 2011/02 D–134, University of Basel. Retrieved from https://ideas.repec.org/p/bsl/wpaper/2011–02.html

Leavitt, H. J. (2005). *Top Down: Why Hierarchies Are Here to Stay and How to Manage Them More Effectively*. Boston, MA: Harvard Business School Press.

Littener, J. (1973). *Organizational Analysis*. New York: Wiley

McManis, G. L. & Leibman, M. S. (1988, August). Succession planners. *Personnel Administrator*, 24–30.

Meier, K. J. (2000). Ode to Luther Gulick. *Span of Control and Organizational Performance, Administration & Society*, 32, 2, 115–137.

Mintzberg H. (1979). *The Structuring of Organizations*. Englewood Cliffs: Prentice-Hall.

Morgan, G. (1998). *Images of Organization*. Thousand Oaks, CA: Sage Publications.

Parker, S. K., & Wall, T. D. (1998). *Job and Work Design: Organizing Work to Promote Well-Being and Effectiveness*. Thousand Oaks, CA: Sage Publication.

Pfeffer, J. (1979/1989). *New Directions for Organization Theory: Problems and Prospects*. New York: Oxford University Press.

Popper, M., & Gluskinos, U. (1993). Is there an inverse "Peter Principle"? *Management Decision*, 31, 4, 59–64.

Sherman, E. (2005). Tweaking HR information systems can help HR stay in compliance with Sarbanes-Oxley rules. *HR Magazine*, online edition: http://www.shrm.org/Publications/hrmagazine/EditorialContent/Pages/0505hrtech.aspx

Snow, C.C., & Snell, S.A. (1993). Staffing as strategy. In Schmitt, N. & Borman, W.C. (Eds.), *Personnel Selection in Organizations*. San Francisco: Jossey-Bass.

Sparrow, P., & Cooper, C. L. (2003). *The Employment Relationship: Key Challenges for HR*. London: Butterworth-Heinemann.

Wallin, L., Pousette, A., & Dellve, L. (2014). Span of control and the significance for public sector managers' job demands: A multilevel study. *Economic and Industrial Democracy*, 35, 3, 455–481.

Whittington, R., Pettigrew, A., Peck, S., Fenton, E., & Conyon, M. (1999). Change and complementarities in the new competitive landscape: A European panel study, 1992–1996. *Organization Science*, 10, 5, 583–600.

Wong, C. A., Elliott-Miller, P., Laschinger, H., Cuddihy, M., Meyer, R. M., Keatings, M., ... Szudy, N. (2015). Examining the relationships between span of control and manager job and unit performance outcomes. *Journal of Nursing Management*, 23(2), 156–168.

Worren, N. (2008). Managing the company's resource pool. *People & Strategy*, 31, 3, 42–49.

Wrzesniewski, A., & Dutton, J. (2001). Crafting a job: Revisioning employees as active crafters of their work. *Academy of Management Review*, 26, 2, 179–201.

Wulf, J. (2012). The flattened firm. *California Management Review*, 55, 1, 5–23.

Zenger, T. R., & Hesterly, W. (1997). The disaggregation of corporations: Selective intervention, high-powered incentives, and molecular units. *Organization Science*, 8, 3, 209–222.

7   Configuring interfaces

Chapter overview

Background	• After establishing sub-units, some interdependencies toward other sub-units in the organization will remain, even if one attempts to group related tasks together.
	• Managing these interdependencies is a core task for managers of sub-units.
Challenges	• The task of managing interdependencies is becoming more challenging as organizations grow more complex:
	– Sub-units are increasingly engaged in multiple projects or working "laterally" across vertical lines of control.
	– Several internal stakeholders may influence a sub-unit's ability to fulfill its mandate.
	• In considering interventions to improve coordination, there is a tendency among managers to focus on one particular type of interdependency while ignoring others.
	• Similarly, both the practitioner and the academic literature tend to focus on one type of interdependency at a time.
Key question	• How should one manage the multiple types of interdependencies that may exist between sub-units in complex organizations?
Proposed approach	• Distinguish between five different types of interdependencies.
	• Describe how the different types of interdependencies can be identified.

- Evaluate the kinds and degrees of interdependencies that will best support effective functioning of a sub-unit.

Introduction[1]

Unit grouping – as we discussed in Chapter 5 – facilitates coordination within the groups that are formed at the expense of coordination across groups (Mintzberg, 1979). Once sub-units have been formed, a key challenge is thus to consider how to create effective interfaces between the different sub-units.

Managing the relationship toward other organizational units has always been a core task for managers of sub-units. But this task is becoming more challenging as organizations grow more complex. Sub-units are increasingly engaged in multiple projects or working "laterally" across vertical lines of control. In a networked, decentralized organization, there may be myriad of stakeholders that may influence the performance of the processes that the sub-unit is engaged in, the resources that it controls, or the decisions that it is formally authorized to make.

Consequently, the key question addressed in this chapter is how managers in complex organizations can design effective interfaces. How can managers identify the different types of interdependencies that exist – or anticipate where they are likely to arise? How can managers determine the kinds and degrees of interdependencies that will best support effective functioning of their sub-units and ensure that their sub-units can fulfill their mandate?

To address this issue, this chapter expands on the concept of interdependency introduced in the previous chapters. We here consider not only the existence (or lack of) an interdependency, but the relative *degree* of interdependency and different *types* of interdependencies between sub-units. Compared to the previous chapters, we also shift the "level of analysis" by formulating a set of design propositions that should be relevant for sub-unit managers. Defining the overall architecture (Chapter 4) and designing the structure of sub-units (Chapters 5) usually require senior management support and occur relatively infrequently. In this chapter, we focus on more frequent, incremental design improvements that leaders of sub-units may themselves initiate once the overall design choices have been made.

ProTech

To illuminate the nature of different types of interdependencies, we describe a simplified case of an IT department in a firm called ProTech, a pseudonym for a multi-divisional engineering company[2] (see Figure 7.1). Until 1999, IT staff in ProTech were organized

1 *Acknowledgement:* Parts of this chapter draw heavily from a working paper that was developed in collaboration with Ron Sanchez of Copenhagen Business School.

2 The author was engaged as a consultant in re-designing the IT function of the company used as an example in this chapter.

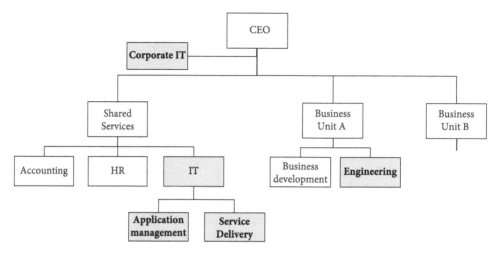

Figure 7.1 Simplified chart showing organizational structure of ProTech (units described in text highlighted).

within the engineering departments in different business units (the IT manager would typically report to the head of engineering in each unit). In 1999, the company decided to introduce the Shared Services concept, and IT staff were transferred to Shared Services together with staff performing transactional processes such as accounting and payroll. The key rationale behind this decision was to derive economies of scale and scope. By consolidating administrative functions into one unit, the company sought to standardize processes, reduce costs, increase its resource flexibility, and also (over time) increase the quality of services. Today, the Shared Services IT unit comprises two teams: Application Development and Service Delivery (i.e., IT Support). These teams serve users employed in the business units. Within a business unit, the engineering department is the main user of the IT department's services, as engineers make heavy use of computer-aided design tools and document management systems. As part of the staff functions at the headquarters, there is also a Corporate IT unit, which develops and implements IT policy for ProTech. In addition, the IT department interacts with external software vendors that develop IT applications (computer programs) to meet the needs of ProTech's business units. The functions of the different sub-units are listed in Table 7.1.[3]

3 The case example has been simplified in that only a small set of sub-units is included, moreover, each sub-unit only performs one function.

Degrees of work process interdependency

An interdependency exists when actions in one sub-unit of the organization affect important outcomes in another sub-unit – for example, quality, cost, or customer satisfaction. Consider the IT department and the Engineering department within ProTech's

Table 7.1 Key functions of IT units in ProTech

Functional requirements	Design parameters			
	Corporate IT	Application management	Service delivery	Software vendor
Develop and implement IT policy	X			
Provide applications		X		
Provide IT support			X	
Develop applications				X

business unit (Figure 7.1). To what extent is Engineering dependent upon IT, or vice versa? To determine the *degree* of interdependency, we consider two factors. The first is *Criticality*, in other words, do actions taken in the IT department affect important outcomes in the Engineering department? This may be the case if engineers make heavy use of software applications to do their work, and if IT is the only provider of those applications. Similarly, IT may be dependent upon Engineering for internal funding for its activities or for support for continual software application development. The second factor is *Uncertainty*, which is related both to *dependability* and to *ambiguity*. For example, can the IT department be relied upon in terms of keeping promises with regard to service levels? To what extent do Engineering and IT have the same understanding of their respective roles and responsibilities?[4] Sub-units enjoy stable and isolated conditions if interdependencies are of low uncertainty and importance. As uncertainty and importance increase, the intensity of communication and collaboration between sub-units increases (and so does the potential for conflict) (Miles, 1979). Interdependencies that are very high in both importance and uncertainty are likely to produce situations that are perceived as chaotic (Figure 7.2).

Traditionally, the key recommendation for coping with an interdependency has been to introduce a *coordination mechanism* (as discussed in Chapters 1 and 5) (Galbraith, 1993; Lawrence & Lorsch, 1967). The appropriate coordination mechanism depends on the degree of criticality and uncertainty. For interdependencies that are relatively low in criticality and uncertainty, it may suffice that managers in the sub-units that are affected interchange information (e.g., via e-mail or phone). For interdependencies that are considered at least moderately critical and uncertain, it may be necessary to set up regular meetings to allow managers of sub-units to coordinate between them. Another approach is to create a "liaison" or integrator role by making one employee responsible for coordinating work between the two sub-units.

The establishment of coordination mechanisms to integrate the work of interdependent units remains a key organization design

4 These constructs may be operationalized and measured. It is possible to ask members of organizational sub-units to rate the importance of interdependencies and to pool their assessments into a variable that can be evaluated for reliability and validity.

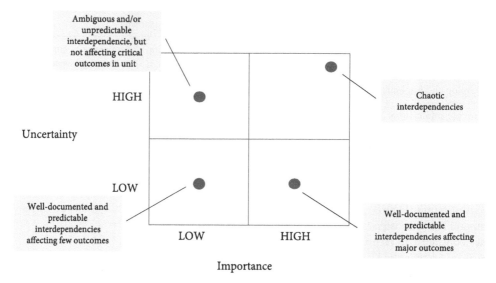

Figure 7.2 Framework for characterizing degree of interdependency between organizational sub-units.

option. However, as mentioned in Chapter 5, it is also possible to intentionally change the degree of interdependency between sub-units – and thereby reduce the need for coordination in the first place (von Hippel, 1990). In addition to introducing coordination mechanisms, three options exist for managing interdependencies between sub-units. One may: a) eliminate an interdependency; b) add a new interdependency, or c) change the degree of an interdependency (i.e., alter its uncertainty or criticality). In this chapter, we examine these options in more detail.

Interdependency types

Traditionally, when using the term interdependency, authors have often referred to what we will here call *activity interdependency*. (An activity is a step in a work process that transforms an input to an output.) Yet interdependencies between activities are only one of several types of interdependencies that sub-unit managers must handle. To configure effective interfaces, they may need to take into consideration four other interdependency types: Activities incur costs and must be resourced, creating *resource interdependencies* toward other units. Moreover, activities within an organization are performed in an "accountability hierarchy" (Jaques, 1989), leading to what we call *governance interdependencies*. However, formal authority is not enough to assure actual performance of activities: Activities are often performed to fulfill either semi-permanent or ad hoc commitments (promises) toward internal or external customers – leading to *commitment interdependencies*. Finally, activities are performed by people who form informal relationships with each other while they are working. When these social relationships affect the decisions made or the performance of work processes, they create what we call *social network interdependencies*. (The five types of interdependencies correspond to the five layers of design parameters introduced in Chapter 1.)

There is an extensive literature on each of these types of interdependencies. However, in most cases, the existing research examines one type of interdependency in isolation. There is a similar tendency among managers when selecting an approach to address a performance problem. In dealing with a lack of coordination between two departments, some managers will tend to focus on governance (and may suggest changing reporting lines as a remedy); others will tend to focus on commitments (and may suggest creating joint goals or agreements between the departments), and so on. Indeed, each interdependency type may represent a *frame* (Bolman & Deal, 1997) that managers use in diagnosing coordination problems and in designing interventions. Being aware of several types of interdependencies may thus provide a potential for reframing the situation by bringing to the fore elements that would otherwise go unrecognized.

Activities

The Activity Type encompasses interdependencies that are directly related to the flow of work across sub-units. Activity interdependencies may exist due to the need for physical inputs from another sub-unit or – more frequently today – a need for *information*. To describe the current Activity dependencies one must first identify the different tasks or activities involved in a given work process. One then maps Activity dependencies by asking the participants in the process who they rely on for information to complete their tasks and who they in turn provide outputs to (cf. Chapter 5). These data may be summarized by using a design structure matrix (DSM) (Figure 7.4). There may be an entire web of activity interdependencies: A typical sub-unit in a large organization may be engaged in several work processes, may receive inputs from multiple other sub-units, and may in turn provide outputs to several internal (and possibly external) clients.[5]

5 One indication of this complexity is that it frequently requires several iterations to arrive at a description that all members can agree correctly represents the way work is actually done in their unit.

The Application Management team in ProTech has a dependency toward the external software vendor, which licenses applications to ProTech. Application Management in turn provides applications as an internal supplier to users in the Business Unit (see Figure 7.3). Service Delivery provides user support to end users; while also receiving information from Application Management about application functionality, on-going upgrades, common errors, known software bugs, etc. In Figure 7.4, these interdependencies are indicated by an x in the appropriate cells of the matrix.

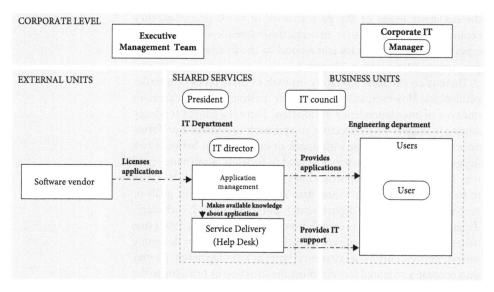

Figure 7.3 Activity interdependencies for the IT department at ProTech.

		A1	A2	A3	A4
Licence applications	A1				
Provide applications	A2	X			
Make available knowledge about applications	A3		X		
Provide support	A4			X	

Figure 7.4 Activity interdependencies for ProTech's IT department documented by means of a design structure matrix (DSM).

The *criticality* of an Activity Interdependency can be evaluated by considering the effect of removing the interdependency on the ability of the sub-unit to perform its function: If work process performance would deteriorate significantly without a specific information flow, for example, criticality would be judged as high. *Uncertainty* can be evaluated by considering the likelihood that the other sub-unit will actually perform the activity (e.g., provide a piece of information) that one is dependent upon and by assessing the likely accuracy of the information provided. A dependency toward a supplier with a poor history in terms of on-time deliverables would be considered uncertain, while a dependency toward a more reliable supplier would be perceived as more predictable and thus less uncertain.

Configuring activity interdependencies

Several project management techniques (e.g., PERT charts and the Critical Path Method) exist that can help managers identify and manage activity interdependencies both within their own units and toward other sub-units in the organization. Moreover, methodologies such as Lean and Six Sigma can be used to analyze, measure, and improve work processes and (thereby) reconfigure activity interdependencies. As an example, a consultant may analyze the work processes in ProTech's IT department and note that Application Management provides outputs to Service Delivery, but that there is no link back to Application Management (cf. Figure 7.3). He may suggest that Service Delivery provides an additional output to Application Management, namely a monthly report with a categorization of the issues that are logged by user support. Application Management is in turn asked to create a plan for how to address commonly recurring technical issues and to present this plan to the IT director. In this manner, *new interdependencies are added* to ensure that the IT department can fulfill its function.

A common challenge in work processes is a mutual dependency between an upstream and a downstream task, which usually leads to multiple iterations before the downstream task can finally be accomplished. Technology management scholars distinguish between two types of iteration: Anticipated and unanticipated (Smith & Eppinger, 1993). A software development team may plan to reconfigure a software application based on feedback from users testing a beta version. But they may also be forced to completely re-design the application if unexpected problems are discovered during the testing. It has been documented that unanticipated iteration may account for as much as 70% of the lead time in product development projects (ibid.). Using tools such as the design structure matrix (DSM), it is possible to reduce the number of iterations by re-ordering activities. But it may also be necessary to *remove interdependencies* that create delays or add coordination costs. As described in Chapter 5, as processes become more mature, it is possible to introduce common standards that remove the need for coordination between employees, as long as the standards are complied to. The removal of interdependencies is the essence of *modularity*, the partitioning of a product design (or work process) into modules separated by standard interfaces (Sanchez, 1995; Sanchez & Mahoney, 1996; Baldwin & Clark, 2000).

In integrating the processes of different sub-units, an important design principle is to define *transfer-points* (Jastram, 1974). It has been observed that process breakdowns often occur during "handoffs" between different sub-units engaged in the same overall process. One approach to avoid this outcome is to create a mutual agreement regarding the deliverables (inputs and outputs) to be contributed by the respective sub-units. For example, in ProTech,

Applications Management and Service Delivery may define at precisely which point the responsibility for handling software errors for a new application is transferred to the Service Delivery team (e.g., only after an application has been rolled out and appropriate documentation have been made available to the team).

Commitments

The basic source of a commitment interdependency is the existence of (or need for) an agreement between actors or sub-units involved in a work process. For example, suppliers agree to deliver specific products or services and clients accept responsibility to pay once the deliverables have been received.

The role of *contracts* in commercial relationships has been studied extensively by economists. The term may cover so-called spot contracts regulating an immediate exchange (e.g., a purchase), classical (formal and written) contracts, or relational contracts, which are implicit agreements between two parties (Kay, 1995). Although formal contracts are usually made only with external customers or suppliers, organizational sub-units may still have written agreements with other sub-units.[6] Typically, such agreements define the services to be delivered, the quality level, and costs. They may also define governance structures for managing inter-sub-unit relations, for example, the mechanisms to be used to monitor performance or to resolve issues that may arise.

However, a sub-unit may hold a large number of commitments that are not formalized in a contract or even a written agreement. Researchers studying communication processes within organizations have considered how commitments are conveyed between actors holding roles such as customer and supplier in a work processes (Winograd & Flores, 1986; Scherr, 1993). They argue that practically all communication in organizations may be reduced to a small set of basic communication acts, such as "requests" and "promises." According to this view, an interdependency is created when an actor makes an explicit promise to produce a certain action (e.g., deliver a service fulfilling the customer's requirements). Commitments are thus formed in a process of negotiation; the key medium is conversations about requirements and deliverables. As the term "conversation" suggests, these agreements are not static: The responsibility to deliver a service or perform a certain role is not "allocated" once and for all; it is formed in an on going, "authorizing" process (Kahn & Kram, 1994) in which people request and agree to perform actions.[7] People may also re-negotiate their commitments if unexpected events occur along the way.

In managing dependencies toward its external software vendors, the IT department at ProTech relies on a formal contract that regulates costs and support levels (see Figure 7.5). With its

6 The main difference compared to contracts made with outside partners is that internal agreements are either "self-enforced" or enforced by means of hierarchical authority.

7 A supplier may also issue a generalized commitment to all customers in the form of a *service guarantee* ("we will resolve all technical issues within 24 hours after notification").

internal clients, ProTech enters into Service Level Agreements (SLAs) that specify service levels, prices, support availability, etc. The SLAs are renegotiated annually. However, within the framework of the SLA, commitments are exchanged between IT employees and users/clients several times a day. For example, every time a user reports an application error, the Help Desk confirms that a software engineer will address the issue and thus commits to delivering a service.[8]

Commitment interdependencies vary in *criticality* and *uncertainty*. Commitment interdependencies are high in criticality if they have direct and significant impact on key work outcomes that a sub-unit is responsible for. For example, commitments regarding reliability and quality made by an IT vendor may be critical for an IT department in terms of its own ability to provide services to internal users according to agreed standards. The uncertainty of a commitment interdependency will tend to be reduced (for the client) when a supplier (internal or external) faces and accepts *consequential accountability* for delivering a product or service – i.e., when a supplier will suffer significant negative consequences if it fails to perform as promised. Commitment interdependency may also become less uncertain if a supplier not only guarantees the delivery of a service or product as specified, but also guarantees a positive outcome for its customer as a result of using the service or product (e.g., a "no cure, no pay" commitment). For example, a real estate agent may make its fee contingent upon obtaining a certain price for

8 In a highly customer-focused organization one would expect the supplier to commit to resolving the issue within a certain time (e.g., within 12 hours for errors with significant impact).

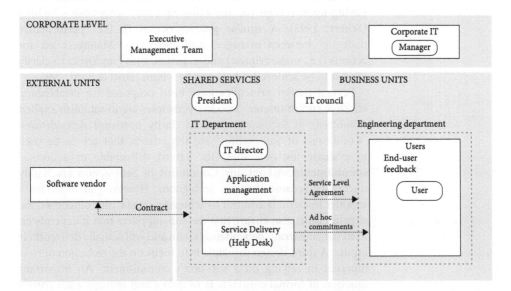

Figure 7.5 Key commitments between the ProTech IT department and other units.

9 Such commitments are relatively rare, however. Doctors normally do not commit to curing diseases (only to deliver treatment) and university professors normally do not commit to produce learning (only to provide teaching).

the house its client is trying to sell.[9] Similarly, managers may ask internal suppliers to commit to producing a positive outcome for an internal client (e.g., "reduce the time engineers use to search for information in the engineering database").

However, as several authors have noted (Scherr, 1993; Haeckel, 1999; Ford & Ford, 1995) communication between members of an organization often falls short of providing explicit commitments to deliver specified actions or achieve predetermined goals. It is more common to define fairly unspecific, activity-based goals (e.g., "provide engineering applications"). Moreover, there is frequently also uncertainty about whether a decision or act of communication signals a "binding commitment" or not. For example, a customer may not clearly understand whether a price quoted by a supplier is just an estimate or a real commitment. Employees may similarly wonder whether management decisions represent broad guidelines or intents, or whether they represent non-negotiable policies and principles. To address such issues, techniques have been proposed to "test" the level of commitment and negotiate more explicit agreements among people collaborating in a work process (Ford & Ford, 1995; Smith, 1999).

Configuring commitment interdependencies

In a work process involving a customer and a supplier, the process of forming a commitment starts with the customer requesting a service. An offer from the supplier may then prompt a negotiation over requirements, timing of deliverables, etc. The intention is to produce an agreement that implies not only that the supplier is committed to deliver but also that the customer is committed to paying upon receipt (or any other mutually acceptable schedule) (Scherr, 1993). A similar process occurs in the "performance dialogue" between managers and employees: Managers ask for actions (i.e., make request) and negotiate with employees to clarify what is to be achieved, when, and by whom (Ford & Ford, 1995).

Several design principles have been proposed for establishing effective commitments. Two key principles are to establish explicit *Conditions of Satisfaction* and to clarify *upstream dependencies*. "Conditions of Satisfaction" are the criteria that are to be used to evaluate the outcomes (the agreed deliverable or action) – commitments without any Conditions of Satisfaction are highly uncertain, because they are ambiguous. However, in order for a supplier to credibly commit to achieving satisfactory outcomes, the supplier must also ensure that the sub-suppliers that it depends on itself (i.e., upstream dependencies) can and will actually deliver their inputs. A third design principle is to focus on the *reduction of risks* inherent in relying on a sub-unit's commitment. An important function of formal contracts is to define and manage each party's risk in a relationship by spelling out the specific obligations created in a commitment, as well as the consequences of non-conformance of these obligations.

Clearly specifying the lateral chain of customer-supplier roles will generally reduce ambiguity and role conflicts. In the example of ProTech, roles designating internal customers and suppliers already exist. In large and complex organizations, however, it is not always clear "who owes what to whom"; specifying who one's internal customers are is often a surprisingly complicated task (Haeckel, 1999). Scherr (1993) proposed a technique – the Commitment Protocol – for mapping customer-supplier roles and commitments at various points in a work process from initial request to final deliverable and acceptance by client (see Figure 7.6). When applying this technique to map processes in organizations, he typically found cases where the customer role was missing or where an individual who performed the role of customer early in a work process would reappear downstream in the role as supplier. In some cases there may even be conflicting demands that prevent a clear definition of customer-supplier roles: Some members of corporate staff functions, for example, may be service providers (e.g. as advisers to business units), while at the same time overseeing policy compliance. However, techniques such as those proposed in Scherr (1993) may be used to re-design work processes and to separate the responsibilities of different individuals in avoid role conflicts. (We will examine this issue in more detail in Chapter 9.)

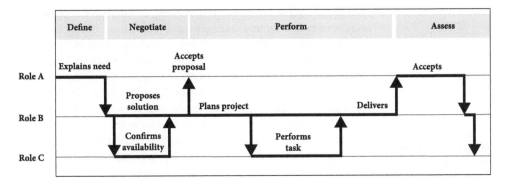

Figure 7.6 Example of a commitment protocol showing customer and supplier roles. (This format for visualizing commitment interdependencies was proposed by Scherr (1993) based on the earlier work by Winograd & Flores (1986).

Governance

The governance type concerns interdependencies related to authority relations in organizations. Governance dependencies arise because of a need for formal approval of a sub-unit's plans or activities by some party or because of a requirement to conduct an activity in conformance with a policy set by superiors. In most cases, managers with a superior position in an authority hierarchy have the right to define tasks, allocate resources, monitor and reward performance, hire or fire, and so on with regard to sub-units occupying lower positions in the hierarchy. Work outcomes at one level are therefore to a significant extent dependent upon decisions made (or not made) by managers or sub-units at higher authority levels in the organization. However, only in the simplest of cases can the issue of governance be reduced to the formal, vertical relations in an organization. One consequence of the increasing use of projects and cross-functional business processes is that decision authority may be distributed among a number of entities. It is common practice, for example, to establish steering groups for larger projects. Whereas the initial ratification of the project proposal is usually the responsibility of line management, the steering group's charter is to monitor and evaluate that the project fulfills its mandate, ensure adequate use of resources, and, occasionally, to assist the project manager in resolving particular issues that require senior management support or intervention. The steering group is usually composed of managers drawn from different functions and departments (sometimes customer or supplier representatives may also be included) (Earl, 1996). In addition, there may also be technology boards, user forums or reference groups that may be able to make certain decisions (or at least provide advice and thus influence decisions) regarding service delivery or functionality. There may also be forums for consultation such as worker-management councils consisting of employee representatives who meet with line managers to discuss the economic situation of the business, working conditions, and health and safety issues. In a large organization, such forums may exist at multiple levels. For example, in a divisionalized firm, there may be worker-management councils at the business unit, divisional, and corporate levels. There may also be multiple decision forums within the same unit or division, depending on the domain: One decision forum that considers investment proposals, another forum that recommends changes to company policy, and so on (Weill & Woodham, 2004).

10 The purpose of an IT policy is usually to ensure that IT management and development are aligned with overall business strategies and that different units follow a consistent set of practices. More specifically, it may include general IT principles, infrastructure strategies, standards regarding IT architecture, and processes for prioritization of investment proposals (see Weill & Woodham, 2004).

The IT department in ProTech is responsible for providing and supporting applications that serve the business needs of internal clients, while complying with the company's IT policies.[10] Although the head of IT reports to the President of Shared Services, there are two other governance interdependencies that significantly affect the IT department (see Figure 7.7): IT Corporate Management develops IT policies to which the IT department must conform, and individual business units like the Engineering department define the user requirements that the IT department must fulfill. The latter governance relationship is mediated by an IT Council, which consists of representatives from both IT and the Engineering department. The IT council escalates larger investment proposals to the Executive Management Team. If approved, the IT Council then monitors and reports on implementation of projects in evaluating whether the expected business benefits of each project are being realized.

The *criticality* of a sub-unit's governance interdependencies will depend on the potential effects of decisions made by other sub-units on the work process of the sub-unit. Interdependencies with sub-units whose decisions determine whether a sub-unit can begin, continue, or terminate a work process are obviously the most critical. The *uncertainty* of governance interdependencies is determined by their degree of stability and ambiguity. Governance uncertainty is affected by individuals that lead the sub-units toward which one is dependent. As March (1988) observed, decision makers may not always have stable preferences; in fact, preferences may shift or even be erratic. Ambiguity with regards to governance interdependencies may also arise due to unclear role definitions, or because of gaps and overlaps in decision rights allocated to various sub-units. One would expect to find the strongest – and least ambiguous – authority relations between sub-units occupying different vertical positions in a hierarchical organization. In project-based organizations that rely on multiple decision forums, however, a sub-unit may face a combination of different governance interdependencies of varying importance. The more complex an organization becomes, the more uncertainty will typically be associated with role and sub-unit

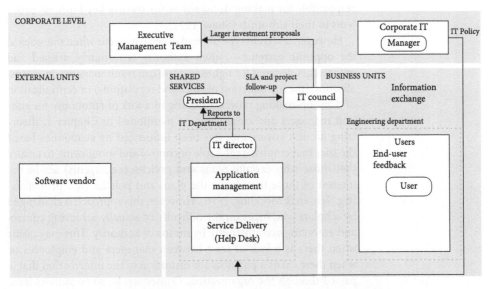

Figure 7.7 Governance interdependencies between ProTech's IT department and other units.

relationships. Jaques (1989) noted, however, that considerable uncertainty may exist even in relatively simple hierarchies. For example, executives at the same level may not agree among themselves who has the authority to allocate certain resources or give instruction to sub-units at lower levels in the organization.

Configuring governance interdependencies

In practice, managers of organizational sub-units are continuously involved in defining and re-defining governance structures and derived interdependencies. The interdependencies affecting a sub-unit may be too few or too weak to enable a process to perform adequately – as for example when a vertical authority relationship or a laterally interrelated steering group does not adequately involve managers of other sub-units whose collaboration is necessary to ensure adequate performance. In other cases, there may be too many interdependencies, resulting in open issues that go unresolved or a loss of time while sub-units wait for management approval for an action. In such situations, managers may need to redefine authority interdependencies to reduce overlaps among different decision domains. Alternatively, they may seek to redefine a sub-unit's mandate to clarify its goals and guidelines so that the sub-unit can act without the need to escalate decisions.

In practice, it is relatively common to observe breakdowns in organizational processes and other organizational dysfunctions that can be attributed to inadequate governance. In today's "networked" and project-based organizations, accountability is frequently blurred: Surveys among employees in large organizations suggest that a high percentage of people are uncertain about who is responsible for making decisions or for solving key business problems in their sub-units (Shaw, 1992).

However, a second type of breakdown can occur when one goes to the opposite extreme – when authority is minutely defined and enforced. A demand for tighter control can result in increasing formalization (the introduction of rules and regulations) or centralization of decision-making power, resulting in a loss of autonomy for sub-unit managers and employees. As mentioned in Chapter 1, theorizing around governance has been influenced by economics-based theories that emphasize the role of control and monitoring to ensure that those who execute plans and policies (i.e., agents) act in the interest of those that define the plans and policies (i.e., principals) (e.g., Jensen & Meckling, 1976). However, this approach is challenged by scholars who focus on the difficulty of actually achieving control and enforcing accountability by means of authority. This may occur when there is a lack of trust between managers and employees or when there exists a potential for distortion of the information that is passed through the organization. Consequently, some authors have argued for more inclusive forms of control, achieved through such mechanisms as mutual monitoring and transparency in decision making (Child & Rodrigues, 2003). A key goal of this approach is to achieve "fair process" (i.e., procedural justice) by clearly communicating expectations, soliciting employees' views before making decisions, and providing explanations for the rationale behind decisions (Kim & Mauborgne, 1996). Some authors have gone even further, in recommending the establishment of democratic organizational structures consisting of governance bodies that include employee representatives (e.g., Ackoff, 1994).

In sum, then, there are three key design principles that sub-unit managers may consider when establishing governance interdependencies. The first is to ensure that governing bodies include adequate *representation*. Second, one may *define roles and responsibilities* in a manner that clarifies accountability while avoiding gaps or overlaps in decision rights. Finally, governance should be exercised in a manner that *maintains or increases trust* between the actors involved.

Resources

Resource interdependencies arise when units share resources or transact with each other (McCann & Ferry, 1979; Pfeffer & Salancik, 1978). In the following, we focus on interdependencies that relate to *financial* resources; however, resources may be of many kinds, including knowledge, personnel, and equipment. One important source of interdependency among organizational sub-units is budgets developed to allocate limited financial resources and stipulate revenues. Financial resource budgeting in large companies is often a complex and political process that create interdependencies between sub-units that control the budgeting process and those that receive budgeted resources (Bower, 1970). Indirect interdependencies are created between sub-units competing for resources in the budgeting process.

Sub-units with profit and loss responsibility usually receive income directly from sales made to external customers. Sub-units that provide internal services may receive their funding from the corporate center or from the business unit that they belong to. Alternatively, they may also receive revenues or charge costs to other sub-units within the organization, particularly if the company has adopted an internal client-supplier model or has instituted a transfer pricing scheme. To understand the resource interdependencies for a particular unit, one must ask where its revenues come from, how costs are allocated (e.g., overhead charge or usage based fees), how any deficits would be covered, where any profits accrue, and how profits may be used.

In ProTech, the IT department pays yearly license fees to the Software vendor who provides software. Because the IT department at ProTech is organized as a Shared Services unit, it invoices the Business Unit depending on the level of usage (e.g., the number of users per application) (see Figure 7.8). In other words, there is a standardized financial transaction – with monthly billings – in the same manner as would occur between any supplier and customer. As a Shared Services function, the IT department is only supposed to cover its costs, and for this reason, does not generate profits that are transferred to the Corporate Level. However, it has received investment funds (a loan) from Corporate to cover procurement of new IT infrastructure.

The *criticality* of a resource interdependency will depend on the relative share of the sub-unit's resources that is provided by a contributing sub-unit. In the simplified example shown in Figure 7.8 the income is received from one internal client (resource provider), but in a real company there will often be a variety of sources of income; any sub-unit that controls a budget may become a resource provider. The *uncertainty* of the interdependency will increase to the extent that the resource flow fluctuates or is subject to competitive pressures from other (potential) suppliers, but may decrease if resource providers lack the ability to switch suppliers (Pfeffer & Salancik, 1978; McCann & Ferry, 1979). For example, business units may be bound by company policy to use only internal providers or use a fixed amount of resources for a given activity. If this is not the case, uncertainty may be decreased by identifying alternative resource providers to offset the potential loss of income from the current clients (e.g., one may consider selling to external clients). In other words, the highest degree of resource interdependency exists

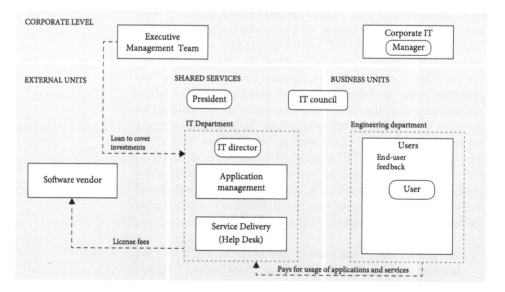

Figure 7.8 The most important resource interdependencies for the IT department at ProTech.

when resource providers supply a great portion of a sub-unit's (internal supplier's) critical resources that cannot easily be substituted by other resource providers. A sub-unit (internal supplier) will have a low degree of interdependency with a resource provider when the resource provided is not essential to the sub-unit's activity or can be obtained from other resource providers.

Configuring resource interdependencies

A key task of managers is to ensure that their sub-units have the resources needed to perform their mandated activities and that resource flows are as predictable as possible in order to avoid a sudden interruption of activities. Another key concern may be to reduce asymmetries in the exchange relationship, that is, altering an interdependency where the exchange is not equally important to both parties. Asymmetry may arise when the units that transact are unequal in size. An application development team consisting of five people in ProTech may use 100% of its capacity on developing a specialized software application for one of ProTech's large engineering departments, yet the team may only be responsible for a small fraction of the engineering department's entire application portfolio (cf. Pfeffer & Salancik, 1978). There are several organizational strategies for adapting to and balancing resource dependencies (ibid.). A manager may attempt to increase the share of the sub-unit's essential resource transfers that derive from reliable resource providers. If an IT unit serves several business units, it may expand the scale and/or scope of services to those sub-units/resource providers that are seen as most reliable in terms of keeping their commitments. It may remove resource interdependencies with high uncertainty – for example, with an unpredictable resource provider whose budget is shared among several units competing for the same budget means. The effect is to increase the criticality of some interdependencies, but reducing their uncertainty. Moreover, managers may try to counterbalance an asymmetrical resource relationship by introducing new resource interdependencies where the power advantage is reversed. The small application development team may utilize its knowledge of ProTech's business processes to develop a software application that has an unique feature that the engineering department will have difficulty substituting with alternative applications. It may also reduce dependency by attempting to add alternative internal or external clients or suppliers (i.e., thereby reducing the criticality of each of the existing resource interdependencies).

Social networks

Social network dependencies exist whenever the performance of a work process is affected by informal ties among sub-units. Ties between organizational sub-units are created by individuals, such as the leader, who represent the sub-unit in his/her interactions with other organizational members (Bonacich, 1991). These ties aid sub-units in obtaining or sharing knowledge across the organization (Hansen, 1999), in influencing decisions related to governance, resources, and activities that may affect the unit (Pfeffer, 1992), and also in developing trust toward individuals in other sub-units, which may increase willingness to form commitments when collaborating in the future.

As with the other types, the *criticality* of social network interdependencies is determined by the effect that these interdependencies have on the outcomes that the work unit is responsible for. *Uncertainty* is related to perceived dependability and reliability of informal ties, which in turn are related to the level of trust that exists between the parties. If the level of trust is low, one does not expect to receive valid or accurate information from the other party, or one may suspect that the other party's support may not be consistent over time (hence, the interdependency would be characterized as being uncertain). Some authors also point out that the particular type of uncertainty differs depending on the form and depth of the relationship. Sheppard and Sherman (1998) proposed a continuum ranging from non-critical or "shallow dependency" to "deep interdependency" between two or more parties.[11] For non-critical interdependencies, the key uncertainty is related to whether the other party will behave in an unreliable or indiscrete manner. As the importance of the interdependency increases, other, more serious uncertainties and risks appear, such as cheating, neglect, and abuse. Sometimes another party may also exploit dependencies by using the risks of such negative consequences as a lever in negotiations. High trust, on the other hand, leads to the expectancy that one will attain positive outcomes based on the actions taken by the other party.

11 For simplicity we only describe two of the four levels of interdependency described in Sheppard & Sherman (1998).

> ProTech's IT director enjoys close relations with his boss (the President of Shared Services) and with the head of Corporate IT (see Figure 7.9). At one point the Executive Management Team was drafting a plan to outsource the entire IT department; however, the IT manager received early warning of this plan from Corporate IT and was able to convince his superiors to change their mind. The IT manager also has informal ties with employees elsewhere in the company that prove useful to the IT department. For example, in order to gauge the quality of services seen from users' point of view, he solicits feedback from a former colleague with whom he frequently socializes and who now works in the business unit that the IT department serves.

Configuring social network interdependencies

There are several ways in which managers of sub-units may be able to develop informal ties and thereby improve their ability to maintain, improve, and expand other interdependency types should

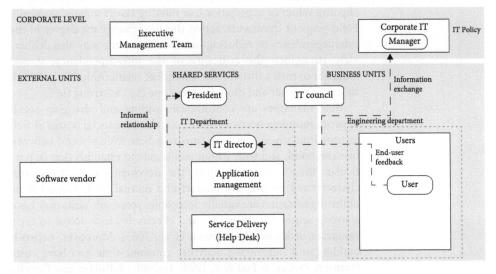

Figure 7.9 Social network interdependencies between the IT department and other sub-units of Pro-Tech.

the need arise in the future. Several authors have demonstrated that a manager's position in a social network, in particular, the proximity to influential people, is a key determinant of the power of the sub-unit that one belongs to within the organization. From a political perspective, the key design principle is thus to achieve *network centrality*. Managers establish informal ties (i.e., add interdependencies) in important networks by seeking out interactions strategically, even social interactions, and making sure that they are "plugged into the structure of communication" within the organization (Pfeffer, 1992, p. 123). They may deliberately lobby for projects and tasks that provide their unit with access to senior people of the organization. Managers may also seek to *enlarge the number* of informal ties. As pointed out by Kaplan (1991), by cultivating relationships with people in other parts of the organization, one creates "a reservoir of trust and goodwill" that can become a crucial resource the day one requires support or help from other units. A third possibility is attempting to *bridge otherwise disconnected networks* inside the organization. As Burt (1992) has demonstrated, considerable influence flows to a person who can bridge so-called structural holes. For example, if corporate staff functions in a firm are disconnected from field operations, a corporate staff manager may initiate a quality improvement program that involves members of corporate staff with manufacturing engineers, and thereby establish a link between operations and staff functions. Finally, managers will be concerned with enhancing the *quality of relationships* (particularly in cases where there already exists an important activity or resource interdependency). This may involve attempts at enhancing trust, aligning values or expectations, or offering favors to build goodwill. Following our framework above, this may change the degree of the interdependency by reducing its uncertainty; one may also deliberately strengthen the criticality of the interdependency, if one manages to turn a distant and infrequent relationship (i.e., a "weak tie") into a closer and more frequent one (i.e., a "strong tie").

Most managers are continuously adding and changing social network interdependencies. However, there are social norms as well as time limitations that may constrain how wide a social network one can build, and with whom one is able to establish ties. In particular, these constraints limit the development of strong ties characterized by frequent contact and mutual trust. Not all parts of the organization are equally accessible: Some sub-units may have a strong sense of territoriality and effectively block access to their resources or knowledge (Brown et al., 2005). Moreover, network building and influencing activities consume time and have costs (Hansen, Pfeffer, & Podolny, 1999). Indeed, McFadyen and Canella (2004) documented that there are diminishing returns as the number of ties is increased.

Yet the greatest challenge may be the removal of a social interdependency. One may simply stop maintaining contact with people; however, norms of reciprocity, loyalty, and stability within networks make social relationships inherently "sticky." As pointed out by Walker (1997) we know little about how social networks are dissolved and one of the few theoretical models that includes the dissolution stage adopts the metaphor of marital divorce to explain how it happens. In other words, reconfiguring social network interdependencies may be a difficult and protracted process.

Discussion and conclusion

In large and complex organizations, significant opportunities for performance improvement are often to be found at the interfaces between sub-units (Rummler & Brache, 1990). However, one often focuses on a single type of interdependency, usually Activities, when considering options for sub-unit performance improvement. In this chapter we have therefore proposed a broader framework that encompasses five different types of interdependencies (Figure 7.10).

An important consideration is whether the different interdependencies that we have described are independent or not. In other words, is the degree of interdependency between two sub-units equal with regard to the different types of interdependencies (Commitments, Resources, Activities, Governance, and Networks)? There are several examples that would suggest that different interdependencies are independent and that they for this reason may be in misalignment to each other. We may again return to the example of ProTech. In the description above, we explained that the IT department is an

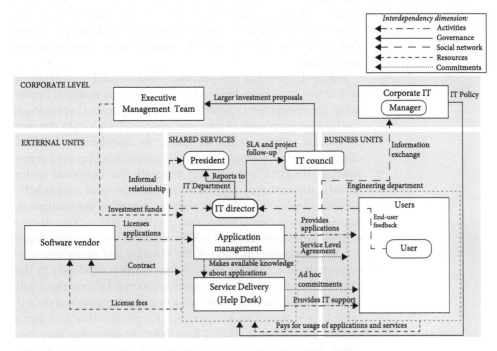

Figure 7.10 Dependencies between the IT department and other units in ProTech.

independent cost center that charges out its costs to the different business units. In other words, the Resource model is decentralized – it follows the Shared Services model intended to supplant hierarchical and functionally oriented departments with customer-driven service provider units. However, consider the situation that emerges if ProTech introduces a governance model where application development choices are centralized to Corporate IT or a second "matrix" reporting structure where the IT manager reports to the vice president of Corporate IT in addition to the head of Shared Services. In these cases, the Governance model would become more centralized, but ProTech may not necessarily centralize the Resource model, that is, transfer IT costs to a central, corporate budget. The same possibilities exist with regard to other interdependencies, for example, social network structures do not always match the formal authority relations, work processes do not necessarily match the resource flows, and commitments do not always match the activities being performed, and so on. Instances of misalignment are probably very common. To some extent, this may reflect the added – and perhaps unavoidable – complexity that arises when organizations try to move from a functionally oriented to a more project- or network-based structure, or when organizations introduce matrix structures that combine e.g., product- and market-based reporting lines. However, we would also speculate that misalignment may be due to a form of "coordination neglect" (Heath & Staudenmayer, 2000), that is, a failure on the part of managers to effectively coordinate the different design parameters that need to work in concert to sustain effective organizational functioning.

Acknowledging the independence, and possible misalignment, of different interdependency types also has some potential implications for management research. The approach that we have outlined can help interpret some of the conflicting empirical results obtained by scholars within contingency theory. As described in Chapter 1, contingency theory sought to establish connections between organizational structure and external demands. The empirical studies aimed at supporting contingency theory have in some cases failed to produce consistent results, for example, regarding the relationship between environmental uncertainty and the degree of centralization of an organization. Pfeffer (1997) concluded that this was largely due to an oversimplification of the meaning and measurement of organizational structure. From the perspective developed in this chapter, it seems clear that an organization may be centralized with respect to one interdependency type (e.g., governance) and decentralized with respect to another (e.g. resources). This may partly explain why different studies have failed to converge: They may simply have measured different aspects of constructs such as centralization, formalization, and differentiation. The implication is that contingency theory research might yield different results if it employs less abstract constructs.

In sum, this chapter has described five interdependency types and proposed a set of generic design propositions for addressing common challenges related to sub-unit interdependencies (see summary below). This framework may serve as a basis for managerial practice as well as for academic research aimed at improving the performance of work processes within complex organizations.

Overall design propositions

Objective	*Enhance organizational functioning by improving sub-unit interfaces.*
7.1	Identify *current* interdependencies (cf. Table 7.2).
7.2	Identify the interdependencies that *should be* created, removed or reconfigured to ensure that the functions of the organization or sub-unit can be fulfilled (cf. detailed design propositions in Table 7.3).
7.3	Implement the required changes to close the gap between the current and the required interdependencies (cf. Table 7.3).

Table 7.2 Diagnostic questions that may be used to identify current interdependencies

Type	Question
Commitment	• To which other sub-units does the sub-unit hold commitments (and vice versa)? • What is the Criticality and Uncertainty of each of these interdependencies?
Activities	• Which other sub-units provide inputs to the activities performed in this sub-unit? • To which other sub-units does the sub-unit provide outputs? • What is the Criticality and Uncertainty of these interdependencies?
Governance	• Who makes decisions that may affect the sub-unit? • What is the Criticality and Uncertainty of each of these interdependencies?
Resources	• Who provides resources to the sub-unit? • What is the Criticality and Uncertainty of each of these interdependencies?
Social network	• What informal ties exist toward other actors/ sub-units in the organization that may affect decisions or outcomes in the sub-unit? • What is the Criticality and Uncertainty of each of these interdependencies?

Table 7.3 Detailed design propositions

Objective	Design proposition	
Configure Activity interdependencies	7.1	Add interdependencies that are required to fulfill the function of the unit/organization
	7.2	Remove activity interdependencies that create delays or add coordination costs (e.g., by standardizing processes, interfaces)
	7.3	Define transfer-points to avoid breakdowns during hand-offs
Configure Commitment interdependencies	7.4	Establish explicit conditions of satisfaction at start of process
	7.5	Clarify downstream dependencies before committing to a client
	7.6	Manage risks in important projects (e.g., by formalizing mutual obligations)
	7.7	Remove conflicting customer/supplier roles in processes
Configure Governance interdependencies	7.8	Ensure that governance bodies include key stakeholders
	7.9	Clarify roles and responsibilities to reduce ambiguity around accountability
	7.10	Establish trust by implementing decision processes satisfying criteria for procedural justice ("fair process")
Configure Resource interdependencies	7.11	Increased the share of the sub-unit's essential resource transfers from reliable resource providers to reduce uncertainty
	7.12	Remove resource interdependencies with high uncertainty to increase predictability of resource flows
	7.13	Reduce the risk in asymmetrical exchange relationships by developing counterbalancing resource dependencies

	7.14	Add alternative internal or external suppliers or clients to reduce dependency on one or a few resource providers
Configure social network interdependencies	7.15	Act to achieve network centrality to increase sub-unit power
	7.16	Enlarge the number of informal ties to build options for future support
	7.17	Increase influence by bridging unconnected networks
	7.18	Enhance quality of important relationships

Review questions

1 How do you evaluate the criticality and uncertainty of an interdependency?
2 What are the key characteristics of the five types of interdependencies described in this chapter?
3 What may managers do to ensure that the members of their sub-units are aware of, and effectively manage, interdependencies toward other units?
4 Select a sub-unit that you are familiar with (e.g., a team in the company where you work, a university department, etc.). Interview a member of the unit and use the questions above to identify the key interdependencies between this unit and other units within the same organization. Draw a diagram to summarize your findings. Comment upon any "disconnects" that you may observe.
5 From the business press or your personal experience, select a case where a company is attempting to resolve a performance problem involving one of its sub-units and its relations to other units within the organization (or toward external constituents). Can you think of alternative ways of resolving this problem, invoking the five interdependency types?

Research questions

1 To what extent could the consideration of current and potential interdependencies sensitize sub-unit managers or employees to uncertain interdependencies and improve the ability to predict interdependencies that may affect them in the future?
2 How could interdependency misalignment be operationalized and measured?
3 What are the performance implications of interdependency misalignment?
4 Thompson (1967) assumed that interdependencies were strongly linked to work processes, yet in many settings, one may be able to alter the work processes in order to change the degree of interdependency. What implications does this insight have for Thompson's framework?

References

Ackoff, A. (1994). *The Democratic Corporation: A Radical Prescription for Recreating Corporate America and Rediscovering Success.* New York: Oxford University Press.

Baldwin, C., & Clark, K. (2000). *The Power of Modularity.* Boston: MIT Press.

Bolman, L. G., & Deal, T. E. (1997). *Reframing Organizations: Artistry, Choice, and Leadership.* San Francisco: JosseyBass.

Bonacich, P. (1991). Simultaneous group and individual centralities. *Social Networks,* 13, 155–168.

Bower, J. L. (1970). *Managing the Resource Allocation Process.* Boston, MA: Harvard Business School Press.

Brown, G., Lawrence. T. B., & Robinson, S. L. (2005). Territoriality in organisations. *Academy of Management Review,* 30, 577–594.

Burt, R. S. (1992). *Structural Holes: The Social Structure of Competition.* Cambridge, MA: Harvard University Press.

Child, J., & Rodrigues, S. B. (2003). Corporate governance and new organisational forms: Issues of double and multiple agency. *Journal of Management and Governance,* 7, 337–360.

Earl, M. J. (1996). *Information Management: The Organisational Dimension.* Oxford: Oxford University Press.

Ford, J. D., & Ford, L. W. (1995). The role of conversations in producing intentional change in organisations. *The Academy of Management Review,* 20, 3, 541–571.

Galbraith, J. (1993). *Competing With Flexible Lateral Organizations.* Reading, MA: Addison-Wesley.

Haeckel, S. H. (1999). *Adaptive Enterprise: Creating and Leading Sense-and-Respond Organisations.* Boston: Harvard Business School Press.

Hansen, M., Pfeffer, J., & Podolny, J. (1999). Too much of a good thing? Social networks, influence behaviors, and team performance. Paper delivered at the Academy of Management Conference, August 6–11.

Hansen, M. T. (1999). The search-transfer problem: The role of weak ties in sharing knowledge across organisation subunits. *Administrative Science Quarterly,* 44, 82–111.

Heath, C., & Staudenmayer, N. (2000). Coordination neglect: How lay theories of organizing complicate coordination in organisations. *Research in Organizational Behavior,* 22, 153–191.

Jaques, E. (1989). *Requisite Organization: The CEO's Guide to Creative Structure and Leadership.* Arlington, VA: Cason Hall & Publishers.

Jastram, R. W. (1974). Notes: Organization by sequential responsibility: Transfer points. *California Management Review,* 17, 1, 124–125.

Jensen, M. C., & Meckling, W. H. (1976). Theory of the firm: Managerial behavior, agency costs and ownership structure. *Journal of Financial Economics* 3, 305–360.

Kahn, W. A., & Kram, K. E. (1994). Authority at work: Internal models and their organisational consequences. *Academy of Management Review*, 19, 1, 17–50.

Kaplan, R.E. (1991). *Beyond Ambition: How Driven Managers Can Lead Better And Live Better*. San Francisco: Jossey-Bass.

Kay, J. (1995). *Foundations of Corporate Success*. Oxford: Oxford University Press.

Kim, W. C., & Mauborgne, R. A. (1996) Procedural justice and managers' in-role and extra-role behavior: The case of the multinational. *Management Science*, 42, 4, 499–515.

Lawrence, P. R., & Lorsch, J. W. (1967). *Organization and Environment: Managing Differentiation and Integration*. Boston, MA: Harvard University.

March, J. (1988). *Decisions and Organizations*. Oxford: Basil Blackwell.

McCann, J. E., & Ferry D. L. (1979). An approach for assessing and managing inter-unit interdependence. *The Academy of Management Review*, 4, 1, 113–120.

McFadyen, M. A., & Cannella, A. A. J. 2004. Social capital and knowledge creation: Diminishing returns to the number and strength of exchange relationships. *Academy of Management Journal*, 47, 735–746.

Mintzberg, H. (1979). *The Structuring of Organizations*. Englewood Cliffs, NJ: Prentice-Hall.

Miles, R. M. (1979). Organizational conflict and management. In Miles, R. H., & Randolph, W. A., *The Organisation Game*. Santa Monica: Goodyear

Pfeffer, J. (1992). *Managing with Power*. Boston: Harvard Business School Press.

Pfeffer, J. (1997). *New Directions for Organisation Theory: Problems and Prospects*. New York: Oxford University Press.

Pfeffer, J., & Salancik, G. R. (1978). *The External Control of Organisations: A Resource Dependence Perspective*. New York: Harper and Row.

Rummler, G. A., & Brache, A. P. (1990). *Improving Performance: How to Manage the White Space on the Organisation Chart*. San Francisco: Jossey-Bass.

Sanchez, R. (1995). Strategic flexibility in product competition. *Strategic Management Journal*, 16 (summer special issue), 135–159.

Sanchez, R., & Mahoney, J. T. (1996). Modularity, flexibility, and knowledge management in product and organization design. *Strategic Management Journal*, 17, 63.

Scherr, A. L. (1993). A new approach to business processes. *IBM Systems Journal*, 32, 1, 80–98.

Shaw, R. B. (1992). The capacity to act: Creating a context for empowerment. In D. A. Nadler et al. (Eds.), *Organizational Architecture*. San Francisco: Jossey-Bass.

Sheppard, B. H., & Sherman, D. M. (1998). The grammars of trust: A model and general implications. *Academy of Management Review*, 23, 3, 422–437.

Smith, D. K. (1999). *Make Success Measurable! A Mindbook-Workbook for Setting Goals and Taking Action*. New York: Wiley.

Smith, R. B. & Eppinger, S. D. (1993). Characteristics and models of iteration in engineering design. *Proceeding of the International Conference on Engineering Design* (ICED'93), The Hague, The Netherlands, 564–571.

Thompson, J. D. (1967). *Organizations in Action*. New York: McGraw-Hill.

Von Hippel, E. (1990). Task partitioning: An innovation process variable. *Research Policy*, 19, 5, 407–418.

Walker, O. C. (1997). The adaptability of network organisations: Some unexplored questions. *Academy of Marketing Science*, 75–82.

Weill, P., & Woodham, R. (2004). *IT Governance: How Top Performers Manage IT Decision Rights for Superior Results*. Boston: Harvard Business School Press.

Winograd, T., & Flores, F. (1986). *Understanding Computers and Cognition: A New Foundation for Design*. Norwood, NJ: Ablex Publishing Corporation.

8 Managing the organization design process

Chapter overview

Background	• Leaders periodically initiate organizational re-design processes in order to improve performance.
	• The quality of the re-design process itself is an important predictor of the quality of the organizational model that is developed – and of its acceptance and implementation.

Challenges	• Unless managed skillfully, re-design processes can easily result in suboptimal outcomes:
	  ○ Omitting the link between functions and structure may lead to *misalignment* between the organizational model that is developed and the strategy of the organization.
	  ○ A failure to fully consider the many interrelated elements of organizational models may lead to *incoherent* designs.
	  ○ Lack of proper involvement of key stakeholders in the re-design process may lead to a *withering of trust*, which in turn reduces voluntary compliance with the new organizational model

Key question	• How can we manage re-design processes in a manner that allows us to *Align* the organization with the strategy, create *Coherent* designs, while building *Trust* among key stakeholders (including employees affected by the change)?
Proposed approach	• Develop a structured methodology that leaders can use to plan, develop, and implement new organizational designs.
	• Ensure that the methodology addresses the challenges related to creating Alignment, Coherence, and Trust.

- Consider how the methodology may be further improved by means of field testing and systematic research on design processes.

Introduction

The more complex an organization is, the harder it is to re-design. Leaders that undertake to re-design their organizations frequently encounter problems that are best described as "messes" – problems that are difficult to solve because of incomplete, contradictory, and/or changing requirements (Ackoff, 1999). Leaders may also be subject to considerable pressure from stakeholder groups and individuals who hold different views and who press for a solution that is favorable, given their interests and position in the organization. How can we structure the organization re-design *process* in a way that enables leaders to handle such challenges in a constructive manner?

Most experienced leaders have personal experience from developing and changing organizations. They may hold strong personal preferences for how they should proceed when initiating a re-design process, based on observations of the success or failure of past attempts. Such personal knowledge is clearly valuable and will always influence how one approaches a re-design process. Yet it is also important to acknowledge the limitations of personal knowledge. Personal knowledge is *tacit* and thus difficult to verify and to disseminate. Relying on tacit knowledge alone makes it difficult to create a cumulative learning process in which organization design principles are gradually refined and improved over time.

The development of a methodology, containing guiding principles, frameworks, and tools, is one way to create *explicit knowledge* about re-design processes.[1] A methodology ensures that an effective way to solve a problem is codified and that it can be shared among a larger group of people. It helps in creating shared "mental models" and may thus contribute to "cognitive coordination" among participants in a design process (Werr et al., 1997). A methodology may also serve as a basis for developing a gradually more sophisticated knowledge base about re-design. The methodology may comprise a set of *design propositions*. As discussed in Chapter 1, design propositions should reflect the current state of academic research but should also be revised and improved based on "field testing", by observing the outcome of actual re-design processes where they have been applied.

The purpose of this chapter is to develop a methodology that may provide a basis for systematic and cumulative improvement of knowledge over time. It goes beyond existing methodologies by incorporating some key elements of the axiomatic design approach described in the preceding chapters, for example, by emphasizing the link between functional requirements and design parameters. The

1 Although there is little research on organization re-design processes per se, management scholars have looked at planning more generally and found that the quality of strategic planning processes is important and may research even predict corporate performance (Hart & Banbury, 1994; Dean & Sharfman, 1996). Research on strategic change has similarly demonstrated that the overall approach that leaders select, as well as the timing and sequencing of specific interventions, are important in securing a successful outcome in change processes (Huy, 2001).

methodology has been developed "in the field" and refined during repeated re-design projects. Yet having a methodology is only the first step. Disagreements do exist among practitioners with regard to some issues, and there is a lack of evidence-based knowledge about re-design processes. We acknowledge this by formulating several research questions that are described in the Discussion section.

Requirements to design processes

In line with the axiomatic design philosophy, one should start the development of a re-design methodology by considering the purpose and the requirements that such a methodology should fulfill. Although there will always be some situation-specific requirements to design processes, we here suggest that there are three generic requirements that practically all re-design processes must fulfill in order to be successful. These requirements are to create *alignment* with strategy, *coherence* and consistency between design elements, and *trust* among stakeholders who participate in the process (or who are affected by its outcomes).

At the most fundamental level, organizational models that are developed during a re-design exercise should aid the organization in realizing its strategic goals. In other words, the organizational model needs to be *aligned* with strategic goals. This in turn requires that the strategic goals are known. Moreover, the strategic goals need to be sufficiently clear to allow a design team to make choices that may prioritize one design criterion (e.g., costs) at the expense of another (e.g., customer service). Yet as observers of organizational decision making have noted (e.g., Nutt & Wilson, 2010; Pfeffer, 1992), leaders sometimes encounter fundamental disagreements about goals. Large organizations consist of several stakeholder groups, with different interests and interpretations of the organization's purpose, mission, and goals. Overcoming such disagreements is often the most difficult part of a design exercise.

A CEO of an engineering firm initiates a discussion in his manage-ment team about how the firm's Research & Development (R&D) unit should be organized. It is currently attached to the Headquarters. He is considering whether to decentralize the unit's resources among the firm's different business units. During the process, this proposal meets with considerable resistance, as the R&D staff believe that decentralization would force them to become more like a support function, driven by the business units' short term needs, making it difficult to maintain its current research capabilities. The CEO concludes that the unit lacks a clear purpose: Should its main purpose be to support product development for the business units, or to develop entirely new technologies?

A governmentally funded body responsible for food certification is reviewing its organizational structure. Half way through the design exercise, it becomes clear that there exists some ambiguity with regards to its mission. Staff members mention difficulty in prioritizing different projects, aimed at different users or target groups. This leads to a discussion of who the primary beneficiary is of the body's services: Is it the consumer, who will be able to enjoy safer and higher quality food? Is it the government, which funds its activities? Is it the farmer, the supplier of the food ingredients? Or is it the super market chains that buy the products from the farmer, and, that should be able to increase both margins and volume when products are certified?

An effective organization design process should enable key stake-holders to identify and improve unclear or conflicting goals that preclude the development of viable designs and, once this has been achieved, ensure that new organizational model is aligned with the strategic goals.

The next challenge is developing a design that is *coherent* and consistent. When organization re-design processes are initiated, the purpose is rarely to optimize one part of the organization in isolation but rather to improve *system (i.e., organizational)* performance. This can only be done by looking both at the individual units and at how they interact in carrying out the organization's processes.

Galbraith (2002) described a consumer packages goods company where each function was allowed to organize according to its own logic. Sales was organized according to geography, marketing by brands, manufacturing by site and process, engineering by product, and purchasing by commodity and vendor. If an engineer wanted to modify a product, the initiative would affect over 20 interfaces in the organization (internal teams or sub-units) and he/she would need to communicate and gain support from in each one in order to proceed with the modification.

A building contractor is introducing a new strategy. The firm designs, installs, and maintains electrical systems, ventilation, and plumbing in office buildings. It currently has three business units: One for electrical installation, one for ventilation, and one for plumbing. The new strategy is to provide "solutions" – that is, to compete for larger and more complex projects that involve combinations of services. The three business units have so far worked independently, and have their own customers, projects, and procedures. The new strategy implies that the three business units must combine their efforts and work together on joint projects. The implementation of the new strategy proceeds slowly. The CEO realizes that the business units have been optimized to run independently. They have been designed to maximize sales and profits of their own services, rather than to target customers with integrated offerings.

Although lower-level units may be empowered to develop the specific designs for their own units, it is necessary to *coordinate* the design processes centrally in order to ensure that the pieces fit together.

Third, the design process should not only ensure that a new and better organizational model is developed – but that it is implemented. As members of organizations, most of us observe intentions that are not realized and plans that are only partially implemented.

> *Hood, Huby, and Dunsire (1985) studied the effects of 10 reorganizations of British government departments. The reorganizations consisted of mergers and some demergers of government departments. The intention of the mergers was to bring separate units under one roof to get people to work together and make government policy more coherent (The Economist, 2009). Yet Hood et al. (1985) observed that the changes had had little effect on the way people worked and how different sub-units would collaborate with each other: "The Ministry of Defence in its current form was stitched together from the separate military departments in the 1960s, and it's often said that even now you can see the joints" (The Economist, 2009, p. 38). Hood et al. refer to the "Law of Inertia" to explain why reorganizations fail to produce the intended effects.*
>
> *A global oil services firm introduced a new product-based, divisional organization. The new structure implied that people who had previously been part of functionally defined units would be transferred to one of three product divisions that were established. An evaluation some months afterwards revealed that the new structure had been implemented in different ways in the various offices worldwide. At the Houston office, the regional president had re-allocated workers' offices to ensure that team members were co-located. At the Oslo office, on the other hand, many people were still in the same offices as before, four months after the new structure had been announced. As one manager remarked: "For us . . . there really was no distinct shift between the old and the new organization . . . people don't feel that they are part of a new team . . ."*

2 The first two factors here are based on research on procedural justice or "fair process" (Kim & Mauborgne, 1996). The third is derived from research on change processes by organizational psychologists (Farr, 1990).

As Russell Ackoff stated (1981), no design has ever been created that humans aren't able to subvert. Yet one may ask what the conditions are that motivate managers and employees to voluntarily comply with, rather than subvert, a design that has been selected as the preferred model by their organization's decisions makers. Both systematic research and practical experience point to three crucial factors that influence the likelihood that employees will actively support the implementation of organizational changes.[2] The first is the degree to which employees understand the rationale for initiating the change, and for the particular design that has been selected. The second is related to the ability to influence the outcome of the process by means of participation in the decision process. The third is the degree to which employees see a pay-off for them personally from implementing the organizational changes, for example, whether a new design will provide roles that create opportunities for learning, growth, or career advancement. In short, managers need to create *trust* in the re-design process and its outcomes.

The challenge of creating *alignment, coherence* and *trust* can be converted into requirements for the design process (see Table 8.1). The purpose of the remaining part of this chapter is to outline a methodology that is intended to maximize the chances that re-design processes in complex organizations will fulfill the requirements – that is, that the participants in the process are able to develop designs that are aligned with strategic goals, which are coherent, and which creates trust and thus are likely to be implemented and complied to by organizational members.

Many managers working in large organizations will be able to recount instances of dysfunctional organization design processes. Their leaders may have been unwilling to consider new options and simply resorted to the same solutions that have been used in the past; decision processes may at one point have disintegrated into political maneuvering among key players, or decision makers may have selected solution alternatives that would obviously fail to address the underlying causes of a widely recognized problem. In fact, such

Table 8.1 Key challenges in re-design processes and how these are addressed by the design methodology proposed

Challenge	Examples of techniques recommended
Creating *Alignment*, i.e., ensuring that the chosen model is aligned with the company's mission and strategies	– Facilitation techniques to clarify mission and purpose – Use of mapping tools to identify correspondence between goals (functional requirements) and organizational variables (design parameters)
Creating *Coherence*, i.e., improving the performance of the entire system, as opposed to optimizing individual parts	– Central coordination of design process – Explicit consideration of the *interdependencies* between sub-units – Sequencing of activities (strategic design before operational design) – Coordinated re-configuration of *Operating model, Resource model*, and *Governance model*
Creating *Trust*, which is necessary for the chosen organizational model to be accepted and implemented by the organizational members	– Methods that allow key stakeholder groups to participate in the design process – Development and use of explicit decision criteria – Careful operationalization of the design and systematic transition planning

problems are so commonplace that many managers and employees probably doubt the feasibility of attempting to create alignment, coherence, and trust. They have come to the conclusion that organizational re-design is primarily a political process that only a handful of key players are likely to be involved in.[3] Others may support the more frequent and gradual adjustments that are carried out to roles and processes within the different sub-units, but be skeptical about creating a re-design project with a broader mandate.

3 The fact that that new organizational models are sometimes imposed in an attempt to gain political control is well recognised in the academic literature (e.g., Morgan, 1986, p. 162, and Pfeffer, 1992).

Obviously, no methodology for conducting an organization design process will by itself resolve such issues; a methodology will only serve its purpose if there is a pre-existing commitment to addressing organization design issues in a systematic and transparent manner. Nevertheless, the overall assertion here is that one is unlikely to achieve a successful re-design of large and complex organization using unsystematic methods or overly political strategies. The first question to a line manager contemplating an organizational re-design is thus what kind of process the line manager envisages. The methodology described in this chapter is primarily intended for those managers willing to articulate their decision criteria, to test their own assumptions, and involve relevant stakeholders throughout the process.

We should acknowledge that the process advocated here is relatively time-consuming and requires some project support. (In a large organization, either internal or external project resources should be assigned to support the process through the different phases described below.) Indeed, a key assumption is that making quick decisions is not a valid goal in itself. What counts – in terms of improving corporate performance – is what one may call "time to value", that is, *the amount of time that elapses before the intended benefits of the organizational model are realized.* A systematic re-design process requires an investment of time. Not only does it take time to perform the actual project activities (e.g., data collection and analysis); the process often requires negotiation between different stakeholder groups and frequently sets in motion psychological processes where new concepts and ideas, that may immediately seem new or foreign, gradually mature and become accepted as potential solutions.

The purpose of the methodology is not to eliminate all "politics" in the process; this would be impossible in any case. However, the methodology is built on the assumption that there are productive and unproductive ways of handling the political aspects of an organization design process. In accordance with theories on negotiation (Fisher & Ury, 1983), it is assumed that it is easier to create productive dialogue if one can first obtain commitment toward general principles and decision criteria, and delay the discussion regarding individual roles to a later stage in the process. It is also assumed that it is easier to discover effective design solutions – and to implement them, once selected – when different stakeholders have been involved throughout the process. It may be impossible to design an "optimal" model, but it may be possible to create a design process in which participants jointly create new designs, evaluate decision alternatives, implement the design, and also adjust elements of the design that do not work as intended.

In the following, a set of tools used to produce "deliverables" that document the outputs of each step of the process is described. Documenting information has a value in itself; for example, it improves the ability to effectively share information among a group of stakeholders. Written records of the design process also allow "traceability", that is, the ability to document on what grounds a given design option was selected. This in turn facilitates learning, as outcomes can be compared more directly to prior decisions and decision criteria. However, even more important is the role that these tools play in shaping the design process itself. To take a simple example, using an organization chart as the main tool in design process is likely to lead to a rather narrow focus on the formal reporting structure. A tool, on the other hand, that explicitly includes other organizational dimensions (such as interdependencies between sub-units) may to a significant degree change what information is collected, how stakeholders perceive the key design challenges, and potentially also widen the range of design alternatives that are considered.

This chapter advocates a "fact-based" approach by describing how data about the organization can inform design decisions. Yet it does not claim that organization design can or should be a fully "analytical" process. As Georges Romme (2003) has pointed out, to create a new design, it is often necessary to transcend the current definition of the problem, and this is particularly the case with "messy problems" (Ackoff, 1999) with contradictory requirements. Such problems require creative re-conceptualization to be resolved. A methodology thus does not remove the need for creativity. A methodology may, however, aid managers in focusing the problem solving efforts on the right issues, in planning and managing the design process, in providing tools for the collecting and analysis of data, and in testing and validating ideas that are generated.

Sequence of activities in re-design projects

The methodology proposed here is divided into three main phases: Analysis, Design, and Implementation. These phases may in turn be divided into nine more detailed steps (see Table 8.2). In the following it is described in more detail how to perform each step using examples from actual re-design projects.

Step 1. Setting the agenda

Organizational re-design processes potentially entail significant costs yet have uncertain outcomes. Even a limited restructuring of a

Table 8.2 Phases and steps of the proposed methodology

Phase	Step
1. Analysis	1. Set the agenda 2. Analyze the current organization 3. Define design criteria
2. Design	4. Develop the organizational architecture (strategic design) 5. Select the preferred model 6. Operational design
3. Implementation	7. Create transition plan 8. Implement 9. Evaluate

single department often takes months to implement, saps time and attention from core activities, and may even result in key members leaving the department, if they are disappointed with their new roles. In a larger, multi-unit organization, the costs and risks multiply: A poorly executed re-design process may cause a deterioration of the organization's long-term financial performance. Experienced leaders are well aware of such risks. How, then, are re-design processes initiated? The risks inherent in changing the organization imply that no re-design will be initiated without a strongly perceived need for change.[4]

For most management teams, there are many issues competing for attention, and it usually requires a strong champion to ensure that "the organization" enters as an item on the decision-making agenda. Key decision makers must be confronted with the issues, reminded of the need to act, and become convinced that organization re-design is an appropriate solution. The key purpose of this initial step, which is called "Setting the agenda", is precisely to create a consensus among key stakeholders about the need for change.

A fundamental insight in organizational behavior is that motivation to change is created when key stakeholders perceive a significant gap between the *current* and the *potential* performance of their organization (or of an organizational sub-unit).[5] To evaluate current performance one may use both perceptual and objective data. There are numerous sources of data that may be consulted. Obviously one should make use of whatever standard measures the organization uses to track the performance of its processes (e.g., time, quality, and cost) and financial results (e.g., profitability of different sub-units). Other useful sources are employee surveys and customer surveys, which document how the organization is perceived and in many cases contain findings that reflect strengths and weaknesses of the current organizational model.[6]

To evaluate what the *potential* performance level is, or should be, it is natural to start with the organization's strategic goals and consider

4 In fact, there is some evidence that suggest that managers frequently wait too long to make required changes (Miller & Friesen, 1980; Tushman & Romanelli, 1985).

5 The individual-level psychological mechanisms creating motivation to change are explained in "self-discrepancy" theory developed by Higgins (1987).

6 A lot of information, down to the sub-unit level, can often be obtained from employee and customer surveys by first considering the statistical results, and then conducting a qualitative analysis of the comments made by respondents to pinpoint more specifically the causes of problems that are suggested by the statistical analysis.

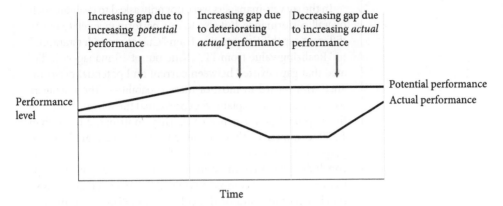

| Increasing gap due to increasing *potential* performance | Increasing gap due to deteriorating *actual* performance | Decreasing gap due to increasing *actual* performance |

Potential performance
Actual performance

Performance level

Time

Figure 8.1 Changes in an organization's actual and potential performance over time[7].

the organizational implications of the goals. One may also compare the organization to other similar organizations, or to an idealized view of what the organization would look like, if it were optimally designed (Sachs, 1999). Of course, the gap between an organization's current and potential performance is not static, and may widen during the design process. The gap may increase because managers perceive that the actual performance is decreasing, or because the potential performance increases (i.e., the ambition level is raised) (see Figure 8.1).

It is helpful to ask managers to evaluate the organization's relative performance level in the early phase of a design process (see Case Example 8.1). If they indicate that there is a gap between their current and their potential performance, one can then examine the factors that prevent the organization from achieving its optimal performance level. In this manner, it is possible to confirm that stakeholders do perceive that there exists a potential for performance improvement, and that an organizational re-design would be the appropriate intervention to realize this potential.

7 The general format for this chart has been borrowed from Sachs (1999).

Case Example 8.1: Assessing the gap between current and potential performance

In a survey distributed to in a large telecom company, 300 senior managers were asked to evaluate the current performance of the company relative to competitors and compare it to the performance level they believed the company would need to attain in order to realize its strategic objectives. The results were visualized in a chart similar to the one shown in Figure 8.2. At the time of the survey, the company was experiencing increased competition from smaller and more nimble competitors.

In the survey, managers were not only asked to evaluate their overall performance, but also to rate performance related to 10 different capabilities, ranging from "Customer understanding" to "Realizing value from IT." Nine out of 10 managers indicated that gaps existed between current and potential performance with regard to most of these capabilities. The managers were also asked to explain what prevented them from achieving their optimal performance level. They contributed more than 1,300 comments. These comments were then analyzed to pinpoint the underlying causes of the capability gaps. It was concluded that a common denominator for many of the gaps was organizational complexity, which led to an inability to take timely decisions, and/or difficulty in mobilizing resources in support of strategic objectives, and/or low productivity. For example, managers were concerned that an inordinate amount of time was spent on internal processes, rather than on external, market-focused work.[8]

8 Of course, a performance gap as defined here may be caused by a number of different factors and these findings may not necessarily generalise to other organizations.

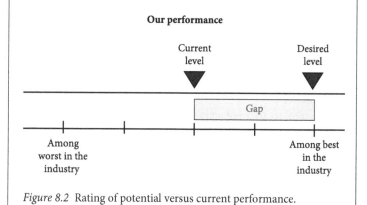

Our performance

Current
level

Desired
level

Gap

Among
worst in the
industry

Among best
in the
industry

Figure 8.2 Rating of potential versus current performance.

It should be emphasized that the goal is not to develop solutions in this initial phase, nor to identify the exact cause of any problems. The goal is simply to consider whether organization design is a contributing factor to a performance gap, and, if this assumption is confirmed, develop a shared consensus among key stakeholders about the need to act. This should allow the creation of a clear *mandate* for a re-design process. By mandate we here refer to an explicit decision to form a re-design project, a clarification of the desired outcomes, and a timeline and overall plan for the project. It is also helpful if leaders at this point can agree on some key principles for how the process should be executed: Who should be involved? How will decisions be made? Do we aspire to a design process that will produce *alignment, coherence, and trust*? It is important to set the tone early about the guiding principles – and ensure that one has a common understanding of what they entail. It is much more difficult to introduce such principles later in the process, if one discovers that processes begin to derail in an unexpected direction.

As mentioned, most leaders will need some kind of support in the re-design process. The type and level of support required will depend on the complexity of the change that is considered. In a large organization undertaking significant change, it is customary to form a dedicated project team with internal and/or external resources. The key responsibilities of the project team is to plan the overall re-design process, collect and analyze data about the organization, facilitate management meetings, develop design options, and support the implementation of the chosen model. In a smaller firm, or in a large firm undertaking less radical changes, it may suffice to have a part-time internal or external advisor supporting the leader. In any case, if multiple units are affected by the decisions that are made, we assume that *central coordination* of the process will be required in order to achieve a coherent design. This does not imply that designs are developed in a "top down" fashion, on the contrary, we shall advocate the use of a highly participatory approach. The need for coherence does mean, however, that decisions cannot be taken in isolation as different sub-units are interdependent; each play a role in the same work processes and changes in the structure of one unit may positively or negatively affect the ability of other sub-units to perform their tasks.

Step 2. Analyzing the current organization

Occasionally, managers may question whether it is necessary to spend time and money analyzing the current organization. Once a project mandate is formed – why not proceed directly to designing the new organization? Indeed, some "re-organizations" simply consist in a quick re-drawing of the formal reporting relationships for the senior executives of the organization. However, the information that is most readily available, such as organization charts, usually provide little or no relevant information about how work processes are performed, how resources are currently utilized, or about interdependencies that exist between units. In addition, it is not uncommon to find that managers have divergent views about how the current organization actually works – something which usually leads to divergent views regarding how it *should* be designed in the future. By investing time in analyzing the current organization, one collects data that are vital in order to take appropriate decisions regarding future designs and also creates a foundation for building trust in the process, by involving managers and employees in identifying improvement areas and potential solutions. This in turn makes it possible to implement the chosen design in less time and at less cost. Thus one should not underestimate the value that can be derived from analyzing the current organization in an early stage of the re-design process.

We have found it useful to provide three key deliverables in this phase. The first is a high-level map that visualizes the *Operating model*, that is, the key units and their main interfaces (see Figure 8.3).[9] It is intended to capture the essence of how the organization currently works, in a user-friendly format, without requiring a full-blown process mapping. The map may be created in a workshop setting, with representatives from the organization or the sub-unit being analyzed, or a consultant may draw the map based on information derived from interviews with managers and employees. In either case it is often necessary with a few iterations before one arrives at a map that everybody feels adequately expresses the current design. Although the resulting map is important in itself, and will become indispensable in the subsequent design steps, equally important are the questions that are raised in constructing the map, and the ability this confers to create shared understanding among the participants in the process.

It is helpful to follow certain conventions when drawing the map. One can mimic a "value chain" logic by placing suppliers on the left of the diagram, the target organization in the middle, and its customers or users on the right.[10] Similarly, one may place management teams and governing bodies (e.g., steering groups) in the upper part of the diagram and more operationally focused units in the bottom part. One should strive to identify the most important interdependencies between the units by focusing on the key outcomes that units are responsible for providing (One will end up with a more complicated drawing if one includes the many cross-unit activities that are performed in order to achieve a certain outcome.) In most cases this type of map makes it possible to

9 Other authors have used similar graphical tools to illustrate the workings of organizations (e.g., Rummler & Brache, 1990; Ackoff, 1999; Haeckel, 1999).

10 However, unlike a value chain or flow chart of work processes, the placement of the boxes on the diagram does not represent a time sequence (e.g., a unit on the left side does not necessarily perform the first step in a process).

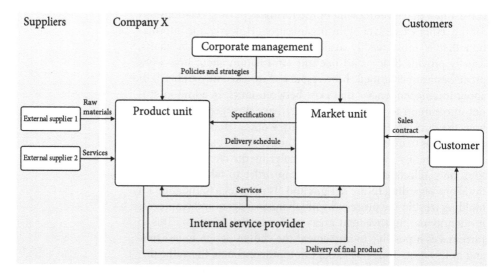

Figure 8.3 Generic template for documenting an organization's operating model

summarize the workings of an entire organization on one page; however, it is of course possible to produce similar maps for different sub-units if additional detail is needed.

The second deliverable is a list of *functional requirements* for the organization. As described in Chapter 1, this term has been borrowed from systems designs terminology, and basically entails defining what the required outputs are. One starts with the overall question: What are the desired results (or outcomes) that this organization is accountable for producing? One then breaks down this top-level requirement into sub-requirements. The format for this deliverable is shown in Table 8.3a and 8.3b. (It is advisable to use verbs in the description of functional requirements and nouns for the design parameters.) As in other fields, such as engineering and IT, requirements express "what" the system should produce, or what outcomes it should be able to provide, and should ideally be *solution neutral,* i.e., the requirements should not presuppose the choice of a given organizational structure or otherwise limit the choice of certain solutions. The challenge of describing *how* requirements are to be fulfilled will be handled in the subsequent phase of the re-design

Table 8.3a Examples of high-level functional requirements (from actual client projects)

Organization	Functional requirements
Software firm	1) Sell software products and services 2) Provide customer support 3) Manage software products 4) Build software products 5) Develop next generation product concepts 6) Support sales and marketing process
Governmentally funded body responsible for food certification	1) Perform farm audits 2) Manage food certification programs 3) Contribute to increased recognition of and market access for food products that have been certified 4) Develop new certification programs and services 5) Plan and administer processes
Geophysical company	1) Market and sell services 2) Develop Multi Client library 3) Perform seismic data acquisition services 4) Provide data processing services 5) Perform data interpretation services 6) Manage projects 7) Provide GeoScience support
IT function in global engineering firm	1) Manage IT Operations (Service Management) 2) Develop applications 3) Maintain applications 4) Provide project support 5) Provide information management services 6) Manage relations with internal customers 7) Manage global IT resources

(Continued)

Table 8.3a (Continued)

HR function in oil services firm	1) Develop individual capability (training and development) 2) Motivate and manage performance (performance management) 3) Shape the workforce (staffing and succession) 4) Build workgroups & culture (survey feedback processes) 5) Perform personnel administration processes 6) Manage employee data 7) Support expatriation process 8) Analyze and report HR data
Metropolitan municipality department responsible for health care	1) Provide support for elected leaders 2) Oversee centers and institutions delivering health services 3) Ensure coordination across municipal districts 4) Develop new services and work processes

Table 8.3b Example of decomposition of a functional requirement

Functional requirement	Sub-requirements
3 Manage products	8.1 Capture customer requirements 8.2 Define Product Road Map 8.3 Follow up implementation of customer requirements 8.4 Perform technical marketing of products 8.5 Monitor customer satisfaction

process, in which organizational units, processes, and roles will be designed that *perform* the functions that have been defined in the current planning step.

In some cases, it may be hard to create consensus around what the functional requirements actually are. The root cause is often compromises that have been built into the current organization due to a lack of clear strategies or priorities, or because of disagreements between different stakeholders. To resolve such issues, it may be necessary to take a step back and reconsider the very mission and purpose of the organization. Stephen Haeckel (1999) suggested a useful exercise, in which the organization's key stakeholders are asked to identify the organization's *reason for being*. The Reason for Being expresses the organization's purpose, or what it exists to do, as opposed to what it must do to exist (specific examples are provided in Chapter 5.) By reducing ambiguity about the organization's overall purpose, one is more likely to succeed in developing a set of clear requirements.

While developing the *operational model* and the *functional requirements*, one should also ask managers to assess strengths and weaknesses of the current organizational design, particularly in light of any new strategic goals or changes in the business environment.

Pre-existing sources of data, such as employee and customer surveys, may also be scrutinized for information that shed light on current organizational functioning. The final deliverable in this step, then, is a list that summarizes these findings and their implications for the new design.

Some additions and variations of the above process may be warranted, depending on the purpose and scope of the re-design project. It may be necessary to consider the current business processes and interdependencies in more detail than the high-level map described above (Figure 8.3) suggests. One may use an electronic survey to collect data from employees in various sub-units. In the survey, employees may be asked about the tasks that they perform and who they collaborate with in performing these tasks. It may also be necessary to collect information about current roles and responsibilities as well as the hierarchical structure within the sub-units. (For "strategic", corporate level re-design projects, it will usually suffice to cover the senior management roles at this stage.) Finally, many re-design projects will involve the re-allocation of resources, for example, if cost reduction has been defined as one of the objectives for undertaking the re-design. In such cases it will be necessary to collect information about current resource utilization. At times, the company's existing databases or Enterprise Resource Planning (ERP) systems do not contain sufficiently detailed data (or do not contain data in the appropriate format) and it may therefore be necessary to collect this information directly from managers, for example, in the form of a survey where managers estimate how resources are utilized across different projects, products and business processes.[11]

11 The organization chart (which usually only shows the permanent positions and reporting structure) is a poor guide to estimating how resources are utilised, as organizations increasingly rely on projects, networks and cross-functional teams.

Step 3. Defining design criteria

Many managers who contemplate the introduction of a new organizational model proceed directly to the solution stage, by outlining different alternative organizational models. If we return to the requirements for the design process (Table 8.1), it is clear that this approach is problematical for both political and psychological reasons. Presenting only the outputs of a thought process – such as a new organizational model – often generates resistance that complicates the implementation of the model. Stakeholders need to understand the rationale behind the choice of the solution and, ideally, be provided with the chance to influence how that rationale is construed.

A key assumption is thus that we should make the decision criteria – which we call *design criteria* – explicit; moreover, that we should enlist extensive participation in defining the design criteria to ensure that they reflect the concerns and interests of the key stakeholders. For this reason the third step that we suggest is to identify a set of design criteria that expresses the desired characteristics of the future organizational model. An example would be "Our future organizational model should help us become more customer-focused", or "The new organization should help us reduce costs" (see Tables 8.4a

Table 8.4a Examples of design criteria

Organization	Design criteria
Software firm	1) Promote integration/interoperability between our products, and with other products used by target customers 2) Allow us to capture the requirements of customers in our target markets 3) Create clarity with regard to accountability (of roles/units) 4) Ensure effective coordination across teams and sub-units 5) Allow the development of next generation solutions 6) Be scalable to support growth
Governmentally funded body responsible for food certification	1) Ensure balanced resource utilization across our different food certification programs 2) Increase the orientation toward our key stakeholders/users 3) Realise synergies between our different areas of work 4) Ensure developmental opportunities for our staff 5) Lessen the administrative burden for the director
Geophysical company	1) Promote business development (e.g., commercialization, mergers & acquisitions) 2) Create clarity with regard to accountability 3) Ensure that customers perceive us as one integrated geophysical company 4) Prevent conflicts between product areas regarding resource utilization
IT function in global engineering firm	1) Contribute to a more flexible cost base 2) Increase "manageability" of IT 3) Increase business focus of IT 4) Support operation as a single enterprise 5) Facilitate cost effective delivery of IT services
HR function in oil services firm	1) Ensure that the Group HR function can effectively support the implementation of key strategic HR initiatives 2) Ensure that units in different business areas receive a consistent service level from HR 3) Establish Group HR as a strategic partner to line managers
Metropolitan municipality department responsible for health care	1) Improve our ability to support the elected leaders 2) Accelerate the development of new services 3) Maintain and further develop our competence base 4) Clarify and simplify roles

and 8.4b for further examples). Some design criteria will likely follow as direct implications of the corporate strategy – for example, an organization that has established a growth strategy will need an organization is capable of delivering growth. Other design criteria can be derived from interviews with line managers, and may relate

to, among other things, issues that they consider to be important in realizing strategic objectives or factors that impede or facilitate organizational effectiveness more generally.

It is important to distinguish between *design criteria* defined in this manner and *functional requirements*[12] (cf. Step 2 above). The main purpose of developing design criteria is to aid decision makers in selecting among alternatives; this means that they are temporary, that is, mainly relevant in the design process itself (in Step 3 and in the evaluation phase, Step 9). Different organizational models will to a greater or lesser extent satisfy the design criteria. Functional requirements, on the other hand, are intended to describe the "functionality" of the organization, or, put differently, the *required capability* of the organization. All of the organizational models that are developed in the design phase should satisfy the functional requirements, otherwise they will not constitute viable decision alternatives.[13]

The main purpose of design criteria is to allow systematic evaluation of different alternative organizational models. However, as the above description should have made clear, the role of design criteria extends far beyond that of serving as a tool for *decision making;* they not only help select between a set of alternatives, once developed, but also aid in the development of the alternatives, and in the subsequent implementation of the preferred alternative. On the one hand, design criteria set boundaries on the solution and – if correctly formulated – ensure that the outcome of the design process will be aligned with strategic goals and current needs of the organization. On the other hand, because design criteria are explicit, as opposed to tacit or implicit, they make it possible to include a large set of stakeholders in a dialogue aimed both at refining the criteria and in building support for the organizational changes that they may lead to. In fact, managers may *test* the validity of the criteria – and the stakeholders' commitment to them – by posing the question: "If we are able to design an organization that satisfies the design criteria – which you have all contributed to formulating – would this organization help us address our current challenges and achieve our goals?" If the response is affirmative, one is ready to proceed in the process; in the reverse case one needs to go through this step one more time.

Some managers may have doubts about the realism of the approach advocated here. One concern is that it is simply too difficult to identify precise and relevant design criteria. Thinking in terms of criteria requires a relatively analytical mindset, and some people will have difficulty articulating criteria, although they may be perfectly able to distinguish between the relative attractiveness of various options, once presented as more concrete solution models. A facilitator in the design process may employ a couple of techniques to address this challenge. One is to avoid asking the participants about the design criteria directly, but rather infer the criteria based on how participants describe strengths and weaknesses of the current organization. Similarly, one may also allow the current step (Step 3) to overlap somewhat with the

12 Design criteria in organization design can be compared to constraints in engineering and architectural design. For an interesting discussion of the role of constraints, see Vandenbosch & Gallagher (2004).

13 Stated more precisely: The organizational models that are considered should all have design parameters (DPs) that satisfy the functional requirements (FRs). They may differ, however, with regards to the number of DPs and the relationships between the FRs and DPs. A generic design criterion (described in Chapter 2) is to minimize coupling between FRs.

subsequent step (Step 4), by "zig-zagging" between the development of the criteria and the development of organizational models (cf. Suh, 2001). The facilitator may ask different participants to first describe an ideal organizational model and then ask them to consider what benefits this model would confer.[14]

A related question is how detailed the criteria need to be. (The examples provided in Table 8.4a indicate that the level of detail will differ from one organization to the next.) Sometimes design criteria are stated at such a high level of abstraction that it is virtually impossible to disagree or challenge the proposed criteria. The key principle here is that the criteria should be specific enough to allow decision makers to differentiate among the alternative models that are being proposed.[15] For example, in one of the examples provided in Table 8.4a, the client was comparing three relatively simple models for organizing the IT function in a global engineering firm. In order to differentiate between the models it was necessary to decompose the criteria to more detailed criteria as shown in Table 8.4b.

Perhaps the most important concern is that "political" considerations will outweigh any design criteria developed through a participatory process. In one company, the manager who led the re-design process expressed doubts that the CEO would in fact make use of the design criteria, derived from extensive interviews with the key managers in the organization (as well as with the CEO himself). It may be counter-productive to initiate a participatory process if there is no real intention to make use of the input provided by the participants. It may in some cases be worthwhile to discuss this issue openly with the executive initiating the re-design process and explore whether it is possible to change the conditions under which the re-design is being conducted.[16] The leader may fear losing control, in that the final outcome may be different from what he or she had in mind when the re-design was initiated, and thus "reserves the right" to short circuit the participatory process by imposing his or her own preferred model. In such cases one should attempt to create a higher level of trust in the process; for example, by revisiting the original intent and discussing the rationale behind the chosen design approach. If the leader's own criteria differ from those of the organization's other stakeholders, it may be worth investigating the cause of the discrepancy. It may be a "political issue"; the leader may possess information related to the choice of organizational model that he/she does not want to share with the followers. But the discrepancy may also be due simply to different interpretations of the organization's

14 This is similar to the "Functions follows form principle" that was proposed by Goldenberg & Mazursky (2002).

15 In some cases it may be helpful to rank the criteria. For example, if one has identified 10 criteria based on interviews with managers, one may in a brief follow-up survey ask the same managers to rank these criteria by importance.

16 Argyris (1990) describes specific interventions that can be used to deal with individual defensive routines in cases similar to the one described here.

Table 8.4b Example of decomposition of design criteria

5 Facilitate cost effective delivery of IT services	5.1 Achieve more effective resource utilization and management
	5.2 Contribute to lower application maintenance costs
	5.3 Facilitate lower infrastructure costs
	5.4 Allow re-use of systems, processes and procedures across units

strategic challenges and their organizational implications. If so, it will obviously be helpful if these interpretations can become the subject of open inquiry among the participants in the design process.

Step 4. Develop the organizational architecture (strategic design)

The purpose of this step is to develop, describe and evaluate altern- ative organizational models. A set of functional requirements was defined in Step 2. The first question in this step is what the design parameters are – that is, the organizational units, processes, and roles that are required to ensure that the functional requirements are fulfilled. (This process essentially *allocates accountabilities* to different organizational units.) As suggested by Ackoff (1999), it may be helpful to distinguish between those requirements that are related to providing *inputs* (i.e., internal services), manufacturing or delivering outputs (i.e., *products or services* to end customers), and to *marketing and selling* products or services. This leads to an initial grouping of the organization into three types of units – input units, output (or product) units, and market units (cf. Table 4.2 in Chapter 4).

Once the accountability for different functions (functional require- ments) has been defined, the main task is to consider the required *linkages* between different sub-units, roles, or processes. For example, two interdependent sub-units may be linked hierarchically, by estab- lishing a reporting relationship to the same manager, or they may report to different managers yet coordinate informally, or be linked in terms of an internal value chain where one unit is defined as the internal supplier and the other as the internal customer. (Different ways of analyzing the linkages and interdependencies between sub- units is discussed more fully in Chapter 7.)

Alternative organizational models that are developed in this phase will likely differ in terms of a number of factors. One of the alternatives may imply a shift in the resource model, in that a unit that is currently a cost center would be transformed to a profit center. Another altern- ative may imply a need to build informal networks across units in order to support information sharing and collaboration. A third alternative may hinge on the establishment of new decision forums (for example, a product innovation board with representatives from different busi- ness units). None of these changes will appear on the usual organiza- tion chart that only displays individual positions or units and their reporting lines.

In Chapter 1, we discussed five "layers" of design parameters (Table 1.6). All of these may need to be considered in an organization re-design process. At a minimum, we would suggest that *each altern- ative model* that is developed in this step should be described in terms of its operating model, resource model, and governance model.

–   A chart illustrating the key units and their main interfaces (cf. Figure 8.2 above) and a table mapping the organizational units against the functional requirements, can be used to document the proposed *operating model*.

– A chart showing the nature of resource flows and a description of each unit's financial accountability (whether the unit is defined as a revenue center, profit center, cost center, etc.) can be used to describe the proposed *resource model*.

– A chart showing the formal reporting relationships and a description of decision processes and governance bodies may be developed to express the *governance model*.

A more complete description of the alternative models would include a definition of customer-supplier roles of the main internal units and a consideration of the informal mechanisms that are necessary for a model to function as intended; for example, whether a model presupposes that different units find informal ways to coordinate their efforts or share knowledge.

A final element that may be relevant is *costs*. At this stage one rarely has the information required to perform a detailed analysis of the cost impact of the alternatives being considered. Nevertheless, one may consider some of the key cost drivers associated with the different models that are developed. As an illustration, different organizational models may differ sharply in terms of *span of control* (cf. Chapter 6) and *the number of locations*. Although one has yet to draw a complete organization chart covering all hierarchical levels, one may still consider the top 4–5 levels of the organization and count the number of management positions per level for each of the alternatives that are proposed. Similarly, one may create a simple table with the key work units and their proposed location in the different alternatives.

The approach that we advocate is clearly broader than the stereotypical process of redrawing reporting lines on the organization chart. At the same time, it should be noted that the required documentation is not necessarily very extensive. The key purpose is to capture the essence and provide stakeholders with sufficient information to evaluate the main alternatives against each other; only the selected model will be specified in detail (in Step 6 described below).

Step 5. Comparison and selection

The purpose of this step is to select the preferred model. The first task is to compare the proposed models against the design criteria. Although the formal leader of the organization normally has the final say, other stakeholders – either the management team or a larger group of participants – may be involved in evaluating the alternative models or in forming a recommendation to the leader.

When attempting to compare the proposed models against each other, one may discover that the design criteria have not been formulated in a specific enough manner to allow meaningful comparison. If a design criterion is "increase customer focus", how is this used to differentiate between alternative models? Is a more decentralized model good or bad for customer focus? The solution is obviously to decompose the criterion further, for example, customer focus may relate to the ability to understand customer requirements, to develop new products, to serve customers in certain regions and segments, and so on.[17]

The same holds for the solution alternatives that one is comparing against each other. It is obviously important that not only the key features but also that *the implications* of each alternative are well understood. It can be helpful to perform a "dry run" to spell out the differences. One may develop specific examples of hypothetical decision processes, or ask managers themselves to consider how they would behave in each of the proposed models:

> "In one of the alternatives we have developed, Sales is organized regionally. If you were the head of Sales, how would you ensure that we coordinate across the regional sales units to serve larger, global accounts?"
>
> "In our first alternative, IT has been defined as an internal service provider and the line organization as the internal customer. In this model, who has the authority to take decisions regarding changes to the IT infrastructure?"

Once one is confident that the criteria are sufficiently precise, and the alternatives well understood, one can start evaluating the alternatives against each other. Most practitioners do not use any advanced sophisticated scoring systems to compare alternatives, other than asking executives to rank design criteria and evaluating the models against the criteria (e.g., using a simple three-point scale, see Case Example 8.2). More advanced methods would certainly add sophistication but the concern is that they would not make up for the loss of transparency and simplicity; more complicated scoring systems require more of an "expert" approach and are less convenient in a group setting.[18] The key priority in this should step should rather be to avoid some well-documented and frequent decision errors, such as making decisions based on insufficient data, a narrowing of focus (the tendency to focus on a small sub-set of alternative choices), and the tendency to view more favorably the decision alternative about which one has the most information (Bazerman, 1994). If one follows the steps proposed here, one should minimize the chances of making such errors.

At this point, some of the participants in the process may have growing concerns about the risks of introducing changes to the organization, while others may express disappointment if none of the proposed new models appear to be "optimal." One may include the current organizational model as one of the alternatives that is considered (as it is always an option not to change anything) and evaluate the current model using the same criteria. Experience suggests that few management teams, when asked to make such a direct comparison,

17 Note that this does not necessarily imply that one needs a higher number of design criteria; one can leave out design criteria that do not differentiate between the solution models and select a limited number of highly specific criteria that do.

18 Nevertheless, there may be occasions where more advanced scoring and evaluation systems are warranted, and there is a large literature on multi-criterion decision making that may be helpful for those seeking guidance on the right approach (for an overview, see Triantaphyllou, 2000).

19 In circumstances where one suspects that there may be pressure to conform to peers' or leaders' opinions, one may reduce bias by asking participants to evaluate the options against the criteria in an anonymous survey, rather than using group discussions (see Anderson & Brown, 2010, for a review of research on this issue).

20 The most senior executives (with the exception of the CEO) will often have most to lose from a radical re-design. In a historical analysis of organizational changes in three major industrial concerns, Gammelsaeter (1991) found that new organizational models had generally been introduced by middle managers, who more easily found support for the changes with the CEO than with members of the executive team.

express that they prefer their current model to the alternatives developed during the re-design process.

In describing the development of design criteria above, we noted that participants may sometimes wonder whether political concerns will override the input that they provide to their leaders during the process. However, in the decision phase, the reverse situation is also likely to arise: Leaders may harbor concerns about the objectivity of the input that they have received from their followers. Re-designs inevitably change the power structure in organizations. Leaders may thus suspect that the preferences that are voiced during the re-design process reflect the personal interests of various stakeholders rather than their professional judgment of the relative merits of different options.

There appears to be three possible ways in which to mitigate this particular concern. By emphasizing design criteria rather than solutions in the early stage of the process, as we have recommended, it should become easier to separate the substantive issues from personal interests. Secondly, by including a larger group of managers in the design process, one ensures that the design criteria also reflect the views of people (including middle managers) outside the current leadership team (although it is clear that allegiances to senior executives in some cases may color their assessments).[19,20] Third, we do not believe that the final decision should be a democratic one, even if a larger group of people are involved in developing and evaluating alternative models. It is the prerogative of the leader to select the organizational model, and vesting the decision authority with the leader is particularly important in situations where one or more of the design alternatives imply a considerable change of status, authority, or economic rewards for one or more of the key stakeholders in the organization.

Case Example 8.2: Developing a new organizational model for SoftCo

The following case may serve to illustrate how one proceeds from having developed design criteria to the selection of a preferred model. The case is drawn from a software firm (referred to as "SoftCo") that provides advanced modeling tools used by large oil companies to estimate the size of oil reservoirs and optimize oil production. Most of the product development resources are located at the firm's headquarters. The firm has small sales subsidiaries in the Americas, Russia, East Asia, Middle East, and Scandinavia. The managing director initiated a re-design of the firm following the formulation of a new strategy. His initial concern was the lack of customer orientation and unclear prioritization of product development resources. The members of the management team agreed with this diagnosis, but they also added other concerns. They felt that the firm needed to focus more strongly on long-term innovation, and said that it was unclear whether anybody was accountable for developing next generation product concepts. They were also dissatisfied with the lack of collaboration and coordination across the different teams and units in the organization.

A slightly simplified version of the firm's current operating model[21] is shown in Figure 8.4. The figure illustrates the key interdependencies between the two main units, Product Development and Regions (i.e., sales subsidiaries abroad). In addition, there was a small marketing team at the company's headquarters. The allocation of responsibilities is listed in Figure 8.5.

An important function in software firms is *Product Management*, which includes marketing tasks such as the identification of customer requirements as well as planning activities such as the definition of product "road maps" (i.e., plans for future software releases) (Cusumano & Selby, 1995). In SoftCo, this role had been allocated to the Product Development unit, rather than to Marketing, Sales, or a dedicated Product Management unit. The Marketing unit focused primarily on providing support for the local marketing and sales activities performed by the regional offices, although it was also formally responsible for feeding back data about customer requirements. The Product Development unit would both define the specifications (FR_3) and manage the software development projects (FR_4) (Figure 8.5). In fact, this dual role would be performed by the same person within the product development unit, namely the *product manager*. However, rather than being an impetus for more customer-focused technical work, the experience with this model was that marketing activities, such as identification of customer needs and the development of marketing materials, were consistently de-prioritized, due to a lack of resources in the product development organization. There was also dissatisfaction due to a lack of transparency and accountability, particularly with regard to the allocation of product development resources. Requests for changes to the existing software and for new features would come from many regional sales offices, as well as from the Marketing unit. Managers felt that the current model made it difficult to prioritize different requests, representing the needs of different market segments; at times the product development organization would seemingly favor the requests from the most vocal sales office rather than features aimed at the strategically most important customer segment. As shown in Figure 8.5, the sales subsidiaries were responsible for both sales and for first line customer support. But this combination was seen as less problematical, and (as indicated in Figure 8.4) the two functions were allocated to two different teams *within* the subsidiaries.

21 The example focuses mainly on the issues related to Product Development; other issues that were considered in the re-design process (e.g., the organization of customer support) have been left out for clarity.

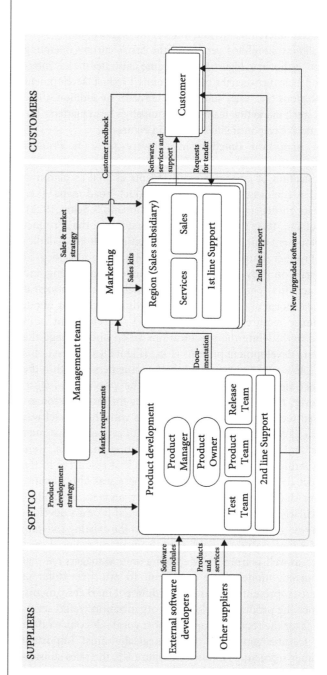

SUPPLIERS

CUSTOMERS

SOFTCO

Figure 8.4 Current operating model of SoftCo.

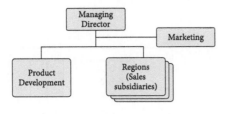

#	Functional requirements (FRs):	Design parameters:		
		Region (sales subsidiary)	Product development	Marketing
1	Sell software products and services	X		
2	Provide customer support	X	x	
3	Manage software products		X	x
4	Build software products		X	
5	Develop next generation product concepts		(x)	

Figure 8.5 SoftCo's current organizational model. In the design matrix, "X" signifies strong relationship, "x" weak relationship, and "(x)" a possible/uncertain relationship.

During the process, two alternative organizational models were developed (see Figure 8.6). The first alternative depicts a relatively common model for software firms, where a product management (or product marketing management) unit identifies the customer requirements for the products and is held accountable for the product's commercial performance. In the second alternative, this responsibility is allocated to the sales unit (or more precisely, to a sub-unit reporting to a senior vice president overseeing Sales & Marketing).

All members of the management team participated in evaluating the models against each other (see Table 8.5). The consensus was that both of the alternatives would strengthen the firm's customer orientation (but Alternative 2 to a lesser degree than Alternative 1). Overall, establishing Product Management as a separate unit (Alternative 1) was viewed as the best option by the majority of the team. There were concerns that organizing Product Management within Sales (Alternative 2) would create a short term focus, with the risk of product management resources being utilized as support personnel for sales managers in busy times (it was mentioned that it would be analogous to the problems, described above, resulting having placed Product Management within Product Development). It was also mentioned that subjugating Product Management within Sales would lead to less clarity

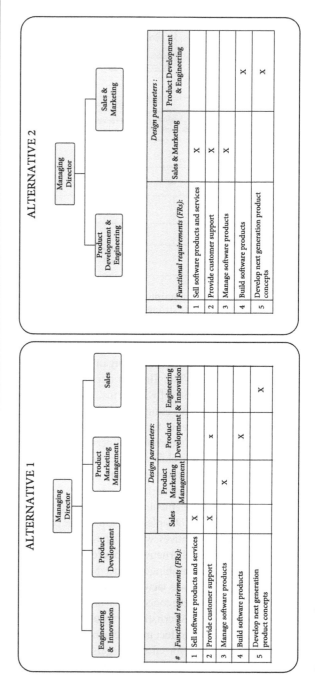

Figure 8.6 Alternative organizational models developed during the re-design process at SoftCo.

Table 8.5 Evaluation of alternatives against design criteria

Design criteria	Evaluation		
	Current model	*Alternative 1*	*Alternative 2*
Increase customer orientation by improving identification and prioritization of customer requirements	☹	☺	😐
Create clarity with regard to accountability (of roles/units)	☹	☺	😐
Ensure effective coordination across teams and sub-units	😐	😐	☺

about roles and responsibilities. At the same time, the team agreed that Alternative 1 involved some risk of creating tension between the teams belonging to the respective units, and that it would be critical to establish effective work processes across product development, product management and sales in this model. Another prerequisite that was mentioned was allocating sufficient capacity to enable a new Product Management unit to fulfill its mandate. It was decided to look more closely at these issues in the transition planning phase (see Case Example 8.2 (cont.) below).

A major advantage of the chosen model was the ability to create distinct internal customer and supplier roles, allowing greater clarity with regard to accountability. The Product Management unit would represent the "Voice of the Customer" – defining "what to build" – capturing market requirements and defining new product features (as well as supporting product roll-outs). Product Development would be the internal supplier, developing software in response to the requirements set by Product Management (determining "how to build it").

Step 6. Operational design

So far in the process, we have been considering organizational models at a relatively high level of abstraction: The purpose of Step 4, for example, was to describe alternative organizational models at a sufficient level of detail to allow decision makers to evaluate the models against each other. Once one has selected the preferred model, however, it is necessary to *operationalize* the model. The main purpose is to reduce the implementation time by clarifying the implications of the selected model as much as possible and create a blueprint that can guide the transition to the new model. This involves detailing the high-level *operating model, resource model,* and *governance model* developed in Step 4.

To complete the *operating model,* one may start by detailing the design of the sub-units of the organization. One may define the mandate for different sub-units of the new organization by describing their key purpose, the outcomes that the units are accountable for, and the key performance indicators that will be used to measure their performance. (More specific techniques for supporting operational level design are discussed in Chapter 5.) One may then consider how the new model will impact working processes, in particular, those that cross unit boundaries. It is rarely necessary to do a full-blown process mapping to implement a new organizational model, but one should identify those working processes that are directly impacted by the organizational change in order to clarify interfaces and specify how different units are to collaborate (e.g., at what step in a process handovers should occur or how two interdependent units are to coordinate their work).

Another important question is *sizing* – how many people are needed in each unit? One can estimate the required size of units based on assumptions about the volume of business and the productivity of teams and individuals. For routine, transactional jobs, it is possible to use the formal methods for calculating required capacity described in the operation management literature (see e.g., Slack et al., 2004). For example, the required number of staff in a customer support center can be calculated based on the expected number of calls and the duration of each call. For more complex jobs such as the ones described in Case Example 8.2, it is difficult to use formal methods, as there may not be a fixed set of inputs or outputs variables. Nevertheless, in most organizations it may be possible, over time, to develop guidelines to support capacity estimation (e.g., "we need 1 test engineer for every 5 developers").

To operationalize the *governance model* one defines the hierarchical structure of the organization, that is, the number of layers, the type and number of roles at each level, and the formal reporting relationships (see Chapter 6 for a detailed discussion). The governance model should also specify the leadership teams and decision forums in the new organization, i.e., their mandate, participants, meeting frequency, and so on.

Similarly, the *resource model* may be operationalized by defining more precisely the financial resource flows in the company. The resource flows will depend on the financial accountability of each unit (i.e., whether a unit is defined as a profit, cost or revenue center) and the transfer pricing principles chosen by the company for transactions between internal units. Some services are likely to be charged on a cost basis, whereas others may be charged out based on a market rate.

In this step one also defines *individual roles and responsibilities*. At a minimum, the requirements of key leadership roles are defined, but depending on the scope of the change and the implementation approach, it may also be necessary to define roles for all levels of the new organization. Experience suggests that relatively short and simple role descriptions will suffice. The definition of individual roles can be seen as a further decomposition of requirements and design parameters. One may thus rely on already existing pieces of documentation from the preceding steps in the process in defining individual roles.

Case Example 8.2 (Cont'd): Operationalizing the selected organizational model in SoftCo

Returning to the case described above, we may consider how SoftCo approached the key activities in the Operational Design phase. An internal working group was formed and charged with the task of defining key roles, clarifying interfaces, and estimating resource needs.

It was mainly the design of Product Development and the new Product Management units that needed further clarification. Both of these units would be led by a vice president (VP), who would be part of the management team. The VP for Product Management would lead a team of product managers, managing the product from a market perspective, whereas the VP for Product Development would lead a team of *technical* product managers, taking ownership of technical product requirements and supporting development projects.

A key question was how to structure the sub-units and roles at the next level. As pointed out by Galbraith (2002), if each sub-unit is designed according to its own logic, managers are forced to work across a high number of interfaces, creating significant barriers to lateral processes. For this reason, a "mirror image" structure was chosen in SoftCo, where both Product Management and Product Development were structured based on (client) work flows, which corresponded broadly to different software packages or modules (or different sets of functionality within the software). For example, some users will use SoftCo's software tools to support seismic exploration, whereas others would use it for reservoir modeling or simulation. With the mirror image structure, each product manager within Product Management would have one primary partner within Product Development (see Figure 8.7).[22] (In addition, other roles were defined, such as the Chief Architect, with responsibility for integration across products.)

22 However, the downside of this structure is that each product manager will potentially interface with all of the sales subsidiaries. But the interdependencies toward the subsidiaries were viewed as less critical.

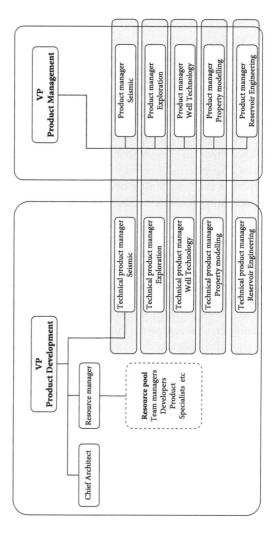

Figure 8.7 New organizational model in SoftCo.

It was estimated that each of these roles would require a full time position. The financial cost of the new structure was then calculated, taking into account that some capacity would be freed up in the current Product Development and Marketing functions (by transferring tasks to Product Management). Even though the establishment of the new function would involve a significant additional cost (through the establish- ment of new product manager positions), this cost was considered in relation to the company's growth projections. Investing in a stronger product management function was seen as critical in order to achieve further growth. (The ability to identify and prioritize customer requirements had been defined as the most important design criterion earlier in the process.) In addition to the increase in capacity, the new model also provided scalability: The size of the organization may be scaled up or down without changing the basic logic. For example, if the workload is less than anticipated for a certain module, it is possible to combine the responsibility for two workflows into one role. If the workload increases, it is possible to add staff members supporting each product manager. It is also possible to add new product manager roles (although it may then be necessary to introduce another vertical layer, in the form of a senior product manager role, in order to maintain a reasonable span of control).

The internal working group also considered how the new organizational model would affect key working processes and

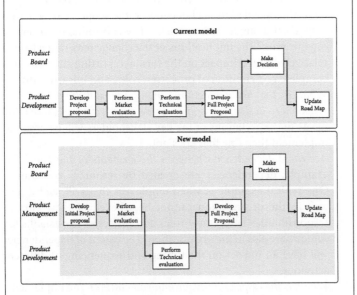

Figure 8.8 Changes in work processes due to new organizational model at SoftCo (excerpt).

interfaces. One example would be the process of updating the product road map based on proposals for new or improved functionality. One clarification that was made was that the product managers should receive the proposals and take them through the different stages of evaluation. It was also decided that the VP of Product Management should present the full Project Proposal to the Product Board (in the current model, this was done by the VP of Product Development). The changes from the current model are highlighted in Figure 8.8.

Step 7: Transition planning and Step 8: Implementation

The purpose of the transition planning step is to select the overall transition approach and to create a plan that minimizes implementation costs and "time to value", that is, the time that elapses before the intended benefits of the new model are realized. Typical implementation activities that need to be prepared include the distribution of information to employees (and possibly customers and other stakeholders), changes in infrastructure (physical facilities, IT systems, etc.), and the recruitment of people to new roles.

There are five – somewhat interrelated – questions that one may consider before selecting the transition approach:

1 *What is the scope of the proposed change?* It goes without saying that the transition approach, and the effort required to implement the new design, will depend on the scope. A new design may affect a single unit or role, a few sub-units, or an entire organization. The implications of the change may range from a relatively limited impact on the formal reporting structure to a complete re-definition of processes, roles, and infrastructure.

2 *What is the likely reaction among key stakeholders to the proposed re-design?* Obviously, a new organizational model that meets the expectations of the key stakeholders will be easier to implement than one that does not.

3 *Are there dependencies between the elements of the plan?* For example, dependencies are created by resources constraints. One typical example is when employees that will staff a new unit in the organization cannot be relieved of their current responsibilities before new roles and processes are established somewhere else in the organization. The extent of dependencies will have an impact on the timing and sequencing of different activities.

4 *Who has the responsibility for implementation?* The implementation may be directed from the center (i.e., the top management team or a project team at the headquarters) or be delegated to

the different operating units (e.g., business units or subsidiaries) in the company.

5   *What approach do we want to take in allocating people to new roles?* In some re-design processes, units are kept largely intact and the change only affects the leaders of units. Other re-design processes, however, lead to a re-allocation of roles within the units and thus affect a larger group of managers and employees. If this is the case, one must consider how staff the positions in the new organizational structure.

From a change management perspective, it is usually desirable to implement a new organization design gradually, in separate phases. For example, many of the large companies that introduced Shared Services organizations during the 1990s did not establish a global Shared Services unit covering all functions from the start, but instead focused on an initial set of core functions (e.g., accounting and payroll), or a limited geographical area, and then gradually increased the functional and geographical scope. Many companies have found that it is most effective to test out new organizational models in a single unit before they are adopted on a company-wide basis. A gradual approach obviously limits the risk of interference with core operational processes of the firm and provides managers with the opportunity to adjust and refine the design solution before it is rolled out on a larger scale.

Yet it is not always possible to use a gradual approach. For example, consider a bank that establishes a customer support center in order to consolidate telephone and e-mail support to customers. The customer center is to be staffed by employees recruited from branch offices. However, these employees currently perform tasks in the branch office that need to be handed over to other employees before they can be released and transferred to the new customer center. And the ability of other employees to take on these tasks may in turn depend on receiving additional support from the customer center. When there are interdependencies of this type, one must implement several elements of the new organizational model simultaneously.

Employee communication is sometimes viewed as the key element of the implementation phase. However, in the approach described here, communication is not an activity that is added at the end of an executive planning process in order to "sell" the proposed change. Communication is rather an on-going activity, and if the preceding steps have been completed, the key requirements for achieving stakeholder acceptance should already be in place. First, it should be possible to communicate a clear rationale for the change, based on strategic consideration and analysis of organizational functioning (Steps 1 and 2). Secondly, it should be possible to present a clear plan for how the process will unfold and the implications for the individual, based the operationalization of the organizational model and the transition plan (Steps 6 and 7). The chances of gaining acceptance for the proposed the chance will have been increased by including representatives from different units in the process (e.g., in developing design criteria and in identifying areas of improvement in Steps 2 and 3) and by allowing the members of sub-units to fine-tune elements of the design during the implementation process.

There are generally two approaches one can take in planning an internal staffing process in those cases where a larger group of people must be allocated to new roles. The traditional approach is that leaders appoint their subordinates in a "cascading" process, i.e., leaders of top level units are appointed first, and they in turn appoint their direct reports, and so on. The main advantage of this approach is speed; an entire organization with several hundred or even thousands of employees can be staffed in the course of a few weeks. However, this approach is sometimes implemented in a manner that compromises trust. People may not be consulted about alternative roles. Managers under time pressure will often select people that they already know rather than take the time to carefully define job requirements and consider alternative candidates. The alternative is to create an internal recruitment process where all new positions are announced (e.g., on the company intranet) and where employees are encouraged to apply for one or more positions. This approach has been used by some firms during large transformations such as mergers. Until recently, the main drawback of this approach was the protracted time (and cost) resulting from having to describe all new positions, distribute information, process applications, and optimize the allocation of people based on their preferences and the company needs. However, software tools are beginning to appear that that allow such internal staffing processes to proceed quickly, even when thousands of employees need to be re-allocated to new roles.[23]

23 An example is a software tool called Organization Weaver, developed by the firm BrightArch (www. brightarch.com)

Step 9. Evaluation

No matter how much care one takes in planning an organization re-design process, there will always be elements of the design that don't work as well as intended. Yet few organizations carry out *systematic, planned evaluations* of organization re-design processes. This means that elements of the design that do not work as intended are not detected and corrected by management, although they may cause great frustration among lower level employees. Worse still, it may create the impression that the new design is cast in stone, and that one should refrain from attempts at improving it. Much has been said about the ability of managers and employees to undermine new organizational models by resisting to fully implement them. Equally common, however, may be the tendency to implement new organizational models exactly as proposed, without informing management of the need for adaptations.

Given the costs and risks involved, one may ask why organizations do not carry out evaluations as a routine aspect of organizational re-design processes. We can only speculate that it may be due to a combination of lack of executive time and attention, and perhaps also individual defensive mechanisms (Argyris, 1990): Leaders who have succeeded in introducing a particular solution may not enjoy being confronted with indications that the solution is less effective than promised. Unfortunately, such an attitude will in itself decrease the chances that the design will be successful in the first place, since nearly all design solutions are dependent upon an openness to adapt to the particularities of the organization and a willingness to improve the design over time.

In addition to correcting elements of the design that do not work as intended, performing evaluations also contribute to *organizational learning*. In evaluating a re-design project, one may both ask to what extent the design is achieving its intended benefits (it is here logical to refer to the design criteria that were defined), and to what extent the re-design *process* was deemed effective. Experience suggests that asking stakeholders to provide their input in such reviews not only uncovers areas for improvement but frequently also help in identifying important accomplishments that deserve recognition. Most managers and employees notice not only the inevitable errors and shortcomings of the processes but also how creating new designs bring out creative ideas, forge new ways of collaboration, and help in implementing long overdue changes to their organization.

Although few organizations explicitly include evaluation as a step in the organization re-design process, an encouraging trend the inclusion of items related to organization design in annual employee surveys. The items being used may not correspond exactly to the design criteria of re-design projects, but nevertheless provide important feedback on issues such as the clarity of goals and accountabilities, customer focus, and process performance; some firms also tap more directly the degree of satisfaction with new organizational models.

Summary and discussion

This chapter has outlined a nine-step methodology for re-designing complex organizations (see Table 8.6 for a summary). The overall goal of the approach is to minimize the "time to value" of new designs. To achieve this, it contains a design process aimed at maximizing *Alignment, Coherence,* and *Trust.* The methodology also incorporates some key element of the axiomatic design approach, in particular, an explicit consideration of functional requirements in relation to design parameters (i.e., organizational units, processes, or roles). The most important techniques and interventions are formulated as a set of *Design Propositions* at the end of the chapter.

The approach presented here builds and extends on existing methodologies and has been successfully applied on a number of client engagements. Nevertheless, the development of this approach

Table 8.6 Proposed steps in the organization design process

Step	Main purpose	Typical deliverables/outcomes
1. Set the agenda	Establish consensus regarding the need for change and the approach to follow	• Decision to re-design organization (or review) • Project mandate and plan
2. Analyze the current organizational model	Create a shared understanding of current organizational functioning	*At a minimum:* • High level map of units and interfaces (operating model) • Requirements /key outcomes for main processes *For operational level design projects:* • Detailed map of processes and interdependencies
3. Define design criteria	Articulate the criteria by which a new design should be selected	• A set of decision criteria, agreed among key stakeholders
4. Develop the organizational architecture (strategic design)	Develop organizational models that satisfies the functional requirements defined in phase 2	• Two or more alternative models (visualized as *operating model* and, if relevant, *resource and governance model*) as well as traditional organizational charts indicating reporting lines. • Estimate of the costs associated with the alternative models
5. Compare and select	Select the preferred model-based on evaluation of alternative models against design criteria	• Evaluation of alternative models • Selected model
6. Operational design	Develop a complete description of the selected model	• Detailed descriptions of the operating, resource model, and governance model • Description of key individual roles and responsibilities
7. Create transition plan	Create a plan for transitioning to new organizational model	• Transition plan (may cover creation of new roles/units, recruitment to new positions; communication with employees, changes in IT systems and infrastructure, etc.)
8. Implement	Implement changes according to the transition plan	• Depending on the selected design
9. Evaluate	Evaluate to what extent the new design fulfills its purpose and make any necessary adjustments	• Evaluation of the effectiveness of the model (given the criteria that were used to select) • Corrective actions

has also raised a number of questions that deserve both academic research and pragmatic experimentation in order to develop even more effective methodologies in the future. Five research questions will be described here.

The first question relates to the development of solution models. Romme (2003) has suggested that one should begin generating solutions models very early in the design process. He argues that one risks locking the thinking of people by focusing too much on the current system. Some consultants also prefer to develop a couple of "straw man" solutions early on in the process to galvanize interest and drive the discussions forward. In this chapter we have advocated a different approach, however, as should be evident by the methodology summarized in Table 8.6. The key assumption is that it is critical to have a good understanding of the current organization before one attempts to re-design it. Another concern is that by introducing solution models too early, one may lead participants to fixate on one particular, seemingly attractive model, before data have been collected about the real challenges that the organization faces. As there are divided opinions on this issue, however, it is suggested that it become a topic for more systematic investigation.

There is also a difference – both philosophical and practical – between those advocating "idealized planning" and those representing an approach to planning and design more characterized by iterative, small steps (termed "muddling through" by political scientist Charles Lindblom (1959)). Russell Ackoff (1999) has been a strong advocate for creating an *idealized model* in the initial phase of the design process. The purpose is to help managers and employees resolve organizational problems by creating a shared model of how the organization would look if they could design it anew, without any constraints. On the other hand, there are occasions when management teams are not able or motivated to engage in "visionary" thinking and where the only chance to gain traction is to initiate the re-design exercise as an incremental adjustment of the current organization. Either approach could be useful in certain situations, however, and it would be useful for practitioners to know more about which approach to select under what circumstances.

As most other design methodologies, the approach described in this chapter makes a distinction between "strategic" and "operational" design. *Strategic design* is concerned with the so-called "umbrella structure" (Nadler & Tushman, 1997), the overall design of an organization, whereas *operational design* refers to the more detailed design of sub-units, roles, and processes. Is this distinction really valid? To what extent can you make "macro" level decisions without "micro" level knowledge? It may be possible in some cases, if the sub-units stay intact. For example, the CEO of a firm may decide to swap managerial roles or make changes in the reporting structure for the top executives, with no intention of altering the boundaries between the sub-units or the work processes at lower levels. However, there are also situations in which changes at the strategic level of a firm inadvertently affect the sub-units one or two levels down in organization (or the interfaces between them). In these situations, one should not make strategic level decisions without some know-ledge about the workings of the sub-units that constitute the organiz-ation. In general, we would expect that the success rate of re-design efforts is higher the more decision makers know about the func-tioning of their organization. New methods are under development that can identify feasible organizational designs based on "bottom up" analysis of roles and interdependencies (Worren, Soldal, & Christiansen, 2017). These methods may erase the traditional distinc-tion made between "strategic" and "operational" design.

A related question is at what point one should staff managerial positions during the design process. Many executives prefer to quickly select managers to staff the key positions once a decision has been made regarding the overall, strategic design. The managers that have been selected are then made responsible for developing the detailed, operational design for their units. Many executives believe sub-unit managers should be accountable for designing their units. Some leaders may also be concerned about breeding uncertainty among the managers in the organization, which could lead some to resign amidst doubts about their future role in the new organization. On the other hand, by nominating leaders for specific positions too early, one risks closing off design options that would have been possible if the positions were not yet filled. By delegating the operational design work to sub-unit leaders one also risks over-emphasizing the unit-specific needs at the expense of the coherence of the overall model. An alternative is involving key managers in the process in temporary working groups, yet delay the formal nomina-tion of leaders to a later stage in the process when the design of the complete model has been determined. In this approach one thus waits until the implementation phase in adding managerial names to the organization chart.

This chapter has highlighted stakeholder involvement as a necessary means to build trust and secure voluntary compliance. This is also a prerequisite for ensuring that the design is based on valid information about current organizational functioning, which in turn influences the extent to which design solutions will be well aligned and coherent. We have assumed that there will be a central design team collecting and analyzing information, developing design ideas, and coordinating the transition process. (In a large organization, the central design team will typically include both internal and external resources.) However, there are consultants that go further and advocate a fully participatory process, where much of the design task is delegated to managers and employees themselves. One example is the large group method described by James and Tolchinsky (2007) and Steil and Gibbons-Carr (2005). The key element in this approach is to gather all key stake-holders (up to several hundred) for facilitated workshops. These workshops essentially deal with all of the steps outlined in this chapter, and in the same sequence, but compressed into 3–5 days of intensive problem solving. The key rationale is that one needs commitment from the members of the organization in order to implement changes, and that people tend to commit to ideas that they themselves have participated in developing. This is undoubtedly true, but one consideration is whether groups are also able to generate high quality solutions. There is some experimental evidence that suggests that groups actually make worse decisions than individuals when asked to allocate roles or sub-divide a task, because they simplify the problem in order to be able to communicate easily with other group members when solving the problem (Raveendran, Puranam, & Warglien, 2016). An important question for future research is thus to clarify to what extent the large group method may constitute an alternative to traditional approaches for managing the design process.

Design propositions

Objective	*Create an effective organization re-design process (i.e., a process that minimizes "time to value")*
8.1 a–c	Develop design options that are *aligned* with organizational goals and strategies by: a) identifying and resolving unclear or conflicting goals at an early stage of the design process; b) ensuring that key stakeholders have a common understanding of the organization's *reason for being*; c) explicitly linking *design parameters* (i.e., organizational units, processes and roles) with *functional requirements*.
8.2 a–c	Ensure that design options that are developed are *coherent* by: a) establishing a central design team to coordinate data gathering, analysis, model development and implementation; b) ensuring that key stakeholders have common view of current organizational functioning, before they consider alternative future designs; c) mapping and evaluating the organization's units and their interdependencies (current and future operating model).
8.3 a–e	Ensure that the process creates or maintains *trust* and that the selected design is voluntarily complied to by: a) sequencing the design process to allow the development of design criteria (i.e., *principles*) to occur before the development of alternative organizational models (i.e., *solutions*);

b) involving key stakeholders in analyzing the current organization, defining design criteria, developing organizational models, and evaluating options;

c) actively communicating to employees the rationale and the benefits to the organization and the individual employee from adopting the chosen model;

d) preparing a systematic and well-structured transition process to implement the chosen model;

e) using a transparent staffing process where individuals' preferences are taken into account when filling positions.

Review questions

1 What are generic requirements to organization design processes?
2 What are the nine steps of organization design processes proposed in this chapter?
3 How do executives or other change agents "set the agenda", i.e., persuade other stakeholders that a re-design is required?
4 What are the advantages of collecting data about current organizational functioning in an early phase of a re-design process?
5 Why should one define explicit design criteria?
6 What is the difference between design criteria and functional requirements?
7 This chapter advocates the use of a systematic, "facts-based" methodology. What are the benefits of such a methodology, and what are the potential concerns some managers may have about it?
8 The chapter argues that involvement of stakeholders is necessary to build trust. Does this imply that the design decisions need to be taken collectively (e.g. by the management team or a larger group of managers)?
9 What are the key questions that one should consider in selecting the transition approach?

Research questions

1 At what point in the design process should one start to develop models of the future organization?
2 In what situations is the "idealized design" approach advocated by Russell Ackoff most effective? In what situations would it be counter-productive?
3 To what extent does knowledge of "operational" issues (such as work process interdependencies) improve the quality of "strategic design" decisions?
4 At what point in the design process should you staff managerial positions?

5 Do large group methods constitute a viable alternative to traditional approaches to re- complex organizations?

References

Ackoff, R. (1981). *Creating the Corporate Future*. New York, NY:
  John Wiley & Sons.
Ackoff, R. (1999). *Re-Creating the Corporation: A Design of
  Organizations for the 21st Century*. New York: Oxford University
  Press.
Anderson, C., & Brown, C. E. (2010). The functions and dysfunctions
  of hierarchy. *Research in Organizational Behavior*, 30, 55–89.
Argyris, C. (1990). *Overcoming Organizational Defenses: Facilitating
  Organizational Learning*. Needham, MA: Allyn & Bacon.
Bazerman, M. (1994). *Judgment in Managerial Decision Making*.
  New York: John Wiley & Sons.
Cusumano, M. A., & Selby, R. W. (1995). *Microsoft Secrets: How the
  World's Most Powerful Software Company Creates Technology,
  Shapes Markets, and Manages People*. New York: Free Press.
Dean J. W., & Sharfman, M. P. (1996). Does decision process matter?
  A study of strategic decision-making effectiveness. *Academy of
  Management Journal*, 39, 2, 368–396.
Farr, J. L. (1990). Facilitating individual role innovation. In M. A.
  West & J. L. Farr (Eds.), *Innovation and Creativity at Work:
  Psychological and Organizational Strategies*. Chichester: Wiley
Fisher, R., & Ury, W. (1983). *Getting to Yes: Negotiating Agreement
  Without Giving In*. New York: Penguin Books.
Galbraith, J. (2002). *Designing Organizations: An Executive Guide
  To Strategy, Structure, and Process*. San Francisco: Jossey-Bass.
Gammelsaeter, H. (1991). *Organizasjonsendring gjennom generas-
  joner av ledere* [Organizational changes through generations of
  leaders; in Norwegian, not translated]. Molde: Møreforskning.
Goldenberg, J., & Mazursky, D. (2002). *Creativity in Product
  Innovation*. Cambridge: Cambridge University Press.
Haeckel, S. H. (1999). *Adaptive Enterprise: Creating and Leading
  Sense-and Respond Organizations*. Boston: Harvard Business
  School Press.
Hart, S., & Banbury C. (1994). How strategy-making process can
  make a difference. *Strategic Management Journal*, 15, 4, 251–269.
Higgins, E. T. (1987). Self-discrepancy: A theory relating self and
  affect. *Psychological Review*, 94, 3, 319–340.
Hood, C., Huby, M., & Dunsire, A. (1985). Scale economies and iron
  laws: Mergers and demergers in Whitehall 1971–1984, *Public
  Administration*, 63, 1, 61–78.
Huy, N. (2001). Time, temporal capability, and planned change. *The
  Academy of Management Review*, 4, 26, 601–623.
James, S., & Tolchinsky, P. (2007). Whole-scale change. In
  P. Holman, T. Devane, & S. Cady (Eds.), *The Change Handbook:*

The Definitive Resource on Today's Best Methods for Engaging Whole Systems (pp. 162–178). San Francisco: Berrett-Koehler.

Kim, W., & Mauborgne, R. (1996). Procedural justice and managers in-role and extra-role behavior: The case of the multinational. *Management Science*, 42, 4, 499–515.

Lindblom, C. E. (1959). The science of "muddling through." *Public Administration Review*, 19, 2, 79–88.

Miller, D., & Friesen, P. H. 1980. Momentum and revolution in organizational adaptation. *Academy of Management Journal*, 23, 4, 591–614.

Morgan, G. (1986). *Images of Organization*. Thousand Oaks, CA: Sage Publications.

Nadler, D., & Tushman, M. (1997). *Competing by Design: The Power of Organizational Architecture*. New York: Oxford University Press.

Nutt, P. C., & Wilson, D. C. (2010). *Handbook of Decision Making*. Chichester (UK): John Wiley.

Pfeffer, J. (1992). *Managing with Power: Politics and Influence in Organizations*. Boston: Harvard Business School Press.

Raveendran, M., Puranam, P., & Warglien, M. (2016). Object salience in the division of labor: Experimental evidence. *Management Science*, 62, 7, 2110–2128.

Romme, A. G. L. (2003). Making a difference: Organization as design. *Organization Science*, 14, 5, 558–573.

Rummler, G. A., & Brache, A. P. (1990). *Improving Performance: How to Manage the White Space on the Organization Chart*. San Francisco: Jossey-Bass.

Sachs, W. (1999). *Adaptation Revisited*. In Proceedings of the Russell Ackoff conference, Villanova University, March 4–6.

Slack, N., Chambers, S., & Johnston, R. (2004). *Operations Management* (4th edn). London: Pitman.

Steil, G., & Gibbons-Carr, M. (2005). Large group scenario planning: Scenario planning with the whole system in the room. *The Journal of Applied Behavioral Science March*, 41, 1, 15–29.

Suh, N. P. (2001). *Axiomatic Design: Advances and Applications*. Oxford: Oxford University Press.

The Economist (2009). *Reshaping Government: Permanent Revolution*. June 13, p. 38.

Triantaphyllou, E. (2000). *Multi-Criteria Decision Making Methods: A Comparative Study*. Norwell, MA: Kluwer Academic Publishers.

Tushman, M. L., & Romanelli, E. 1985. Organizational evolution: A metamorphosis model of convergence and reorientation. In L. L. Cummings & B. M. Staw (Eds.), *Research in Organizational Behavior*, 7, 171–122. Greenwich, CT: JAI Press.

Vandenbosch, B., & Gallagher, K. 2004. The role of constraints. In R. J. Boland & F. Collopy (Eds.), *Managing as Designing*. Stanford, CA: Stanford University Press.

Werr, A., Stjernberg, T., & Docherty, P. (1997). The functions of methods of change in management consulting. *Journal of Organizational Change Management*, 10, 4, 288–307.

Worren, N. Soldal, K., & Christiansen, T. (2017). Organizing from the ground up: Developing a DSM based tool for organization design. Paper presented at the 19th International Dependency and Structure modelling conference, Espoo, Finland, September 11–13.

9 Resolving organization design dilemmas

Chapter overview

Background	• Organizational complexity is increasingly regarded as a key managerial challenge.
	• Practical tools and methodologies are needed that can be used to manage and/or reduce organization designs that stakeholders perceive as excessively complex.
Challenges	• Organizational theory is frequently criticized for being too abstract to provide guidance to practitioners intending to improve the design of their organizations.
	• The practitioner-oriented literature has so far failed to produce effective advice due to inadequate definitions and generalization of simplistic solutions.
Key question	• How can we develop a more rigorous approach that can lead to the development of specific tools and methods that practitioners can use to simplify organizational designs?
Proposed approach	• Use specific cases of complex organization designs as the starting point.
	• Identify possible generic causes that create complexity in these cases based on a mapping of functional requirements and design parameters.
	• Propose generic solutions (design propositions) that can be translated into specific solutions for handling similar challenges in other organizations.

Introduction

Organizational complexity is increasingly regarded as a key managerial challenge. One implication is that we need to consider practical tools and methodologies that can be used to manage and reduce complexity. Unfortunately, neither the academic literature nor the practitioner literature provides much guidance to practitioners on this issue. As noted in Chapter 1, current theories in the organizational sciences are generally too abstract to serve as a basis for designing specific managerial interventions. The practitioner literature has recently started to focus on complexity reduction, but the actual prescriptions do not always address the underlying causes of complexity. One issue is the definition of complexity that is used. A common recommendation is to *reduce variety* that create internal complexity, for example, cutting the number of product variants, centralizing operations, or reducing management layers (e.g., Ashkenas, 2007). In some cases, these may well be relevant options to consider. Yet it is not variety per se but the *interdependencies* between elements (roles, units, etc.) that create complexity (cf. Chapter 2). There is also a tendency to prescribe general principles for simplification rather than on developing diagnostic frameworks that can help practitioners analyze the particular problem they are confronted with and identify the most appropriate approach to resolve it. Moreover, recommendations for how to simplify organizations tend to focus on structure in isolation, instead of considering what the structure exists to do – that is, its *function*. What are the key outcomes or results that the organization, its sub-units, and individual roles are accountable for? The question is not how to simplify organizational structure per se, but how we can reduce organizational complexity *while at the same time* maintaining or even improving on the "functionality" – the ability of the organization to attain key business goals (related to financial results, process performance, costs, customer satisfaction, etc.).

This chapter builds on the key assumptions in axiomatic design theory (AD). AD assumes that *problem definition* is the key to successful design. This means that we first need to find ways to *identify and characterize* complex organizational designs, before we can consider how to simplify them. As described in Chapters 1 and 2, Suh (2001) has demonstrated how it is possible to capture the structure of a particular design solution by mapping functional requirements against design parameters. Moreover, he has indicated how one can identify common features *across* different concrete instances and identify generic principles that one can make use of when re-designing a particular system. The approach is similar to that developed by Altshuller (1985), a Russian inventor, who analyzed thousands of patents in order to identify common problem-solution relationships. Altshuller identified approximately 200 patterns common to the patents that he studied, and he termed

1 The author was either the project manager or a project participant on these projects. The methodology that was followed was to document the situation that was observed during the consulting project. For example, one tool that was used was an "issue log" where key observations, quotes from interviews, and the like were noted down throughout the project. After the project was completed, this information was summarised and a meeting with the client manager was arranged where the client manager could provide feedback on draft descriptions of the cases. In order to protect the anonymity of the individuals and organizations involved, some details in the description of the companies have been omitted or changed, while preserving the basic structure of the challenge facing the managers

these patterns for "standards." These standards are now being taught as inventive principles to designers facing similar problems (the approach is called TRIZ, which is an acronym for a Russian term meaning "The theory of inventor's problem solving") (see Figure 9.1).

Altshuller's (1985) approach was intended for engineers designing physical products, yet may also serve as a guide for developing similar frameworks in other design disciplines. The approach has already been used by marketing researchers who have identified "inventive templates" that can be used by marketing professionals to generate ideas about new product attributes and business models (Goldenberg and Mazurski, 2002).

This chapter is built around a set of brief case examples, drawn from consulting projects with firms in different industry sectors.[1] Each case describes challenges associated with a particular organizational model. The information in each case is analyzed by means of an AD design matrix and/or the design structure matrix (DSM) and formulated as a generic problem. A generic solution is then proposed, which is summarized as design propositions at the end of the chapter. The cases are tentatively categorized into five categories, based on the most salient issue in each: 1) responsibility overlaps, 2) role inconsistencies in horizontal processes, 3) excessive interfaces, 4) conflicting requirements, and 5) interdependency misalignment.

The main purpose of this chapter is to introduce a systematic approach to complexity reduction that is pragmatically valid (i.e., usable by practitioners) as well as testable (i.e., contains design propositions that may be confirmed or disconfirmed by observing the outcome of interventions in organizations) (Worren et al.,

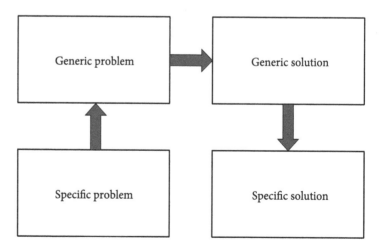

Figure 9.1 The TRIZ problem solving method.

2002). The chapter concludes with a brief discussion of how the approach may be further refined and improved. and employees in the organization described.

1. Responsibility overlaps

Central to all organizations is the concept of division of labor: In all large organizations, the responsibility for performing different tasks is allocated to different internal units (or individuals). But the allocation of responsibility is rarely perfect. One frequently occurring problem is that two or more units or individuals may have been given responsibility for the same task or process (or for the same set of decisions or objectives). There are several possible causes of such overlaps. Those with the authority to design formal structures may be unaware of the issue or may not have had the time or capacity to remove the overlap. At times, responsibility overlaps emerge gradually and may be difficult to prevent before they begin to cause friction between the units or individuals concerned.

To what extent should we be concerned about responsibility overlaps? Up to a certain point, we may have to tolerate the existence of responsibility overlaps as an unavoidable fact of organizational life, and leave it to managers to sort them out. Much of a manager's daily work is indeed spent compensating for such overlaps, by actively communicating and co-ordinating with other units that they share responsibility with for completing a task or performing a process. (There are also cases where responsibility overlaps are the result of a deliberate effort to "force collaboration" between individuals or units by creating joint goals.) On the other hand, it also seems clear that responsibility overlaps negatively affect performance in some cases. A company may have ignored defining the dividing line between sales teams responsible for two different products, resulting in internal competition and uncoordinated marketing efforts toward potential clients. The head of the IT department and the head of the Finance department may both believe that they have the required authority to select a new software package supporting finance and accounting processes. Such disagreements may slow down decision making, and often require escalation to higher level managers for resolution. If this happens intermittently, it may be deemed acceptable, but if it occurs more frequently, it may be a source of concern. Responsibility overlaps can also make it difficult to make individual managers accountable, and to reward them appropriately: Poor performance may always be attributed to the lacking effort or capability of others who participate in the same process. For this reason, it should be a general design principle to minimize responsibility overlaps as much as possible.

Let us consider the situation in an oil services company of around 500 employees. This company design and manufactures process equipment used on oil platforms, such as modules for water injection, hydrate inhibition, water/oil separation, and water treatment. It carries out engineering and production in each of its five country subsidiaries (in Canada, France, Norway, Malaysia, and the UK). The original strategy was to allocate geographical territories to each subsidiary. For example, the unit in Malaysia would serve Asian clients, the French unit would serve southern European clients, and so on. However, over time, clients had become more global, and no longer perceived the ability to carry out engineering projects locally as a prerequisite for awarding a contract to a supplier.[2] This in turn led to increasing competition among the five country subsidiaries.

A team of managers from each subsidiary were asked to participate in a project team facilitated by an internal consultant[3]. The team identified seven common product categories across the units. A key observation was that most of the subsidiaries would deliver the entire product/technology portfolio (see Table 9.1).

The main solution that was recommended was to allocate responsibility so as to minimize overlaps (Table 9.2). The subsidiaries were asked to concentrate on those areas in which they had demonstrated technological and commercial capabilities, and to drop technologies for which they did not have sufficient capabilities to gain a strong competitive position. The proposed solution had two key advantages. It would capitalize on the strengths of each unit while eliminating competition between the units.

The re-allocation of responsibility only concerned the design and engineering processes in the company. It was recommended that the sales function in each country would continue to offer the entire product range and interface with the client. (This solution is consistent with the organizational models described in Chapter 4 of this book, with sales units defined geographically, or by market

2 At the time of the project, the company that is described largely targeted large, international oil companies. Today, this firm targets national oil companies to a greater extent, and national oil companies often do require suppliers to carry out manufacturing locally.

3 I acknowledge the help of Matt Grootveld (the internal consultant on the project team) who contributed documentation and discussed this case with me.

Table 9.1 Product categories delivered by different subsidiaries in oil services firm

	Country subsidiary				
	Norway	Canada	UK	France	Malaysia
Deliver oil treatment systems	X	X	X	X	X
Deliver gas treatment systems	X	X	X	X	X
Deliver produced water systems	X	X	X	X	X
Deliver seawater treatment systems	X	X	X	X	X
Deliver utility equipment	X	X	X	X	X
Deliver internals (components)	X	X	X	X	
Deliver hydrate inhibition systems	X	X	X	X	

Table 9.2 Product categories delivered by different subsidiaries in oil firm after re-allocation of responsibility

	Country subsidiary				
	Norway	*Canada*	*UK*	*France*	*Malaysia*
Deliver oil treatment systems		X			
Deliver gas treatment systems		X		X	
Deliver produced water systems	X				
Deliver seawater treatment systems	X				
Delivery utility equipment					X
Deliver internals (components)			X		
Deliver hydrate inhibition systems	X				

segment, while product units are defined in terms of product or technology.)

A key prerequisite for splitting or re-allocating areas of responsibility in this manner is obviously that the underlying processes for which different actors or units are made responsible are in fact separable. It is assumed that the seven technology areas shown in Tables 9.1 and 9.2 are relatively independent, so that each country subsidiary may develop, design, and manufacture products related to the technology without too many operational dependencies toward the other country subsidiaries.[4] (If there is uncertainty about whether this assumptions holds, one may employ the techniques discussed in Chapter 5 in order to map interdependencies and find an appropriate grouping of activities.)

In this particular case, the solution that was selected was to *re-allocate* responsibilities among the units. However, responsibility overlaps can be resolved in several different ways. We should therefore review the options that exist *in principle* for handling similar cases. For this purpose, let us consider a simplified example of a technology company with a somewhat different structure (Figure 9.2).

Unlike the oil services company discussed above, this company had maintained engineering design and manufacturing activities at its home base, while expanding its activities by establishing pure sales subsidiaries in various countries. The products were sold based on bids submitted in response to RFQs (Requests for Quotations). Initially, both the central engineering unit and the sales subsidiary shared responsibility for the sales and marketing process. The main reason for the shared responsibility was that the sales subsidiary was highly dependent upon the engineering unit's participation in terms of evaluating technical specifications, developing a proposed solution, and estimating a price taking into account the production

4 This is one limitation of the so-called RACI matrix, a widely used tool for defining responsibilities (RACI is an acronym for Responsible, Accountable, Communicated, Informed). The RACI is a simple matrix that lists processes or decision areas on one axis and the names of units or individuals that have a role in making decisions or performing a process on the other. It does not contain any design rules or principles for how to align the responsibilities with the processes.

cost. A decomposition of the high-level functions against design parameters would look like the one shown in Table 9.3.

The initial strategy to deal with a perceived overlap of responsibility is often *specification*: One may attempt to describe the processes and areas of responsibility in more detail to see whether it is possible to isolate the more specific areas affected by overlap. In this particular case, it was found that the sales representatives in the country subsidiary were the ones that called on potential clients, identified leads, and received the RFQs; however, that the RFQs were channeled to sales engineers in the engineering unit, who developed proposals based on the client's requirements. The engineering unit and the sales subsidiaries collaborated in developing the marketing plan, and representatives from both units participated in trade fairs, distributed brochures, and placed advertisements in industry magazines. This leads to the decomposition shown in Table 9.4.

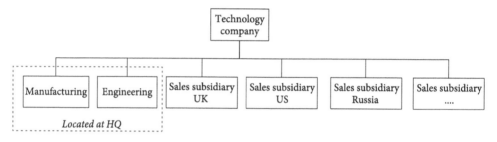

Figure 9.2 Structure of technology company discussed in text.

Table 9.3 Design matrix for sales process in technology company

Functional requirements	Design parameters	
	Engineering unit	Sales subsidiary
Perform sales and marketing process	X	X

Table 9.4 Specification of responsibilities

Functional requirements	Design parameters	
	Engineering unit	Country subsidiary
Develop marketing plan	X	X
Identify new prospects		X
Develop proposals based on RFQs	X	
Set prices	X	X

As one specifies in more detail how responsibility is defined, one does not remove the overlaps themselves, but one may at least create some clarity regarding where the overlaps actually occur. Instead of simply stating that sales and marketing is a shared responsibility, it allows the company to allocate the responsibility for identifying new clients to the country subsidiary, while the engineering unit could be made accountable for developing proposals. One may not approve of this particular split of responsibilities, but it would probably be fairly effective in terms of creating clarity of accountability: One can imagine separate (and relatively independent) indicators being developed to measure performance, such as the number of new leads identified by the country subsidiary, and the "hit ratio" (sales made to proposals developed) for the product unit.

A second approach, which can be termed *Standardization,* could be applied to handle the overlapping responsibilities with regard to pricing (cf. Table 9.4). If there are frequent disagreements between the country subsidiary and the engineering units regarding pricing, one could develop standard guidelines or norms for how pricing decisions are to be made. For example, it is common among car manufacturers to centrally develop price guidelines for car models, while national car importers or dealerships are able to adjust prices within a certain range based on the local market conditions.

One responsibility overlap listed in Table 9.4 remains to be clarified, namely the shared responsibility for the marketing and sales plan. This overlap could be handled in the same manner, by detailing different aspects of the plan (e.g., focused on the global, regional, segment level) and specifying what aspects of the plan each unit would be responsible for. On the other hand, the development of a marketing and sales plan is often an annual event. For this reason, an approach we may call *sequential separation* is possible: The two units may jointly participate in this activity, if it can be conducted prior to – and be considered an input to – the other activities that they are responsible for. It may therefore be treated differently from the other, more continuous processes that are listed in Table 9.4.

The possibility of *re-allocating* the responsibilities remains (that is, changing which unit or actor is responsible for a given activity, process, or decision). In this case, sales subsidiaries interfaced with clients yet the engineering unit developed the actual proposals to them. This may work well in some companies where client needs are expressed as written, technical requirements. Splitting the initial sales and the subsequent proposal development process would be less appropriate in firms where customer needs are more implicit, so that direct client interaction is required, or where clients for other reasons prefer to interact directly with the technical experts. Different options for re-allocating responsibilities exist in such cases. One option is to give the responsibility for the entire sales process to the market unit (i.e., the Sales subsidiary). (This would not necessarily involve the transfer of technical personnel from the engineering unit to the subsidiary: The technical experts in the engineering unit could be considered internal suppliers to the country subsidiary's sales people in the proposal development process.) It would then be the country subsidiary that would request assistance and also be held accountable for sales revenues.

One also has the option of re-drawing the formal boundaries between units, an option we could call *restructuring*. For example, if two units are jointly responsible for the same activity, one has the option of merging the two units into one. A country subsidiary and a product unit may be merged into one. This could be an appropriate option if the product in question is only produced for one national market. By merging two units, one also removes the responsibility overlaps, viewed at the top level, as shown in Table 9.5. Of course, the issues will remain *within* the units that are merged, unless one follows the same process as above in terms of clarifying responsibility at a more detailed level.

2. Role inconsistencies in horizontal processes

The marketing and sales process that we have described above is one example of a "horizontal" business process that depends on the collaboration and negotiation between units performing different roles in the internal value chain. A number of processes that were once managed by means of vertical hierarchical governance are now managed in this manner. Another example is IT: Whereas IT staff in large companies used to be organized in IT departments within different business units, many companies have consolidated IT departments into Shared Services organizations that provide services to business units based on service level agreements (SLA) that stipulate quality levels and costs (Table 9.6). Although this model has gained widespread adoption, many firms encountered – and still encounter – significant challenges in the attempt to transform hierarchical relationships into effective customer-supplier processes underpinned by formal commitments such as SLAs. One important challenge is to appropriately define the role of customers, responsible for requesting services and monitoring service delivery, and internal suppliers, who are supposed to perform the work needed to deliver the services.

In this section, we will consider the situation confronting the Chief Information Officer (CIO) of a large engineering firm with a

Table 9.5 Design matrix for merged units

	Design parameter
Functional requirements	*Engineering unit and country subsidiary*
Perform sales and marketing process	X

global IT function of altogether 500 people. A couple of years prior to taking on this role, the IT function had been split into two parts. The responsibility for hardware (servers, networks, etc.) and IT support was allocated to an IT department organized within the firm's Shared Services unit, whereas the responsibility for software related to core processes (application management and mainten-ance) had been allocated to IS departments, organized within the business units. The rationale behind the model was that the software teams needed to be organized as part of the line organization, as their work typically involved configuring software to the unique needs of engineering projects. When establishing the Shared Services unit, the leaders of the business units had been skeptical of introdu-cing another boundary between the application developers and the users, and had argued that the people providing software that supported core processes should remain in the line organization.

At first sight, this particular split of responsibilities does not appear to be illogical (see Table 9.7). However, when examining how this design intent had been decomposed further, several prob-lematical areas were discovered.

In order to evaluate the model, both IT managers and the internal clients were interviewed. The overall finding was that the Shared Services unit generally failed to deliver services to the expected level. Representatives from the engineering projects complained that it was unclear who they should contact in order to fix problems and that it took an inordinate amount of time to respond to change requests (i.e., requests for changes in the features or functionality of applications). An IT manager that was interviewed remarked that the organization was "messy." Meetings with representatives from IT, IS, and the business units were characterized by "fire fighting" to resolve technical issues, and little time was left to discuss how to

Table 9.6 Design intent behind the Shared Services model

	Design parameters	
Functional requirements	*Business units*	*Shared Services*
Define, request, and approve services	X	
Provide services		X

Table 9.7 Design matrix for firm that split IT and IS

	Design parameters	
Functional requirements	*IT (Shared Services)*	*IS (Business unit)*
Perform IT operations	X	
Provide core applications		X

address more longer term needs. There were also concerns about high costs due to inefficient work processes and a lack of standardization of applications across different internal units.

It was concluded that the mess was caused by several interconnected problems, such as unclear goals and performance standards (i.e., the SLA), inappropriate grouping (i.e., suboptimal boundaries), and lack of effective governance (including diffuse and overlapping accountabilities). A particularly interesting implication of the split between IT and IS was the effect that this design decision had had on horizontal customer and supplier roles. It was found that the particular allocation of responsibilities in this company meant that IS sometimes was a supplier to IT, a client of IT, a joint supplier, or a link or mediator between IT and the line organization. This is represented in the design matrix shown in Table 9.8.

Just as the same individual may have more than one role assigned to him or her (e.g., the same person may be manager and sales representative), an organizational unit may also perform multiple functions. One challenge in conceptualizing this problem is that the roles or functions may be logical when considering a single work process separately, yet they may be inconsistent when considering how they have been defined *across* different work processes. Three examples are illustrated in Figure 9.3 a–c using the visual formal of the so-called commitment protocol described in Chapter 7. When establishing or revising the SLA, it was IS, on behalf of the business unit, who would negotiate the terms (Figure 9.3a). (There was no service level agreement that covered the services that IS provided to the business units.) In other words, in this case IS performed the role as "customer," which was natural, in that IS departments were organized within business units. At other times, however, IS would be a kind of supplier to IT, for example, in resolving a software application error (Figure 9.3b) or creating access to applications (Figure 9.3c). It was also observed that the help desk, which was organized within IT, would log requests (and thereby allocate capacity by assigning the task to an IT specialist) not only for its own personnel but also for personnel belonging to IS. In other words, the purported supplier (IT) "managed" the client's (IS) resources in this case.

As pointed out in Scherr (1993), the existence of multiple roles sometimes occurs legitimately, but it can also be a source of confusion and even represent a conflict of interest. In this particular case,

Table 9.8 Actual design that was implemented (compare to Table 9.6)

Functional requirements	Design parameters	
	Business units	*Shared Services*
Define, request, and approve services	X	
Provide services	X	X

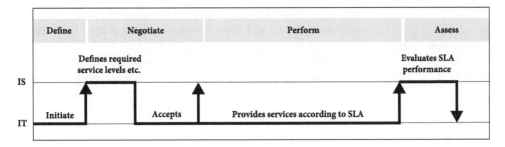

Figure 9.3a Commitment protocol for SLA management process.

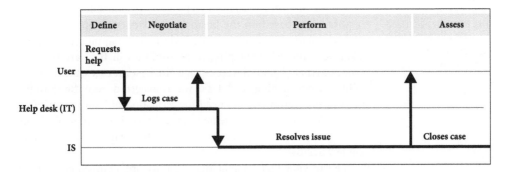

Figure 9.3b Commitment protocol for software error resolution process.

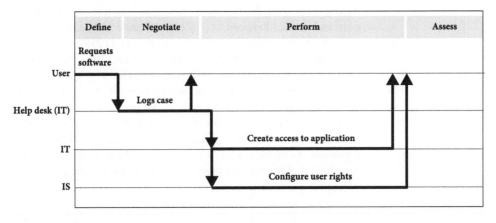

Figure 9.3c Commitment protocol for process used to create access to application.

end users were uncertain about who to contact for help and they also experienced that IS and IT were poorly coordinated. As illustrated in Figure 9.3c, both units would independently send a message to the user confirming that requested software had been installed or that access had been created. As already mentioned, responsibility overlaps not only create unnecessary hand-offs but may make also make it difficult to create clear accountability for process performance. One example in this company was that the unit performing the customer role (IS) was asked – in its role as "SLA manager" (Figure 9.3a) – to monitor, evaluate, and approve outcomes that it itself has been an active participant in producing (Figure 9.3b–c).[5]

A large restructuring project was initiated by the CIO to address these issues. The solution proposed by the restructuring team was to integrate the IT and IS units, that is, transfer the IT personnel to the Shared Services organization. By implication, the services provided by both units would then be included in the SLA. Moreover, a new role of "customer manager" was defined that would be responsible for all IS/IT deliveries to a business unit. To create a clear customer role it was also proposed that each customer manager should relate to a Business Information Officer (BIO) responsible for defining requirements based on the business unit's current operations and business plans. Finally, more detailed process mapping was undertaken to remove overlapping responsibilities in the various work processes that IT and IS were engaged in. In some cases, the responsibility for performing work tasks was transferred from the IS to the IT sub-unit, removing the need for escalation of issues from IT to IS. The design matrix for the new organization is shown in Table 9.9 (Note that this decomposition preserves the design intent shown in Table 9.6 above.)

We can view inconsistent roles in horizontal customer-supplier processes as a special case of overlapping responsibilities as described in the cases in the first section of this chapter. In addition to the overlap of responsibility, however, we are here also dealing with a potential *conflict* between two roles performed by the same person or unit. As mentioned in Chapter 8, Scherr (1993) developed a methodology that can be applied in such cases. The first step is to define the internal suppliers and customers. By creating a chart that shows the requests and the commitments made in a work process involving suppliers and customers (cf. Figure 9.3a–c) one can then "test" the consistency of the design by considering the roles at various steps in the same process as well as across different work processes. As we have seen in this example, if inconsistent roles are identified it may require a regrouping of tasks/roles, the creation of

5 We may add that such role reversals are not unique. Scherr (1993) noted that a client that engages a consulting or accounting firm is the paying customer, but also performs the role of supplier of information about the client's operations. However, the "client-as-customer" role is usually performed by a different individual than the "client-as-supplier" role.

Table 9.9 Revised allocation of responsibility between business units and IT/IS

	Design parameters		
	Business unit	Shared Services	
Functional requirements	*(BIO role)*	*IT*	*IS*
Define, request, and approve services	X		
Perform IT operations		X	
Provide core applications			X

new roles, and/or the transfer of responsibilities between internal units.

3. Excessive interfaces – "Everybody connected to everybody"

Organization design methodologies have traditionally placed a strong emphasis on the importance of effective coordination and integration. As discussed in Chapter 8, one frequently discovers "disconnects" in large organizations, that is, poorly functioning or lacking interfaces between sub-units (i.e., there are latent interdependencies that are not identified and/or enacted). Yet the emergence of higher levels of internal complexity has also created the opposite phenomenon: The existence of too many interdependencies. The question in such cases is not how to introduce more or better coordination, but how to expend less effort on unnecessary coordination.

A telecom company with around 9,000 employees created a team to deliver strategic HR services to the organization. Ten strategic HR advisors were recruited, whose main role was to serve as project managers in developing and rolling out various HR systems and initiatives, such as leadership development programs, performance management tools, and employee surveys. The company was comprised of eight different divisions. In addition to serving as project manager for a particular initiative, each strategic HR advisor had therefore been asked to take on an additional role, that of client relationship manager, in which they each served as the advisor to one of the divisions. The key responsibility in this role was to build and maintain effective relations with the internal clients in the divisions (line managers and HR managers) and ensure that programs, tools, or processes were adapted to the current needs in the divisions. The key responsibilities of the ten HR advisors are summarized in Table 9.10.

One of the initial observations[6] was that members of the unit seemed to spend quite a lot of time in meetings. It was also noted that many different members of the strategic HR team seemed to be involved in the same process, and that it was difficult to identify who the real "owner" was of a given process or activity. To understand the organizational design of this team, it is helpful to map interdependencies of the various members of the team against each other (see Figure 9.4).

When looking at Table 9.10 and Figure 9.4 it becomes apparent that the dual roles had created a complex structure with a high number of interdependencies. For example, the project manager for the annual employee survey (Advisor #1 in the matrix) would need to communicate with the HR advisor representing each of the divisions (Advisor #2-#8) in order to perform his/her role. (Typical issues to coordinate with the divisions would include how to communicate the purpose and timing of the survey, how to provide feedback about

6 Many of the services were delivered in collaboration with external consultancies or training and development providers. The author was asked to serve as the external project manager for one of the projects during the autumn of 2007. The author was given a desk and worked side by side with the members of the unit for about five months.

Table 9.10 Allocation of responsibilities in Strategic HR team

	Strategic HR team									
	Advisor 1	Advisor 2	Advisor 3	Advisor 4	Advisor 5	Advisor 6	Advisor 7	Advisor 8	Advisor 9	Advisor 10
Plan an implement employee survey	X									
Plan and implement performance management process		X								
Plan and implement leadership development process			X							
Plan and implement competency management process				X						
Plan and implement succession planning process					X					
Assist in planning and development of performance management process						X				
Assist in planning and implementing leadership development process							X			
Assist in planning and implementing employee survey								X		
Assist in planning and implementing employee survey									X	
Assist in planning and implementing competency management process										X
Serve as client manager for Division 1	X									
Serve as client manager for Division 2		X								
Serve as client manager for Division 3			X							
Serve as client manager for Division 4				X						
Serve as client manager for Division 5					X					
Serve as client manager for Division 6						X				
Serve as client manager for Division 7							X			
Serve as client manager for Division 8								X		

the results to different leadership teams in the division, and so on.) The project manager is herself the customer contact for one division, so there is one divisional representative to meet with. There is also one colleague who assists in the project (Advisor #9) (Figure 9.5). Advisor #1 thus has dependencies toward all but one of the other team members, and the situation is similar for the other advisors – the distribution of roles is one that ensures that "everybody is connected to everybody." (This situation was exasperated by the unit's norm of always communicating with a division through the customer contact.) This design leads to high coordination costs: There are 56 interdependencies in the matrix (out of 90 potential bilateral interdependencies), or 5.6 on average per advisor, and that is only counting the strongest, most critical interdependencies between the advisors – the matrix does not show potential, weaker interdependencies that may exist between the advisors or dependencies

	Advisor 1	Advisor 2	Advisor 3	Advisor 4	Advisor 5	Advisor 6	Advisor 7	Advisor 8	Advisor 9	Advisor 10
Advisor 1		X	X	X	X	X	X	X	X	
Advisor 2	X		X	X	X	X	X	X		
Advisor 3	X	X		X	X	X	X	X		
Advisor 4	X	X	X		X	X	X	X		X
Advisor 5	X	X	X	X		X	X	X		
Advisor 6	X	X	X	X	X					
Advisor 7	X	X	X	X	X					
Advisor 8	X	X	X	X	X				X	
Advisor 9	X							X		
Advisor 10				X						

Figure 9.4 Work process interdependencies between members of strategic HR team.

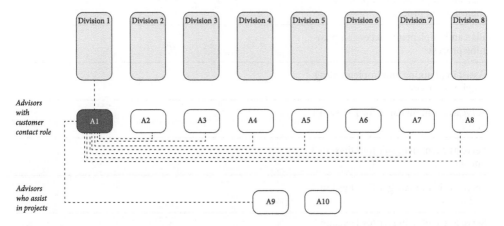

Figure 9.5 Situation for Advisor 1 in the original structure (8 internal interdependencies plus 1 with the division that he/she is the customer contact for).

toward entities such as external service providers, other corporate functions, etc.

There are two main approaches that one can take to reduce the number of interdependencies in such a case. The most obvious solution is to remove the dual roles, which we could call *specialization*. The distribution of roles would depend on the expected workload for each role, but as an example, we could create two teams. The first would have six process owners or specialists, each working on only one strategic HR process: The employee survey, performance management, leadership development, succession planning, or competence management. The second team would consist of four customer contacts, each responsible for two divisions. The resulting matrix (Table 9.11 and Figure 9.6) shows that this rather simple structural change would reduce the number of interdependencies by around 25% (from 56 to 42). For Advisor 1 it would reduce the number of interdependencies from nine to five (Figure 9.7). Such a

Table 9.11 Revised allocation of responsibilities within Strategic HR team

	Strategic HR team									
	Advisor 1	Advisor 2	Advisor 3	Advisor 4	Advisor 5	Advisor 6	Advisor 7	Advisor 8	Advisor 9	Advisor 10
Plan an implement employee survey	X									
Plan and implement performance management process		X								
Plan and implement leadership development process			X							
Plan and implement competency management process				X						
Plan and implement succession planning process					X					
Assist in planning and implementing employee survey						X				
Serve as client manager for Division 1 and 2							X			
Serve as client manager for Division 3 and 4								X		
Serve as client manager for Division 5 and 6									X	
Serve as client manager for Division 7 and 8										X

	Advisor 1	Advisor 6	Advisor 2	Advisor 3	Advisor 4	Advisor 5	Advisor 7	Advisor 8	Advisor 9	Advisor 10
Advisor 1	▓	X					X	X	X	X
Advisor 6	X	▓								
Advisor 2			▓				X	X	X	X
Advisor 3				▓			X	X	X	X
Advisor 4					▓		X	X	X	X
Advisor 5						▓	X	X	X	X
Advisor 7	X		X	X	X	X	▓			
Advisor 8	X		X	X	X	X		▓		
Advisor 9	X		X	X	X	X			▓	
Advisor 10	X		X	X	X	X				▓

Figure 9.6 Work process interdependencies after revising the allocation of responsibilities.

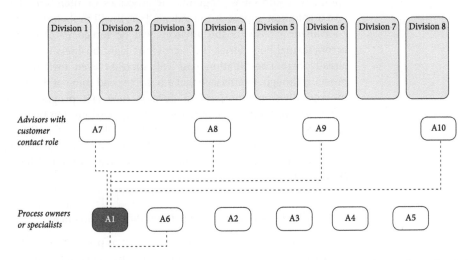

Figure 9.7 Situation for Advisor 1 after revising the allocation of responsibilities (5 interdependencies).

change implies a considerable decrease in coordination cost – which translates directly into added capacity that can be used on the core tasks that the unit is responsible for. It is important to note that this improvement does not come at the cost of added dependencies at the other end: Each business unit will still have one common inter-face toward the Strategic HR team.

This solution has the additional advantage of creating greater role clarity for the individual advisor: One would be either be a specialist, focusing on a certain service or initiative (at least for a period of time), or a generalist, consulting with the internal clients and planning how to roll out the programs and processes.

One disadvantage with this solution is that it may reduce task variety for the individual. It also increases the distance between the specialists and the internal clients that the specialists serve in the divisions. This may be a concern among some HR professionals, who would prefer a model that places them in direct contact with their internal clients more often (Kates, 2006). One approach that would address this concern would be to step outside the matrix, so to speak, and distribute the roles among the eight divisions. The strategic HR team would then be reduced in size (or even disbanded) and the ten HR advisors would instead be transferred to the divisions, where they might report to the divisional HR manager. This solution could be appropriate as part of an initiative to decentralize resources. It adds capacity to roll out the programs and processes in the divisions at the expense of capacity in the corporate center dedicated to the development of common new programs and processes. Distributing the strategic HR roles among the divisions will be more problematical in the absence of such a rationale. If the company requires new programs and processes, or intends to maintain a common approach to strategic HR, it will probably increase coordination costs as the advisors will be forced to coordinate across formal boundaries (i.e., across the eight business units): An already high coordination cost will increase even further. It is possible, though, to envisage that advisors spend some of their time in cross-divisional projects to develop new HR programs and processes even if they are organized within divisions. On the other hand, once they have been transferred to a division, the division may be reluctant to see the experts work on projects outside the division (as long as the division is allocated the cost for the HR heads) (Kates, 2006).

4. Conflicting requirements due to resource dependency

Dependency on a common resource – such as production facilities or distribution channels – is a common source of coupling in functional requirements. We will use a key dilemma facing a seismic surveying company to illustrate this form of complexity. Seismic survey companies basically help oil companies in the search for oil by collecting seismic data (both offshore and onshore) that are then analyzed and interpreted by geologists in the oil companies. In the particular company that we will examine, offshore (marine) surveys were conducted by a fleet of around 12 specialized vessels, while the onshore surveys were carried out by a separate business unit with field crews, working on projects around the globe. The CEO initiated a review of the organizational structure of the company. One important design criterion that was identified was to differentiate more strongly between two parts of the offshore business. Offshore seismic surveys are done either on the request of a particular oil company, which then becomes the sole owner of the data collected (so-called "contract" surveys), or as an investment by the seismic survey company itself, in building up a library of data that can be sold to multiple clients over time (so-called multi-client surveys). The income from contract surveys are received upon completion of the survey, whereas the income from multi-client surveys are spread over several years, depending on the sales of the library data. Historically, these two areas had been combined in the company both in terms of managerial accountability and operations: The same senior managers would be accountable for both contract and multi-client work, and would often try to schedule multi-client work in between contract work in order to utilize vessel capacity effectively (however, at lower levels of the organization, one would find sales teams dedicated to each product). Yet the CEO had come to believe that these two areas in fact represented fundamentally different business models. Consultants working for the company had observed that contract work had a tendency to drive out multi-client work in the short term, hurting the company's longer-term prospects. They recommended a stronger separation of the two areas, in fact, they had tentatively drawn a new organizational chart showing an entirely product-based organization, with "Contract" and "Multi-Client" as two separate business areas.

The key managers in the company were intrigued by this idea, but wanted to spend some time clarifying what the objectives of a re-design should be and to evaluate the implications of a possible change in structure. During interviews with managers in the different business units, it quickly became clear that there were some challenges related to a possible split between Contract and Multi-Client. The simple reason was that both relied on the same production resource, namely the vessels. Although Contract and Multi-Client clearly represented two different business models, they were highly interdependent from an operational point of view, in that the same vessels, with the same crews and equipment, would do both types of work. In times of high demand for both products, and limited vessel capacity, management would have to carefully allocate capacity between the two product areas.

The proposed organization design would lead to a decomposition of functions as shown in Table 9.12. It is indicated (with an "x" in parenthesis) that there may be coupling with regard to the revenue goals. One cannot maximize revenues for Multi-Client projects without considering whether there is capacity to carry out the surveys, which depends on how many Contract projects that are sold and scheduled, and vice versa. The underlying challenge is thus related to the shared use of the production resources (vessels). It is similar, in principle, to the case where two product lines are manufactured in the same factory. In a seismic surveying company, the added challenge is that the "factory" – the vessels carrying out the seismic survey – are moving objects and that it requires considerable time and cost to switch a vessel from one region to another.

7 With a few exceptions, there was little overlap between the two product lines in terms of customers: Only rarely would the sales teams for both contract and multi-client target the same customer. If this had not been the case a more appropriate design would be a three-dimensional structure as discussed in Chapter 4.

There are three generic solutions to this challenge. First, a company may simply separate the production resources. The seismic survey company may divide its vessel fleet into two groups, one handling Contract, and the other Multi-Client projects (see Table 9.13).

This is an uncoupled design according to axiomatic design principles, in that it does allow the achievement of each functional requirement without compromising the other.[7] Other factors being equal, an uncoupled design is clearly preferable. It not only removes the production resource interdependency but also creates a situation where the two business units can sell their respective products in an autonomous fashion. Removing the resource interdependency removes the need for complex internal coordination mechanisms, such as matrix reporting structures.

Table 9.12 Allocation of functions with product-based organization

Functional requirements	*Management*	*Vessels*	*Contract Business Unit*	*Multi Client Business Unit*
		Design parameters		
Allocate vessel capacity	X			
Perform contract surveys		X		
Perform multi client surveys		X		
Maximize revenue from contract projects			X	(x)
Maximize revenue from multi client projects			(x)	X

Table 9.13 Design matrix showing allocation of functions with separation of production resources

Functional requirements	*Management*	*Vessels 1–6*	*Vessels 7–12*	*Contract Business Unit*	*Multi Client Business Unit*
		Design parameters			
Allocate vessel capacity	X				
Perform contract surveys		X			
Perform multi client surveys			X		
Maximize revenue from contract projects				X	
Maximize revenue from multi client projects					X

On the other hand, there may be design criteria or constraints on the desired solution that will need to be met. For example, minimization of costs could be one constraint. Separating a manufacturing process by product may result in higher costs due to slack (one may not be able to utilize the production facilities fully), in addition there is the initial investment of creating the extra assembly line. Since the production resources in this case are moving objects, operating around the globe, this solution would imply a significantly higher fuel cost, as one would need to cover a lot more distance with only six vessels at one's disposal compared to 12.

A second option would be not to split the company into two business units, but instead create one unit responsible for the sales of both products (Table 9.14). With this option, vessel capacity is shared between the product areas, and one avoids the conflicting interdependencies described above (Figure 9.12).

Rather than structurally merging the two sales units (Contract and Multi-Client), the same effect may be achieved by *aligning the incentives* of the two units. The intention would be to ensure that the sales units focus simultaneously on sub-unit performance and overall corporate performance, by finding a production mix that maximizes overall profitability. However, it is important to note that neither of these two alternatives would solve the underlying problem, they simply delegate the resolution complex trade-offs to managers further down in the organization.

Finally, a third alternative is to use market mechanisms to increase access to production resources. Namely, one or both business units may be allowed to outsource production (i.e., lease vessel capacity), either for all projects or only in times of high demand (obviously, a key assumption is that adequate vessels would be available on the market.) This may be an uncoupled design (see Table 9.15).

Although this approach should be effective from a structural perspective, there are some potential disadvantages as well. Market

Table 9.14 Design matrix showing allocation of functions if the two product lines are combined

Functional requirements	Design parameters		
	Management	*Vessels*	*Contract and Multi-Client Business Unit*
Allocate vessel capacity	X		
Perform contract surveys		X	
Perform multi client surveys		X	
Maximize revenue from contract projects			X
Maximize revenue from multi client projects			X

Table 9.15 Design matrix showing allocation of functions if the product units are allowed to outsource production (i.e., lease vessels)

Functional requirements	Design parameters				
	Management	*Own vessels*	*Leased vessels*	*Contract Business Unit*	*Multi Client Business Unit*
Allocate vessel capacity	X				
Perform contract surveys		X			
Perform multi client surveys			X		
Maximize revenue from contract projects				X	
Maximize revenue from multi client projects					X

sourcing is often more expensive than using internal production facilities. In a cyclical industry like the seismic surveying business, the rates for hiring a vessel moves in step with overall demand, and when the market is at a peak there may not be any additional available capacity available. Moreover, one may not be able to remove the interdependency entirely as suggested in Table 9.15. For example, if one business unit chooses to outsource production, while the other continues to source internally, the latter may have to tolerate a higher unit cost (as the overall volume decreases). A potential solution to this problem may be to allow the production resources (the vessels in this case) to also produce for other companies when there is available capacity. (This would be akin to adopting a full internal market where units may both sell and buy externally.) However, a company is likely to consider such a move only if it does not consider its production technologies to be a core competency (in addition to its design, project execution, and marketing capabilities). In many industries, production resources often become gradually more commoditized over time. This is partly the case in the seismic surveying business; recently geophysical companies have emerged that do not own any vessels but rely entirely on market sourcing, i.e., hired vessels. However, so far, these are mainly low-end vessels that are not fitted with the latest technologies used by the seismic surveying companies operating their own fleet.

5. Misalignment of interdependencies

In Chapter 8, we discussed five different types of interdependencies that may exist between organizational sub-units, related to activities, governance, resources, commitments, and social networks. We also noted that these interdependencies may not always be in alignment with each other. This creates a special form of complexity that often presents managers with considerable challenges. This type of misalignment may occur for a number of reasons, but a fairly common cause is the partial transfer of responsibility or the establishment of dual reporting lines.

> The Chief Operating Officer (COO) in a large multidivisional company is planning the development and roll-out of several new quality improvement programs, such as Lean manufacturing and Six Sigma. To succeed with these initiatives, he believes he needs the support of the internal consulting team in the company. However, this team is not part of the COO's corporate staff, but organized within the Shared Services unit, a separate, legal entity within the company. The COO believes he needs several full-time project managers for the quality initiatives and therefore considers merging the consulting group with the corporate staff group at the company's headquarters. However, the CFO of the company is concerned about the (the appearance of) overhead costs and is skeptical about any increase in the number of corporate staff. As a compromise solution, the COO announces that the head of the internal consulting unit will report directly to him, with only a dotted line relationship to the pre-existing line manager (i.e., the head of the Shared Services unit). No other formal changes are made to the design of the unit, which continues to appear on the organization chart as a sub-unit within Shared Services.

In reality, a "hybrid" model is created by this change (Figure 9.8). According to the organization chart, the internal consulting team is a

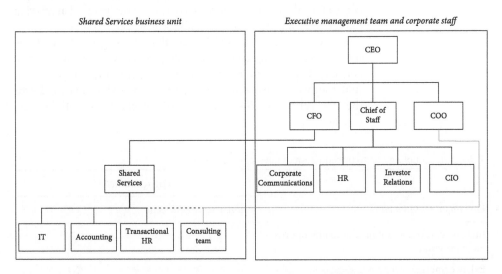

Figure 9.8 Organization chart depicting new reporting line (in light gray) for internal consulting team.

sub-unit within Shared Services. Yet it becomes a corporate staff function in terms of its governance interdependencies (the formal reporting relationship). For example, after the change, all hiring decisions were authorized by the COO rather than the head of the Shared Services unit. In terms of its resource interdependencies, the internal consulting unit remained an internal supplier unit, like other Shared Services units, as its costs were still expected to be covered from fees generated from internal clients, rather than from the corporate staff budget. (The funding for the quality programs was partially created by charging the business units a fee for the use of various quality improvement tools, participation on training courses, etc.)

Although this change was implemented simply by drawing a new reporting line crossing two legally separate units, it increases complexity in some subtle ways.

The change creates asymmetry in terms of the reporting relationship as well as misalignment between the resource and the governance dimension of the organization (cf. Chapter 8), which carries the risk of creating role and incentive conflicts (see Table 9.16). The Shared Services director is faced with the challenge of having a subordinate who reports to a manager more senior than him/herself. The risk is that the more powerful manager on one dimension (in this case, the COO) bypasses the manager on the other dimension. In fact, the COO went on to launch several quality improvement programs for which there was insufficient funding, yet which the director of the Shared Services organization nevertheless felt obligated to accept, and which consequently led to a deficit in the accounts. (It subsequently required significant time and energy to clarify who was responsible for covering this deficit.) Alternatively, in a scenario where the managers on the two axes are more equal in status and power, one can easily imagine a situation where activities become stalled if the manager controlling the resources refuses to cover the costs involved in carrying out the work mandated by the unit's formally defined superior.

It was eventually acknowledged that the organization of the internal consulting team was suboptimal, and when external consultants later were brought in to reorganize the corporate staff unit, they were also asked to develop a new organizational model for the internal consulting team. In this process, three options were considered:

Table 9.16 Coupling due to introduction of new reporting line

	Design parameters	
Functional requirements	*Shared Services director*	*COO*
Increase corporate support for quality improvement programs		X
Balance internal revenues and costs	X	(X)

- Reverting to a pure Shared Services model (i.e., eliminating the dual reporting relationship)
- Transferring the members of the internal consulting team to the corporate staff unit
- Transferring the members of the internal consulting team to other parts of the organization (i.e., the business units).

A combination of the last two measures was eventually chosen by this company. The internal consulting team was split in half, with some consultants transferred to the divisions, while the remaining half was transferred to the corporate staff.

This case shows how a seemingly innocuous change in formal reporting lines may introduce considerable complexity in an organization. In addition to the contradictory functional requirements (Table 9.16) it also led to power asymmetries and ambiguity with regards to roles and responsibilities.

Conclusion

In this chapter, five cases have been described that all exemplify different forms of complexity, but the causes and the consequences of differ. Table 9.17 summarizes some key features of the cases described.

Table 9.17 Summary of cases representing complex organizational designs

Case	Main issue	Consequences
1. Overlapping accountabilities	• Lack of definition or separation of responsibilities between two or more roles, units	• Competition among sub-units, roles • Unclear accountability • Frequent escalation of issues
2. Role inconsistencies in horizontal processes	• Inconsistent unit mandates • Role conflicts (e.g., same person performs and approves outcome of process) • Missing customer or supplier role	• Poor service quality as perceived by customers • General lack of oversight, accountability • Interdepartmental conflicts
3. Excessive interfaces	• Excessive number of work process interdependencies due to dual roles	• Information overload • Excessive time and effort used to coordinate work • Low productivity
4. Conflicting functional requirements	• Coupling between strategic or operational goals due to resource dependency	• Competition for resources • Interdepartmental conflict • Suboptimal performance compared to similar systems without coupling
5. Interdependency misalignment	• Misalignment of different interdependencies (such as those relating to governance and resources)	• Unclear governance; accountability • Conflicting priorities • Power asymmetries

The cases demonstrate how complex organization designs may be described and analyzed by considering the relationship between different functional requirements and/or design parameters as suggested in Suh (2001). The solutions that have been proposed illustrate various ways of simplifying the designs. The intention has been to maintain or improve the system's functionality (i.e., the ability of a sub-unit or an entire organization to realize its goals and strategies) while minimizing internal complexity by de-coupling functional requirements and/or design parameters. Put differently, the proposed solutions are intended to serve as directions for simplifying the structure of the system that delivers an outcome, not to change or simplify the outcome itself.

The proposed approach may be further developed and validated in different ways. As the cases were derived from a limited number of consulting projects, it is necessary to confirm, and if necessary, revise the framework proposed here. One question is the validity of the categorization. The cases were tentatively grouped into five categories; further analytical and empirical work may extend or revise this conceptualization. Secondly, the consequences of complexity that have been described (and summarized in Table 9.17) were mainly based on the author's own observations. More systematic research may identify in a more precise manner the consequences of complex designs on organizational functioning. Finally, it is important to verify that replicable *solutions* have been identified, in other words, that the design propositions that are proposed can be used to resolve similar issues encountered by managers in other organizations. This may be done by collecting data from organization re-design projects where the design propositions are employed and where data are collected to evaluate the outcome. It is also possible to use experimental methods (see Goldenberg and Mazurski, 2002), by asking one group of participants in an experiment to re-design a structure by applying the design propositions, and compare with the results from a second group that either uses an alternative approach (or purely intuitive means).

Although we are far from having a system as rigorous as that developed by Altshuller (1985) in the physical domain, the approach that has been outlined will hopefully serve a starting point for managers in selecting interventions and for scholars in further developing theory, methods and tools that address the challenge of organizational complexity.

Design propositions

Objective	*Reduce or eliminate responsibility overlaps between units, roles.*
9.1	Depending on the specific design goals and circumstances, select one or more of the following actions:

a. *Specify* responsibilities for individual process steps or decision areas.
b. *Standardize* process, for example, by establishing common guidelines for resolving issues.
c. *Sequentially separate* activities in time to allow units to reach a joint decision or form a policy together.
d. *Re-allocate responsibilities* to ensure that related activities are conducted within the same unit.
e. *Restructure* formal boundaries to merge units responsible for interdependent activities together.

Objective	*Ensure that customer and supplier roles in horizontal business processes are consistently defined.*
9.2	Depending on the specific design goals and circumstances, select one or more of the following actions: a. Ensure that lower level grouping is in accordance with higher level design intent (i.e., avoid coupling when decomposing the design). b. Establish explicit customer and supplier roles. c. Analyze processes as a series of commitments between customers and suppliers. d. Re-design processes to remove inconsistent roles and ensure that there are "complete" commitment protocols (also see Chapter 7).
Objective	*Reduce coordination costs caused by an excessive number of interdependencies within a unit (or between different sub-units that form part of a larger unit).*
9.3	*Specialize* roles if there are dual responsibilities.
9.4	*Group roles* into sub-groups (see Chapter 5).
Objective	*Reduce or remove coupling between functional requirements that is due to dependency on shared resources.*
9.4	Depending on the specific design goals and circumstances, select one or more of the following actions: a. *Separate resources* by splitting them into independent groups. b. *Restructure* formal boundaries between sub-units. c. Introduce *market sourcing* to increase flexibility and the range of resources accessible to the firm.

Objective	*Avoid interdependency misalignment.*
9.5	When considering a change in one design parameter of the organization (e.g., governance), assess the impact on other design parameters (e.g., resources, commitments, activities, and social network) and evaluate whether there exists design options that preserve interdependency alignment.

Review questions

1 In general, how can one map the structure of a design that stakeholders perceive as excessively complex?
2 Why do responsibility overlaps emerge in many large organizations?
3 How can horizontal customer-supplier roles be consistently defined?
4 How can you reduce the number of interdependencies between individuals or teams?
5 What options are available when one wants to simplify an organization where functional requirements for different sub-units (i.e., business goals) are in conflict?
6 Why are different interdependency types (or dimensions), such as governance versus resources interdependencies), sometimes misaligned?

Research questions

1 What would be an appropriate research methodology to verify that the categorization of issues proposed in this chapter is representative, or alternative, identify an improved conceptualization?
2 How could one more systematically test out, and further improve, the proposed interventions aimed at reducing complexity (i.e., the design propositions)?

References

Altshuller, G. S. (1985). *Creativity as an Exact Science*. New York: Gordon and Breach.

Ashkenas, R. (2007). Simplicity-minded management. *Harvard Business Review, 85*, 12, 101–109.

Goldenberg, J., and Mazursky, D. (2002). *Creativity in Product Innovation*. Cambridge: Cambridge University Press.

Kates, A. (2006). (Re) Designing the HR organization. *Human Resource Planning, 29*, 2, 22–30.

Scherr, A. L. (1993). A new approach to business processes. *IBM Systems Journal, 32,* 1, 80–98.

Suh, N. P. (2001). *Axiomatic Design: Advances and Applications.* New York: Oxford University Press.

Worren, N., Moore, K., & Elliott, R. (2002). When theories become tools: Toward a framework for pragmatic validity. *Human Relations, 55,* 10, 1227–1249.

Glossary

This list primarily include terms that are used across several of the chapters in the book.

In some cases there are multiple entries, either because the meaning of the term differs depending on the setting or because different definitions are used.

Accountability   1. A situation where an individual can be called to account for his or her actions by another individual or body authorized both to do so and to give recognition to the individual for those actions. Accountability is *assigned to a role* (usually by a superior) – when a person accepts the role, he/she is accepting accountability for doing his or her best to fulfill role expectations, achieve goals, and work within the boundaries of the organization's policies and values (derived from Jaques, 1989).
Note difference from **Responsibility**.
2. A particular type of commitment between people in an organization (potentially at the same hierarchical level), where one person commits to delivering a specific outcome (result) for another person (possibly within certain conditions of satisfactions, e.g., regarding time and quality) (derived from Haeckel, 1999).

Agency theory   A theory explaining the relationship between an *agent* who makes decisions on behalf of a *principal.* The principal and the agent have different risk preferences and goals, creating a conflict of interests. The typical relationship that is studied is that between shareholders (principal) and corporate management (agent).

Agent	Someone (e.g., CEO) who acts on behalf of a principal (e.g., owner of a firm). See **Agency theory**.
Authority	The right a role holder has been given (usually by a superior) to make decisions and control resources (within a given area). It may also include freedom to reject or approve requests and proposals and/or give instructions to subordinates.
Axiom	A principle that is fundamental (i.e., it cannot be proven) but for which there are no counterexamples.
Business areas	A division in a divisional (or multidimensional) firm. Usually, a business area contains multiple business units.
Business units	Sub-units in a divisional (or multidimensional) firm. In a large firm, business units may be grouped within **business areas** (divisions).
Capability	An organization's internal resources and competences (managerial, technical, financial, etc.) that contribute to competitive advantage in a given area.
Chief Executive Officer (CEO)	The head of a corporation (in the UK, the term "Managing Director" is traditionally used).
Clustering	The grouping of elements (e.g., roles) into clusters (teams or sub-units) in a manner that maximizes the number of within-cluster interdependencies and minimizes the number of between-cluster interdependencies.
Contingency theory	A theory that claims that there is no best way to organize a firm, lead a company, or make decisions. Instead, the optimal course of action is contingent (dependent) upon the situation (e.g., the type of external demands that the firm must address). There are contingency theories in several sub-fields of management (e.g., related to leadership styles, decision making, and organization design).
Coordination costs	The cost of processing and sharing information between interdependent roles or sub-units within the organization in order to achieve coordinated action. *Note difference from **Transaction costs**.*
Coordination mechanism	Method used to achieve coordination or integration between roles or sub-units (e.g., communication via e-mail or phone; meetings).

Cost center	A sub-unit within a firm (e.g., department) that is not accountable for its profitability but for some or all of its costs.
Coupling	A conflict between two or more functional requirements (or functions). When there is coupling, efforts at fulfilling one functional requirement will undermine (or will have a certain probability of undermining) efforts at fulfilling one or more of the other functional requirements.
Criteria	**1. Grouping criteria** **2. Design criteria**
Decentralization	1. The delegation of decision rights to lower levels of the organization. 2. The delegation of decision rights to local units (in an organization with multiple locations). 3. The transfer of resources from central to local units (in an organization with multiple locations).
Decision rights	Authority within a given area (e.g., the right to approve expenditures up to 1m USD).
Decomposition	The sub-division of a system into smaller elements that are placed at a lower hierarchical level.
Design	1. [Verb] The process of developing design parameters (the "how") to achieve functional requirements ("the what"). 2. [Noun] The outcome of a design process (e.g., a product, building, or organizational structure).
Design criteria	1. Firm-specific criteria that are used to evaluate alternative organizational models against each other in a design process. 2. Generic criteria that may be used to evaluate the design of any organization or organizational model. *Note difference from **Grouping criteria**.*
Design matrix	A table or matrix where **functional requirements** (FRs) are mapped against **design parameters** (DPs).
Design parameter	A specification of a role, unit or process that will satisfy a **functional requirement** (FR).
Design proposition	A prescriptive hypothesis, i.e., a guideline or rule describing how one can achieve a given goal in a given situation.
Design structure matrix (DSM)	A square matrix where interdependencies between **design parameters** (DPs) are mapped.

Dimension	**Grouping criteria** or organizing principle.
Division	An organizational unit in a firm (usually medium sized or large) that contains several smaller sub-units (e.g., departments).
Divisional organization	An organization with **divisions** structured according to products, markets, or geographies
Economies of scale	Cost advantage that arises with increased output (larger production quantity) of a product
Economies of scope	Cost or revenue advantage by sharing or combining resources across multiple units
Executive	A senior manager, such as a vice president, executive vice president, or chief operating officer.
Fit	A situation in which the organizational structure (or another characteristic of the organization) matches the contingencies that the organization is facing (i.e., the external or internal demands). A key term used in **contingency theory**.
Formalization	The extent to which work roles, procedures, and processes are defined and documented in an organization.
Function	1. A **functional requirement**. 2. The **mandate or mission** of a unit. 3. A sub-unit in a **functional organization**.
Functional organization	An organization structured according to skills and knowledge (i.e., containing sub-units, or functions, for Sales, Manufacturing, Distribution, etc.) *Note difference from **Functional requirement**.*
Functional requirement	A desired outcome that an organization or sub-unit should produce.
Goals	Objectives (usually time bound) that are assigned to a person or unit to ensure that the function (mandate, mission) of a unit is fulfilled. *Note difference from **Functions** and **Functional requirements**.*
Governance	1. Processes related to the exercise of authority and control within organizations (e.g., allocation of decision rights, approval of decisions, monitoring of performance, etc.) 2. Principles and processes by which corporations are controlled and directed by the board of directors and other stakeholders [Usually referred to as "Corporate Governance"].
Grouping	1. [Verb] The process of sorting or allocating different roles and sub-units to groups (e.g.,

roles into teams and sub-units into departments or divisions) based on some **Grouping criteria.**

2. [Noun] The outcome after having sorted roles and sub-units into groups.

Grouping criteria   A criterion used to sort or allocate roles or sub-units to groups (e.g., "All accountants are to be placed in the Finance department"). *Note difference from* **Design criteria.**

Hierarchy   1. Arrangement of roles in an organization according to levels of authority and accountability.

2. A layered system of clustering, where a cluster at one level combines and integrates the functions of lower level units.

Implementation   The process of putting a plan or model into effect; execution.

Interdependencies   A relationship between two or more elements (e.g., roles, units, work processes) that are linked or mutually reliant on each other

Interface   The common boundary between two interdependent roles, processes, or units

Job   A position in an organization that may contain several **roles**.

Level of analysis   The organizational level (or level of detail more generally) that one is considering or analyzing at the moment. For example, one may choose to analyze roles, sub-units, or the overall organizational structure.

Manager   A person who is accountable for the results of others (i.e., the subordinates).

Mandate   1. The authority that has been assigned to a sub-unit.

2. A task or goal that has been assigned to a sub-unit.

Matrix structure   An organization with dual reporting relationships; i.e., where a significant proportion of the employees or managers report to more than one boss.

Minimal critical specifications   Specifications that define precisely what needs to be done, without defining how it should be done.

Misfit   A situation in which the organizational structure (or another characteristic of the organization) does not match the contingencies that the organization is facing (i.e., the external or internal demands). A key term used in **contingency theory.**

Mission	An organization's or sub-unit's purpose or "reason for being."
Multidimensional organization	An organization that consists of sub-units that have been defined based on different grouping criteria (e.g., function, product, geography) at the same hierarchical level.
Organization	A purposeful (i.e., goal directed) system consisting of interrelated roles that are hierarchically differentiated (i.e., that contain levels of roles with different levels of authority).
Organization design	1. [verb] The process of developing and selecting the organization's structure (i.e., formal and semi-formal features such as roles and accountabilities, reporting relationships, sub-units, management layers, as well as interfaces and coordination mechanisms) in order to satisfy functional requirements (strategies, missions, or mandates).
	2. [noun] The outcome of the design process (i.e., the structure of the organization).
	3. [noun] A field of study concerned with developing theories, methods, and tools to achieve improved organizational effectiveness by changing organizational structure
	4. [noun] A practitioner discipline aimed at applying systematic principles, methods, and tools to achieve improved organizational effectiveness by changing organizational structure
Organizational architecture	The design of the overall organization (e.g., organizational structure, coordination mechanisms, and interdependencies) developed to ensure that it fulfills its mission and strategy. Organizational architectures should be *purposeful, future oriented, coherent,* and *provide context* for individual action.
Organizational complexity	1. Coupling between functional requirements, which leads to unclear accountability and a low probability of goal achievement (see **Coupling**).
	2. A large number of interdependencies between different design parameters (process steps and/ or sub-units in an organization), which leads to high coordination costs and/or increased risk of errors and delays.
	Note difference from **Task complexity.**
Organizational economics	A set of theories that use concepts and methods from the field of economics to

understand organizations. The most well-known theories are transaction cost theory, agency theory, and contract theory.

Organizational model
A specification of an organizational structure or architecture.

Organizational structure
The grouping of an organization into sub-units and the formal reporting relationships that define roles and authority at different levels of the organization.

Organizational theory
A field of study and knowledge concerned with describing and explaining the nature of organizations, how they function, and how they develop over time. Well-known theories in this field include institutional theory, contingency theory, resource dependency theory, social network theory, population ecology theory, and critical theory of organizations. Many scholars in this field are sociologists. Note difference from **Organizational economics** and **Organization design**.

Principal
Someone (e.g., owner of a firm) who appoints an agent (e.g., CEO) to work on his behalf. See **Agency theory**.

Process-based organizational structure
An organizational structure that has been sub-divided based on the organization's main work processes (as opposed to functions, products, or geographies). In a process-based organization, "process owners" are appointed in addition to (or instead of) functional managers. The process owners have responsibility for an end-to-end process that may cross several functional areas.

Process maturity
The extent to which work processes are explicitly defined, managed, measured, controlled. A high level of process maturity also implies there is a system in place for continuous improvement of the processes.

Process dependencies
Sequential interdependencies between activities in a work process, or between different work processes (due to a need for information, resources, approval, etc.).

Profit center
A sub-unit within an organization (e.g., a business unit or division) that is accountable for both revenues and costs, and therefore, profits

Re-design
1. [Verb] The process of changing the organizational structure.
2. [Noun] The outcome of having changed the organizational structure.

Reporting line	The indication of an authority relationship between one or more subordinates and a manager (i.e., on an organization chart the reporting line indicates to whom a subordinate reports; usually a manager one level above in the hierarchy)
Requisite	Deliberate and logical (opposite of arbitrary). *Related to the requisite organization approach developed by Jaques (1989)*
Requisite variety	The principle that internal variety (or complexity) must match the external variety (or complexity) that an organization is subject to. *Proposed by Ashby (1956), also known as the First law of cybernetics.*
Responsibility	1. An individual's sense of obligation to perform at a certain level or in a certain manner, or to take certain actions (generally connected to the accountability in a role) 2. [Casual usage] Accountability.
Revenue center	A sub-unit within an organization that gains revenue from product sales or service provided. The manager in revenue center is accountable for revenue only.
Roles	1. A description of a set of activities that has been assigned to an individual in an organization 2. The purpose behind the set of activities that has been assigned to an individual in an organization 3. [For units within the organization] Mandate or mission.
Span of control	The number of subordinates that a manager is responsible for.
Specialization	A focus on a limited set of skills or activities.
Standardization	The process of ensuring that components, products, services, or work processes conform to common specifications to ensure consistency and repeatability
Standard interface	An interface of an organizational sub-unit that makes it possible for the sub-unit to interact or transact with a large number of other sub-units (or external parties) at a low cost, because it interacts in the same manner (or utilizing standard procedures and tools etc.) and does not have to customize its approach to the individual sub-unit or party with which it is interacting.

Strategic choice	The idea that managers have an influence on organizational structure (as opposed to the view in **contingency theory** that contingencies represent imperatives) (Child, 1972).
Subsidiary	A unit of a multi-national firm that is located in one country and carries out the firm's business in that country.
System	A set of interrelated elements. Thus a system is composed of at least two elements that are connected to each other in some way. There are different types of systems, including mechanical, biological, and social. Moreover, one distinguishes between closed systems, which are completely self-contained, and open systems, which interact with their environment (Ackoff, 1971).
Tacit knowledge	Knowledge that someone has that is not verbalized or codified, making it difficult to transfer to other people.
Task complexity	The extent of ambiguous information, multiple or uncertain alternatives, unknown consequences of action and/or multiple or uncertain means-ends connections inherent in a task. The higher the task complexity, the more knowledge and the higher the competence level that is required to perform the task successfully.
Transaction costs	Costs that are involved in making and carrying out a transaction between two parties or more (e.g., related to searching for information about goods or services, bargaining and reaching agreement between seller and buyer, and enforcing contracts) *Note difference from* **Coordination costs**.
Vertically integrated	Arrangement by which the supply chain of a firm is owned by that firm rather than by suppliers or distributors.
Work process	A set of activities performed in order to develop, produce, and deliver a product, provide a service, or manage an organization. Work processes may be informal or they may be documented and managed systematically.
Working capacity	Competence or cognitive ability to handle work tasks. Also see **Task complexity**.

References

Ackoff, R. (1971). Towards a system of systems concepts. *Management Science*, 17, 661–671.

Ashby, W. (1956). *An Introduction to Cybernetics*. New York: Wiley.

Child, J. (1972). Organizational structure, environment and performance: The role of strategic choice. *Sociology*, 6, 1–22.

Haeckel, S. (1999). *Adaptive Enterprise*. Boston: Harvard Business Review Press.

Jaques, E. (1989). *Requisite Organization: The CEO's Guide to Creative Structure and Leadership*. Arlington, VA: Cason Hall & Publishers.

Index

For Product Safety Concerns and Information please contact our
EU representative GPSR@taylorandfrancis.com Taylor & Francis
Verlag GmbH, Kaufingerstraße 24, 80331 München, Germany